D1068695

THE CHRONICLE
OF NOVGOROD
1016–1471

THE CHRONICLE
OF NOVGOROD
1016-1471

TRANSLATED FROM THE RUSSIAN

BY

ROBERT MICHELL

AND

NEVILL FORBES, Ph.D.

Reader in Russian in the University of Oxford

WITH AN INTRODUCTION BY

C. RAYMOND BEAZLEY, D.Litt.

Professor of Modern History in the University of Birmingham

AND AN ACCOUNT OF THE TEXT BY

A. A. SHAKHMATOV

Professor in the University of St. Petersburg

CAMDEN THIRD SERIES
VOL. XXV

AMS PRESS
NEW YORK

Reprinted from the edition of 1914, London
First AMS EDITION published 1970
Manufactured in the United States of America

International Standard Book Number: 0-404-04799-8

Library of Congress Catalog Number: 70-137264

AMS PRESS INC.
NEW YORK, N.Y. 10003

TABLE OF CONTENTS

GENERAL INTRODUCTION

I. THE REPUBLIC OF NOVGOROD

" LORD NOVGOROD THE GREAT," *Gospodin Velikii Novgorod,* as it once called itself, is the starting-point of Russian history. It is also without a rival among the Russian city-states of the Middle Ages. Kiev and Moscow are greater in political importance, especially in the earliest and latest mediaeval times—before the Second Crusade and after the fall of Constantinople—but no Russian town of any age has the same individuality and self-sufficiency, the same sturdy republican independence, activity, and success.

Who can stand against God and the Great Novgorod?—*Kto protiv Boga i Velikago Novgoroda ?*—was the famous proverbial expression of this self-sufficiency and success.

From the beginning of the Crusading Age to the fall of the Byzantine Empire Novgorod is unique among Russian cities, not only for its population, its commerce, and its citizen army (assuring it almost complete freedom from external domination even in the Mongol Age), but also as controlling an empire, or sphere of influence, extending over the far North from Lapland to the Urals and the Ob. The modern provinces of Novgorod, Olonets, and Archangel, with portions of Vologda, Perm, and Tobolsk, represent this empire.[1]

The great Novgorod of the Middle Ages, the quiet, decayed cathedral town of to-day, lies on both sides of the deep and broad Volkhov, on its way from Lake Ilmen to Ladoga and the Baltic. Here we are about one hundred miles south-east of St. Petersburg.

As in the Middle Ages, the *Side* or *Quarter of St. Sophia* still lies on the left of the Volkhov, the *Commercial Side* on the right. The eleventh-century cathedral of the Holy Wisdom, " Saint Sophia," is still one of the historical monuments of Russia, while the walls of the Kremlin of Novgorod show how slender was the fourteenth-century Russian skill in fortification.[2]

But the mighty turbulent Republic is no more. The modern town, of some 26,000 people, has little more than a tenth, perhaps, of its old numbers, when to Ghillibert de Lannoy, coming from the Low Countries in 1413, it appeared " of prodigious greatness."[3] The Hanseatic Market is a memory. The ancient earthern ramparts are in ruins, and of their stone towers only one, *The White,* still stands on the south of the city. Quite as ruinous is the Tower of Yaroslav, overlooking that Court of Yaroslav, which was once the favourite meeting-place of the popular assemblies. The great bell which summoned the citizens to these assemblies, or to riot, hangs there no longer. More than from Florence or from Ghent has the old life departed, which made Novgorod a Slavonic counterpart of the city-states of Italy or of Flanders.[4]

Novgorod, in the days of its power, is in name an elective Principality, in fact something like a democratic Republic. The *Veche*, or General Assembly of the citizens, is the ultimate and irresistible authority, though its ordinary activities are of course limited by other forces, ecclesiastical, commercial, aristocratic, and princely.

(i) The power of these Electoral *Knyazes* or Princes rests mainly on their own personality, and their capacity of maintaining popularity and organizing support. In modern language, Novgorod is largely governed by the party system. While the Prince can command a majority, or at least avoid open defeat, he is secure, except against surprise: as soon as his party is the weaker, the result is inevitable. In the language of the Chronicle, they " show him the way out."

From the earliest times the citizens are noted for their " free spirit." At the beginning of Russian history we have their traditional revolt against the very Rurik they had just called in to found the new Slav-Scandinavian people of *Rus*—" Our Land is great, but there is no Order or Justice in it; come and . . . rule over us." A century later, Svyatoslav proposes to govern Novgorod by ordinary officials, but the city insists on a son of the Grand Prince. " We know how to find another *Knyaz*." The menace is heeded (964-72).

Yaroslav the Lawgiver (1016-54), one of the real statesmen of Russian history, fully recognizes the power and value of Novgorod. Above all his other favours, tradition singles out the Charters or Privileges granted by him to the city—a Russian parallel to the " Good Laws of Edward the Confessor," or the German Town Charters of Charles the Great.[5]

As the old Russian Federation, under the Grand Princes of Kiev, falls to pieces in the twelfth century, Novgorod republicanism develops. The sovereignty is treated as purely elective, and deposition becomes well-nigh parallel to election. A prince installed one year may be " shown out " the next.

Thus in 1136 (taking examples only from the time of Stephen and Henry II of England) the men of Novgorod seize and imprison Prince Vsyevolod in the Archbishop's palace " with his wife and children, and his mother-in-law," and finally expel him.

The next prince reigns less than a year; his successor is driven out after "twenty-one months." In 1141 the city "sat without a prince" nine months, and the man next chosen is put in the Archbishop's Palace and "let go" after a few weeks.

Again in 1154 Novgorod turns out its prince, and "fetches in" another, who soon goes to reign at Kiev, leaving his son David in his place. David is "shown the road" before the close of this same year (1154).

In 1157 David's successor, despite the support of the *Commercial Quarter*, has to fly under cover of night. The prince next appointed (in 1158) is shown the way to Ladoga in 1160—only to be restored, "with his full liberty," after "a year less than a week," when his rival and supplanter is "fetched away." And in this way examples might be tenfold multiplied.[6]

There is another side to the picture. In the changeful line of Novgorod princes, we meet sometimes with men who rule. Yaroslav the Lawgiver, in the eleventh century, is such a sovereign; Alexander Nevsky, in the thirteenth, is another. From 1240, when he gains his "eponymous" triumph upon the Neva, till his death in 1263, Alexander dominates Novgorod. He even makes the Republic diplomatic. After the intoxicating victories of the Neva over the Swedes (1240), and of Lake Chudskoe over the German Knights (1242), it was hard to submit to the Mongol taxgatherer (as in 1259). But Alexander realizes that to defy the Horde is to complete the desolation of Russia. The hero of Novgorod at last persuades her of the humiliating truth. He rides out with the Mongol emissaries, whom he had guarded day and night from mob violence, and under his protection "the accursed ones" go "through the streets, writing down the houses of the Christians." To save the Russian remnant, Alexander journeys repeatedly to the Western Tartar army (or *Golden Horde*) upon the Volga—once at least to the Great Khan in Mongolia (1246–50). Death overtakes him on his way home from the Golden Horde in 1263. The news reaches Novgorod as the Eucharist is finishing; turning to the people, Archbishop Cyril tells the disaster—"The sun of the Russian land has set, my children." "Grant, Merciful Lord," exclaims the Chronicler, "that he may see Thy Face in the age to come, for he has laboured for Novgorod, and for the whole Russian land."[7]

Yet even this hero of the North, fresh from the victory of the Neva, has for a time to leave Novgorod, "with his mother and his wife . . . having quarrelled" with the citizens. Better thoughts come with reflection. At the beginning of the next year Alexander is recalled (1241).[8]

As time goes on, and Eastern and Western Christendom see the growth of more powerful monarchical states, the Novgorod princedom further declines, and at last we find the citizens doubting only whether to become frankly Muscovite or disloyally Polish (1471).[9]

(ii) The crisis of 1471, ended by the victory of Moscow, brings into relief the second person in the temporal polity of the Republic—in " the accursed " *Posadnitsa* Martha, wife of the *Posadnik*, Governor, or Burgomaster Simon Boretsky. This remarkable woman, a Russian parallel to Elizabeth of England, Catherine de Medici, and the rest of the brilliant female offspring of the Classical Renaissance, almost succeeds in detaching Novgorod from Russia and the Eastern Church, and is therefore not greatly flattered by the Chronicle of the city, in a last section thoroughly pervaded by Muscovite influence. The hatred of her opponents shows the influence which one *Posadnik* at least is able to exercise. But usually the *Posadniks*, like the princes, are creatures of the popular will. They are set up and cast down almost as frequently, and their fate is harder. Deposed princes are " shown the road," but deposed or unpopular governors are often killed. Thus in 1134, 1146, 1156, 1161, 1171, 1172, 1175, 1189, 1205, 1219, we hear, within one century only, of *Posadniks* expelled or restored; in 1167 and 1209 of *Posadniks* executed or proscribed.[10]

The *Posadnik* riots of 1209 give us a vivid picture of the city in uproar. " The men of Novgorod held a *Veche* over *Posadnik* Dmitri and his brethren . . . And they went to plunder their courts [houses] and set fire to . . . [them], seizing their effects, and selling their villages and servants . . . taking of their treasures a countless quantity." Later Dmitri is brought in dead, and Novgorod would have thrown the body from the bridge, "but the archbishop forbade." " And they kissed the Cross that they would not keep Dmitri's children " in the city.[11]

Strong governors perhaps appear more often than strong princes. And such governors play a leading part in home and foreign politics, as in 1135, 1214, 1215, 1264.[12]

At times, as in 1218, the Novgorod Democracy keeps a *Posadnik* in office, in defiance of the Prince. " He is blameless, and we will not give in to this." Yet next year the fickle monster may displace its favourite, only to replace him the same winter.[13]

(iii) As everywhere in Old Russia, the Church in Novgorod is of the first importance. Vast as is the sphere of the Latin Church in Western history, the Greek Church in Russia is only less prominent because of the absence of Papalism, of religious war, and (in comparison) of ecclesiastical encroachment.

As early as 1034 *Nestor* mentions one of the *Vladykas* or Archbishops, whose succession is so carefully recorded, and in 1045 the historic Cathedral of the Holy Wisdom, the *Hagia Sophia* or *Sophiisky Sobor* of Novgorod, is built by Yaroslav the Lawgiver and his son Vladimir.[14]

St. Sophia becomes the symbol of the freedom, prosperity, and power of the city. "Where St. Sophia is, there is Novgorod," exclaims Prince Mstislav in 1215. "Come to your patrimony, to St. Sophia," the citizens beseech Prince Yaroslav. " With the aid of St. Sophia," Novgorod conquers in battle. Sooner than submit to the Mongol census (in 1259) the people resolve to " die honourably for St. Sophia." " I bow down to St. Sophia, and to the men of Novgorod," says Mstislav, when negotiating for his installation as prince (in 1210). " I make my greeting to St. Sophia . . . and to you: God grant I may lie by my father in St. Sophia "—is the farewell of the same prince to Novgorod.[15]

An accused Archbishop who has been exiled rights himself " through God and St. Sophia." " The Devil crushed by God and St. Sophia," is the Chronicler's exclamation, at the end of a riot, when " brethren come together . . . and kiss the Cross."[16]

The Novgorod Chronicle, a work of ecclesiastics, abounds in references to church matters. Almost every other year we read of the consecration or adornment of a church or monastery, " a refuge for Christians, a joy to Angels, and ruin to the Devil." Often it is St. Sophia itself, Novgorod's Westminster, which is repaired or beautified, or which becomes the burial place of another prince.[17]

These ecclesiastical notes constantly throw light upon political and social conditions. From some we learn of a *Varangian* or Scandinavian Church; from others, of a merchant's daughter becoming an abbess; from others, of the Archbishop's palace used as a prison for deposed princes or other great offenders; from others, again, of the *Vladyka's* influence in heading embassies, stopping riots, reconciling parties, and allaying popular fury.[18]

The Archbishops, usually chosen by the Prince and citizens—

but needing confirmation by the " Metropolitan of all Russia " at
Kiev, Vladimir, or Moscow—ultimately depend on popular favour.
Thus in 1211 Mitrofan is exiled, " bearing this gladly, like John
Chrysostom," and after eight years is recalled by the same popular
voice (1219).[19]

Monasticism, which began in the Eastern Church, and has always
played so great a part in Russia, is strong at Novgorod. Many a
time it is recorded how a Bishop, Igumen, prince, or rich man,
founds a monastery—" a refuge for Christians and a delight to the
faithful ":[20] like the " Bishop's Court," the Russian monasteries
serve at times as guard-houses for prisoners of state.[21]

As in the West, so in the East. The greatest soldiers and statesmen may take refuge in the cloister. Alexander Nevsky himself,
when he feels his mortal illness, is " shorn " as a monk (Nov. 14,
1263).

And abundant are the examples of prominent ecclesiastics of the
Republic being " shorn into " (or " for ") the *schema*, " choosing
to lead a life of silence."[22]

(iv) " Mediaeval society (many still believe) included only soldiers,
churchmen, and peasants." Mediaeval Russia, and especially
Novgorod, gives as much help against this superstition as any
Westernland.

The burgess, the responsible citizen, who possesses a stake in the
Republic, and who deliberates, votes, and fights for its freedom and
greatness, is constantly in evidence.

But beyond the ordinary business and business man of the
average prosperous mediaeval town, the merchant and his trade
play an exceptional part in Novgorod. For here was one of the
four capital factories of the Hanseatic League in non-German
lands.

Before, or during, the time of Frederic Barbarossa, foreign traders
are noticed at Novgorod (1142); Bremen merchants appear
in Livonia (1157); and direct commerce between Cologne and
Russia is recorded (1165). The agreement concluded at the close
of the Crusading Age (1269) between Novgorod, Lübeck, and Gothland, shows that the *Nemtsy* had long possessed a regular commercial status on the Volkhov. And the famous *Skra* or code of the
Nemetski factory here goes back to the early thirteenth century
(1225).[23]

Half the town is known, we have seen, as the *Commercial Side*.[24]

Here the foreign traders had their quarters, their guildhall, their church (of St. Peter), their shops, stores, and dwelling-houses. This *Court of the Nemtsy*, or *Court of St. Peter*, was built, like the Hansa settlements in Bergen and London, for defence as well as for trade, and was closed and guarded at night. At its head was a Council of Aldermen, with a President, the " (Chief) Alderman of St. Peter's Court." Common Rooms (very unlike those of Oxford) were maintained for all the Hanseatics, " summer and winter travellers " alike—both the privileged seafarers, and the landsmen who, as enjoying an easier life, had fewer privileges in the factory. The junior clerks and apprentices had plenty of freedom in the " children's room."

The *Nemtsy* of St. Peter's Court had their own brewery, bees, and forests. Their organization was largely governed by the sound principles of keeping their good things to themselves, and guarding against fraud by their customers, as well as against the intrusion of non-Hanseatics into the Russian trade.[25]

In the early days of this factory, the annual profits are stored at St. Mary's Church in Visby—another indication of Gothland influence. The original authors of the *Skra* are probably Gothland merchants, and the Novgorod " court of the *Nemtsy* " is perhaps at first a dependency of Visby. But in the fourteenth century the Gothland domination is first rivalled, then replaced, by that of Lübeck. Thus from 1346 the Hanseatic President in Novgorod is chosen, by representatives of the Hanse towns, *from among Lübeck and Visby merchants*.[26]

The growth of Hanse trade in Russia, during the Mongol Age (1220-1460), is not only due to the business ability of the German merchants. It is aided by the disasters (and consequent dependence) of the Russian people at this time—by Tartar, Lithuanian, and especially Teutonic, conquest.

Except in Flanders, no field of non-German trade gives so wide a Hanseatic picture, shows so many Hanse centres engaged in the local commerce. Merchants of Brunswick, Dortmund, Duisburg, Magdeburg, Munster, and pettier towns appear in Russia, especially in Novgorod, often travelling by the dangerous overland routes. And even mediaeval Russians sometimes venture far overland in search of customers.[27]

The Annals of Novgorod abound in notices of trade. Already in the twelfth century (as in 1137, 1141-2, 1195) the mercantile interest makes itself felt in war and politics.[28]

Commercialism further develops in the thirteenth century, when we hear of extortions from merchants, in 1209; of merchants sent, with the *Posadnik*, to call in a new prince, in 1215; of merchants plundered by this new ruler in the same year; of gallant tradesmen (kettlemakers, clockmakers, silversmiths) killed in battle (in 1216, 1234, and later years); and of terrible fires on the *Commercial Side*, with destruction of *Varangian* and *Nemetski* merchandise, in the *Varangian* church, or in *Varangian* Street (in 1217 or 1299).[29]

In the fourteenth century commercial matters, and especially interference with trade, are among the prominent causes of quarrel between Novgorod and Sweden, the Teutonic Order, and Moscow.[30]

Lastly, in the fifteenth century, foreign values and coined money are introduced into Novgorod traffic, and the old tokens superseded. Thus in 1410 " the men of Novgorod began to trade in *Nemetski artugs* and Lithuanian *groshes* . . . doing away with skin-tokens," and in 1420 they " began to deal in silver coin," and sold the *Nemtsy* their *artugs* again.[31]

(v) Every rank, power, and interest in Novgorod rests upon the sovereign people. As no dynasty can establish itself permanently, still less any aristocracy of western type, the Republic preserves with peculiar purity the ancient democratic ideas and institutions. Down to the Muscovite conquest, the city is more powerful than any of its lords, officials, or classes.[32] The great popular assembly, comparable to that of Athens in power, is supremely characteristic of Novgorod among Russian states. The *Veche* invites a new prince, and arraigns, imprisons, or expels him when it pleases.[33] It elects and deposes *Posadniks* and the lesser officers of state.[34] Within the limits of the sacred lot, and of Orthodox feeling, it elects, as it can depose, the *Vladykas* or Archbishops.[35] It decides peace and war, and punishes criminals. A bad character, or unpopular personage, may be hurled from the Great Bridge—or otherwise put out of the way—at the conclusion of a *Veche*.[36]

Like the Polish Diets, the Novgorod *Veches* nominally respect the primitive Slavonic principle of necessary unanimity. But there is no real *liberum veto* on the Volkhov. Minorities in Novgorod are bludgeoned, ducked, drowned, " put to the edge of the sword," or expelled from the city. Prince or *Posadnik*—or any respectable party among the nobles or commons—can legally or practically summon the *Veche*, which usually meets either " at " (i.e. outside) St. Sophia, or in the *Court of Yaroslav* on the *Commercial Side*. Sometimes rival parties call rival *Veches*, which finish with a conference upon the Great Bridge, or with fighting.[37] Matters of religion and morality are an important part of the work of the *Veche*, which banned pagan superstitions, punished the black art, designated the favoured few from whom a new archbishop might be chosen, or deposed an unpopular prelate.[38]

II. THE EMPIRE OF NOVGOROD.

ON any general view of European history, there are few incidents more suggestive than the territorial expansion of Russia—the eastern vanguard of western civilization. However we may criticize the Russian people, it is certainly the pioneer and representative of Christendom in the north-east of Europe and in the north of Asia. And nowhere in the Old World has the dominion of the higher races been so widened as in the lands from the Black Sea to the White, and from the Baltic to the Sea of Japan, which have been gradually conquered and colonized by the Slavonic-Scandinavian *Rus*.

The primitive Russian homeland did not include more than a fraction (mainly in the West-Central zone) of the present Russia-in-Europe. It was the political, mercantile, and adventuring ambition of Russian states, traders, and freebooters, which gave so noteworthy an extension to the Russian name.

The first discovery of those two Siberias—European and Asiatic—which lay north and north-east of the primitive Russians, as far as the Polar Ocean and Tobolsk province, was the work of Novgorod. Probably about the time of the First Crusade (1096), and certainly before the Second (1147), the Republic had already come into touch with the country just beyond the Ural Mountains.

Long ere this, perhaps as early as the age of Cnut (1000–30), the Novgorod pioneers had penetrated to Lapland, the White Sea, and even the Urals. One of the North Ural passes most likely corresponds to those *Iron Gates* where the men of Novgorod suffered disaster in 1032—" Few returned, but many perished there."[39]

In 1079 we have the earliest reference of the Novgorod Annals themselves to these distant regions: " They killed Prince Gleb *beyond the Volok* " (in the Northern Dvina country) " on the 30th of May."[40]

The time of Henry I of England shows Novgorod communicating with the Asiatic lands beyond the dividing range. Speaking of a year which apparently answers to A.D. 1112, the *Fundamental Chronicle,* usually known as *Nestor's,* tells how one Guryata Rogovishch of Novgorod sent his servant to the Pechora, how the Pechora folk then paid tribute to *Novgrad,* and how from the Pechora the messenger went on to *Yugra.* We may doubt the Yugrian report of a mysterious people enclosed in lofty mountains by the sea, vainly struggling to break out, and accessible only by an opening through which they screeched their unknown lingo, thrust out an iron finger, and bartered furs for iron. But we need not doubt the historical statement which introduces this legend, or see in Nestor's *Yugra* anything very different from the *Yugra* of later time—the north-west corner of Asia, and especially the valley of the Lower Ob.[41]

Now this Siberian connexion is not a passing incident, like the early Russian dominion on the Azov or in the Crimea, or the early Russian raids towards and beyond the Caucasus. On the contrary, it appears fairly persistent throughout the central and later Middle Ages; when Novgorod is displaced by Moscow, the Muscovite power continues and develops the Russian overlordship in *Yugra.*

A tribute-gathering expedition in 1169 shows Novgorod active in the *Trans-Volok* or Northern Dvina basin, and may have been concerned with payments as far as Asia; and the foundation of Vyatka in 1174 carries permanent Novgorod settlement far nearer to Siberia, along a more southerly track. But in 1187, on the eve of the Third Crusade, *Yugra* appears tragically; both here and in lands west of Ural the natives rise and massacre their Russian masters or customers. The punitive expedition of 1193–4 ends in disaster.[42]

How and when intercourse with Asiatic Siberia is resumed we are not told; but this resumption possibly took place before the end of the Crusading Age, for in the agreement of 1264 between Novgorod and Prince Yaroslav, *Yugra,* like Perm and the Pechora, appears among the domains or " claims " of the Republic.[43] Sixty years later, in 1323 and 1329, Novgorod complains of outrages on its citizens travelling to *Yugra.*[44] These outrages were often the work of Russian enemies (as at Ustyug) in the Northern Dvina basin, planted on the flank of the north-east trade-route from Novgorod, and a constant danger to its commerce. Again, the demand of Moscow, in 1332-3, for " tribute in silver " for the lands beyond the Kama— the first sign of coming Muscovite overlordship—probably has a special reference to the mines Novgorod had long exploited in the Northern Ural.[45]

Lastly, in 1445, within a generation of the ruin of the Republic, we hear of a last vigorous effort to assert Novgorod rule in *Yugra*. Again the *Chronicle* tells of initial successes; then, as before, victory ends in ruinous defeat.[46]

In 1471 Moscow crushes Novgorod, and takes over the Novgorodian empire. But even before this, the founder of the Moscow Tsardom, Ivan the Great, on his way to the subjugation of Novgorod, begins the conquest of the Asiatic Siberia with which Novgorod had dealt so long.[47]

To the connexions between Novgorod and her less remote provinces there are fuller references. We have noticed the death of Prince Gleb in 1079, the tribute-gathering expedition of 1169 in the Trans-Volok, the foundation of Vyatka in 1174, and the Muscovite demand for " silver-payment " on the Trans-Kama lands in 1332-3. The Northern Dvina, the most valuable region *beyond the Volok*, appears more definitely in 1337, when Ivan Kalita attacks it to enforce his Trans-Kama silver claims, and is " brought to shame there "; in 1340, when Novgorod warriors raid Ustyug; in 1342, when rebel adventurers conquer all the Trans-Volok; in 1355-9, when Ivan II of Moscow corresponds with the Dvina Governor and notables; in 1366, when Novgorodians " coming from the Dvina " are seized by Muscovite forces; and in 1393, when Moscow compels Novgorod to yield to the Metropolitan.[48]

Ivan Kalita had first turned Muscovite policy towards the Arctic Dvina; besides its wealth in furs and timber, he aimed at winning an outlet to the ocean.[49] Some seventy years later, his schemes are momentarily realized. In 1397 all the Dvina people are seduced from Novgorod, and " kiss the cross " to Moscow. The Grand Prince issues ordinances for his new subjects (in 1398-9), which are the earliest Muscovite laws known, and the first Russian laws preserved since Yaroslav (1016-54).[50] Yet in 1411, 1417, 1419, 1445, we find Novgorod again in possession of most of Siberia-in-Europe.[51]

But finally the overmastering power of Moscow, which in 1452 chases an enemy through the Dvina lands, and in 1458-9 conquers Vyatka, achieves under Ivan the Great the complete destruction of Novgorod power on the Dvina, as elsewhere (1471).[52]

Later Russian progress in the Kama and Pechora regions is

specially connected with the Russian Church.   About 1376 the monk Stephen, afterwards canonized as the apostle of Perm (" Stephan Permsky "), founds the earliest church in the Upper Kama.   It was a venture of some risk, for a former missionary in this country had been flayed by the natives, " while they were yet but infants in the Faith."[53] Yet before his death in 1396 Stephen had overthrown the local idolatry of the *Golden Old Woman*, stopped the sacrifice of reindeer, secured the triumph of Christianity, and founded Muscovite influence in a region whence, two centuries later, Moscow overruns the Siberian Khanate.[54] Under Stephen's successors the Russian Church took root in the Pechora country (1397–1445)—as it did on the White Sea during the same period, through the foundation of the greatest monastery of the Far North, in Solovetsky island (1429).[55]

Last among these distant fields of early Novgorod expansion comes Lapland, the westernmost region of Siberia-in-Europe. Neglecting any alleged treaties of the tenth century, or other evidence of Novgorodian power here before 1264, we now find Kola included with *Yugra*, the Trans-Volok, and the Pechora, among lands of Novgorod influence.[56] Again, the peace concluded between Novgorod and Sweden, in 1323, fixes the Varanger Fiord as the boundary between the two powers in Lapland.   As elsewhere, religious influence accompanies mercantile and political control; like Stephen in the Kama, Iliya of Novgorod and Theodorite of Solovetsky appear as apostles of faith and culture to Kola and the Lapps.[57]

We may here remember that the early Russian expansion in the North is led, not by an absolute monarch and his soldiers, but by a fickle, half-theocratic democracy, whose chief activity is commerce, and to whom the right of insurrection is sacred.   We may also recall that the free life of Old Novgorod has left widely-scattered traces in North Russia.   Thus the colony planted in the well-stocked and beautiful woodland of far-away Vyatka, in 1174—though no longer governed by elected civil magistrates, sharing power, in Novgorod fashion, with Church dignitaries—yet still keeps much of the manners and customs, the domestic architecture, the head-dress, and even the dialect, of the mother-city.   On the other hand, when autocratic Moscow displaces its liberty-loving rival, popular government has clearly been found wanting in Russia.   If Novgorod had not fallen before Moscow, she would have submitted to Poland.

Ivan the Great conquers her, in the name of Russia and Orthodoxy, to save her from treachery and *Latinism*. And Moscow certainly substitutes a clearer political reality for the vague and fluctuating dominion, often no more than a commercial monopoly, of the Novgorod merchants.

Again, to understand this Russian expansion, the influence of rivers must not be overlooked. The history of Russia, like that of French America, is largely a river-history: her conquest is often a progress from end to end of a river-basin, from one river system to another. The slight elevation of the northern plains aids the inland navigator from Novgorod to Ural, from Ural to Pacific.

Once more, if the Ural were not in some places, despite length and breadth, so insignificant a range, the Novgorod connexion with Asia might be cited as another disproof of the fallacy that mountain chains form an absolute barrier between states and races.

Lastly, the empire of Novgorod is largely commercial; her discoveries and conquests are often the victories of a remarkable trade-expansion. The mercantile side of history has often been treated with contempt. But what form of man's energy has done more to bring about the discovery of the earth, to " clear the mind of cant," to break down the obstacles of ignorance, fear and prejudice which once hemmed in mankind and separated lands and races?

III. THE FOREIGN RELATIONS OF NOVGOROD.

THE relations of Novgorod with its neighbours, its friends, and its enemies, form the last section of our subject.

I. And first as to the chief RUSSIAN STATES.

(*a*) NOVGOROD AND KIEV.

With Kiev, the so-called " Mother of Russian cities,"[58] the acknowledged head alike in politics and religion, during all the early centuries (*c.* 880–1169), the relations of Novgorod are naturally long and intimate. During most of this time the Grand Prince of Kiev nominates the Princes, and sometimes the *Posadniks*, of Novgorod, subject to the popular approval. And the Metropolitan of Kiev, with the same limitations, ratifies the episcopal elections.

Oleg, as Prince at Kiev, and chief of the Varangians in Russia, is said to have imposed a regular yearly tribute on Novgorod, about 881. His successor, Olga, " wisest of all persons," the pioneer of Christianity among the *Rus*, visits the city, from Kiev, in the next

century, and establishes " depots for commerce," and " tolls and
dues " on some of its waterways. (c. 947–950?). Olga's son, the
Great Vladimir, becomes Prince of Novgorod in 970, before he
reigns in Kiev.[59]

Through much of the eleventh and twelfth centuries, the Novgorod
Chronicle records events at Kiev (especially the succession of Kiev
Princes and Metropolitans, or the embassies of Novgorod representatives) as matters affecting the metropolis of Russia, and
interesting to all Russians.[60]   The very name of *Rus* is long used to
designate the Kiev region.[61]

Yet the downfall of Kiev in 1169, when the Russia of the Forests
humbles the Russia of the Steppes,[62] is unnoticed in the Novgorod
Annals.   Even the final calamity, the Mongol storm of 1240, is only
mentioned indirectly.   On the other hand, the lesser disasters of
1203 and 1235, when heathen Kumans or Polovtsi, aided by traitor
Russians, waste the city, are properly bemoaned by the Novgorod
historian.[63]

(b) NOVGOROD AND MOSCOW.

The intercourse of Novgorod with Kiev begins with the beginnings
of Russian history, and is only important in the pre-Tartar period,
the period of Kievian greatness.   But with Moscow the Northern
Republic does not much concern itself before the fourteenth century, when the *White Stone City* claims the headship of the Russian
principalities.   It is in 1238, when Russian allies are vainly struggling
to save Ryazan from the Mongols, and " the men of Moscow ran
away," that we have the earliest notice of " Mother Moskva " in
the Novgorod Chronicle.   The fall of Moscow itself, a few weeks
later, before the " lawless Ishmaelites " of Batu, is next recorded—
but here, as in 1293, Moscow is merely named, in passing, as one
of the less important victims—and after this we hear little of Muscovite interest from the Novgorod Annals for almost a century
(1238–1325).[64]

But at last, in 1325, we find the Archbishop of Novgorod visiting
Moscow " for confirmation by the Metropolitan."   For Ivan Kalita
had just induced the Russian primate to move his *Stol* from
Vladimir, and Moscow had definitely taken the place of Kiev as the
Canterbury or the Mainz of Russian Christianity.

In 1335, again, we find the Republic, despite " colonial " quarrels,
recognizing the *Knyaz* of Moscow—this same " John of the
Purse "—as Grand Prince, the secular head of the Russian people.

Ivan visits Novgorod and " has a friendly talk "; Novgorod notables go to be honoured at Moscow.[65]

When the Moscow sovereign or Metropolitan visits the Tartar Court on any special occasion (as in 1336), or when anything uncommon happens at Moscow—such as the fire of 1337, or the death of the Grand Prince in 1340—it is duly recorded at Novgorod.[66] Still more, when (as in 1332) the Muscovite begins to aggress upon Novgorod; and most of all (as in 1337) when history records the discomfiture of the aggressor, " regardless of the kissing of the Cross," who, by the " power of the Cross," is " brought to shame."[67] In 1346 we first hear of the enthronement of the Moscow Grand Prince in Novgorod, as its Russian suzerain—though the Khan of the Golden Horde is still " Tsar," supreme even over Semeon the Proud, who after enthronement in Novgorod goes to " the *Low Country* on the Tsar's business." Yet Novgorod still struggles against Muscovite ascendency, appealing to the Tartar, on Semeon's death, to give the Grand Princedom to Vladimir-Suzdal once more (1353); and though the intrigue is now unsuccessful, it momentarily succeeds a few years later (1360).[68]

But in 1366 the Muscovite—now the famous Dmitri of the Don— is again Suzerain Prince, and quarrelling vigorously with the Republic about a Volga raid of Novgorod adventurers who had plundered Moscow merchants. Peace is made in 1367; the lieutenant of Dmitri is installed in Novgorod; and Novgorod helps Moscow against the hated Tver (1375), and accepts her decision in a dispute about the Metropolitan chair (1376).

On the other hand, Dmitri Donskoi confirms all the old rights of Novgorod in the year of his Tartar triumph at Kulikovo " in a clean field beyond the Don, on the birthday of the Mother of God," when, " preserved by God, he fought . . . for the Orthodox Faith, and for all the Russian land " (Sat., Sept. 8, 1380).

As the Tartar flood subsides, Moscow presses on Novgorod afresh, and in 1386 the Republic pays Dmitri a heavy fine (8,000 roubles) " for the guilt of the Volga men."[69] Towards the close of the fourteenth century we find Novgorod (in 1391) again struggling to free itself, if not from the political suzerainty, at least from the ecclesiastical jurisdiction, of Moscow. But before the end of 1393 (and this is prophetic) Novgorod yields, and concludes peace " on the old terms."[70]

More serious trouble follows from the reiterated Moscow aggressions in the colonial field, as in the Northern Dvina basin (1397

1401, etc.). Diplomacy effecting nothing, the Republic makes vigorous reprisals, usually (till the fatal age of Ivan the Great) with fair success.[71]

II. NOVGOROD AND THE SCANDINAVIANS.

The history of Novgorod and of Russia begins with the Scandinavian settlement which civilized, and in the higher sense created, both. And during the earlier centuries the Scandinavian connexion is naturally close (c. 862–1060).

Novgorod is often mentioned in early Scandinavian records as *Holmgarth*—" probably because it stood on a holm," or low flat river-bank, near where the Volkhov issues from Lake Ilmen.[72]

According to *Nestor*, Rurik settles first in Novgorod, when he enters Russia to rule the tribes that had invited the *Rus*. " And the Russian Land, Novgorod, was called (i.e. called *Rus*) after these Varangians; they (i.e. the *Rus*) are the Novgorodians of Varangian descent; previously the Novgorodians were Slavs."[73]

The mastery of the *Rus* over the Slavs begins, therefore, with their settlement in Novgorod; but the great northern town soon ceases to be their capital. After some twenty years, Rurik's successor, Oleg, takes Kiev and makes it his capital, and even the name of *Rus* now vanishes from Novgorod, and is usually, for centuries, connected with Kiev.

Yet, though abandoned by the sovereign clan of the *Rus*, Novgorod maintains its distinctive position. In reality it is the chief rival, and in commerce ultimately the superior, of Kiev among the early Russian states (880–1220). In Novgorod the Scandinavian element is stronger even than in Kiev—so strong indeed that *Nestor* considers it a Varangian town.[74] Elsewhere we hear of the Varangian Church, of the Guildhall of the Gothlanders in twelfth-century Novgorod, and of other matters which prove the early prominence of Scandinavians, and especially of Swedes, in Novgorod traffic. But in the later Middle Ages the Scandinavians gradually give way to the Germans, and the Hansa comes to control Novgorod trade.

From the eleventh century we find less evidence of Scandinavian intercourse, though Scandinavian blood and spirit continue to work at Novgorod.

And when we next hear of Scandinavian influence, as in 1142, it is purely hostile.[75] Towards the close of the Crusading Age comes the decisive struggle of 1240, when, " through the power of St. Sophia and the prayers of the Mother of God," *Svei* and Northmen are routed by that prince of Novgorod, who, from this day, is known as " Alexander of the Neva " (July 15, 1240).[76]

After this Novgorod runs no serious danger from Scandinavia for another century, although at times there are rumours of wars. Thus in 1300 the Swedish attempts on the Neva are renewed: " The accursed came in strength, with . . . a special master from the great *Pap of Rim* (Pope of Rome), and they founded a town at the mouth of the Okhta, in the Neva, and strengthened it indescribably . . . calling it *Landskrona* (The Crown of the Land). But by the power of St. Sophia . . . that fortress came to nothing," being captured by the Novgorod men in 1301.[77]

In the early fourteenth century, perhaps the greatest period of Novgorod power, the Scandinavian states secure the friendship of the Republic, at the cost of former ambitions. Thus, while Denmark concludes a treaty in 1302, Sweden, in 1323, acquiesces in a Novgorod colony at the Neva estuary on Orekhov island, and signs an " everlasting peace," which is renewed in 1338.[78]

But in 1348 Sweden becomes threatening once more: " The *Sveiski* King Magnush " invites Novgorod to send its " philosophers" to a congress to decide between Roman and Greek Christianity. " If your faith is pronounced better, then I will adopt yours; if mine, you will adopt ours." Otherwise there must be war. Novgorod refers the royal proselytizer to Constantinople, and dispatches an embassy to " discuss grievances," but in vain. " He had no grievance," Magnus explained, " but Novgorod must embrace his faith." Fighting accordingly begins, but Novgorod holds its own well, gaining the victory in several encounters.[79]

The slight revivals of Swedish and Norwegian aggression in 1395-6, in 1411, and in 1445—in the Neva region, in Korelia, and in the Far North—meet with no remarkable success.[80]

And, indeed, the whole subject of Novgorod's dealings with the Scandinavian peoples, after the thirteenth century, has no special importance.

III. NOVGOROD AND THE MONGOL TARTARS.

The case stands very differently with the next of Novgorod's neighbours and enemies, the " Mongols whom we call Tartars."

Novgorod is the only Russian state, or city, of importance, which escapes full subjugation by the Mongols of the thirteenth century. And even Novgorod, saved from siege and sack behind her marshes, in a summer of providential wetness, becomes the vassal of the Tartars.

The great Asiatic irruption which alters the whole course of Russian history, and so sharply divides the life and polity of the *Rus*, before the age of Batu, from the life and polity of the same people, after that age (Novgorod is the only noteworthy exception) breaks upon all Eastern Europe with the force of sudden terror. Novgorod is no exception here. " In the same year (1224), for our sins, unknown tribes came. No one knows accurately who they are . . ., what their language is, or race, or faith, but they called them *Tatary* (Tartars) . . . God alone knows . . . and very wise men who understand books, but we do not. . . ." The battle of the Kalka (1224) is vividly described in the Novgorod Annals, and the dramatic departure of the victors, for a season. " We know not whence they came, nor where they hid themselves again. God knows whence he fetched them against us, for our sins."[81]

And when the Horde returns, after twelve years (1236), and these " accursed godless strangers," these " lawless Ishmaelites," swarm " like locusts " into the Russian land, " cutting down every one like grass," the annalist traces their advance with mournful fidelity to within sixty miles of Novgorod. Moscow and many another Russian town, greater than the Moscow of those days, sees its men and women, its priests and monks, yield " their souls to the Lord " in a " bitter and a wretched death," but before the Heaven-protected Novgorod the Mongols pause. God, and the apostolic Cathedral of the Holy Wisdom, and the prayers of the Orthodox archbishop, of the faithful princes, of the venerable monks, guard the city. At the cross of *Ignati*, 100 versts away, the invader turns back south-eastwards, weary and disgusted with the vast morasses and incessant rains which confront and impede him. For all this summer it " stood with " wet.[82]

But Novgorod, though saved for the moment, would soon have shared the fate of other Russian cities, if she had not averted the danger by prompt, ready, and undeviating submission. The princes and officials of the Republic now obey the " Tartar Tsar " in all things, visiting the Horde when summoned (as in 1247), doing homage, punctually paying tribute, admitting Mongol assessors and tax-gatherers (as in 1257). The orders of Batu brook no evasion or delay; and the hero, Alexander Nevsky, statesman no less than warrior, is specially prominent in his obedience.[83]

Thus in 1259, after Lithuania had been devastated,[84] when " the accursed raw-eating Tartars came, taking tribute for the accursed," the Republic, we have seen, bows to the statesmanship of its leader. Novgorod rages and trembles; the greater men " bid the lesser be counted for tribute "; the citizens gather in force—" they will lay their heads by St. Sophia "—but the city submits at last, without a blow.[85]

In 1315, after seventy years of peaceful, if hateful, vassalage, Novgorod is forced into momentary conflict with the Mongols, through the treacherous ambition of the rival Russian state of Tver. The Republic suffers a serious defeat, but repulses an attempt upon the city (1316). In the retreat the enemy lose their way among the lakes and swamps that protected Novgorod, and nearly perish of hunger, eating their horses and leather shields. Finally, an appeal to the Khan of the Golden Horde ends the trouble. In 1327 " a mighty Tartar host took Tver . . . and wasted all the *Rus* land, Novgorod alone being spared "—on payment of a round sum.[86]

As we have seen, the first victories of Moscow, under Dmitri Donskoi, over the Tartars, are exultantly recorded at Novgorod (1380). Nor is the Mongol recovery under Tokhtamysh forgotten, when Moscow is burned, and the hero Dmitri flies before the " godless Tartars " (1382, etc.). And finally Novgorod catches a glimpse of the strange, enigmatic figure of Lame Timur, that champion of Islam, who by his overthrow of the Golden Horde prepares the way for the liberation of Russia and the expansion of Slavonic Christendom, just as by his defeat of the Ottomans he gives a last opportunity to Christian Constantinople. Needless to say, no perception of the real benefits of the conqueror's levelling work is apparent in the Chronicle of the Republic. There is merely an account of the triumph of Tamerlane over the Lithuanians (1398–9) arising out of his earlier triumph over the Golden Horde.[87]

IV. NOVGOROD AND THE LITHUANIANS.

The Lithuanians, the last important pagan race of Europe, the " godless *Litva* " of the Novgorod annals, had something to do with the great Russian city of the North from early times,[88] but it is only after the Mongol conquest that they vitally concern Novgorod in particular, or Russia in general.

In 1258 the Tartars " took all *Litva* land and killed the people "—
it reads like the end of the Lithuanian danger—but we know what
these great phrases mean to annalists of many countries. And here
it is more than usually misleading.

For in the fourteenth century the *Litva* first become a serious
political power under their Grand Prince Gedimin the Conqueror,
who in 1326 appears as mediating between Novgorod and the Germans, and in 1331 as trying to appoint the bishop, as he had appointed the prince, of Pskov, " without regard to Novgorod . . .
being carried away with presumption."[89]

Gedimin and his successors do, in fact, succeed in tearing away
from Russia all the west and south-west of *Rus*, with Kiev itself.
And thus is enacted the first chapter of that injustice which by
the Partition of Poland is gradually transformed into a fresh wrong
still more grievous, now weighing upon the old oppressor.

Against this new power, both before and after the conversion of
Yagielo and the Union with Poland (in 1386), Novgorod struggles
incessantly, and not ingloriously. Pskov submits to the *Litva* in
1342, but the *Elder Sister* of Pskov defies them. A fierce attack in
1346 follows upon some plain language from Novgorod to Gedimin's
successor—" Your *Posadnik*," complains Olgierd, " has barked at
me; he called me a hound." It was a dangerous dog to bark at—
for Olgierd brings Lithuanian power to its zenith, penetrating (as
in 1370) almost to Moscow, and for a time bringing back the Metropolitan of the Russian Church from Moscow to Kiev, now " in
Litva" (1376).[90] The abusive *Posadnik* is executed by his own
fellow citizens at a *Veche*—(the Novgorod democracy treats its servants rather like Carthage)—" for it is owing to you that our lands
have been seized.[91]

The death of Olgierd in 1377, and the consequent domestic
troubles, are a real relief to the Russia now pressed so hard between
Tartars, Lithuanians, and *Nemtsy*.   And the union of Poland and
Lithuania in 1386 does not immediately increase the danger. For
the federated state, though threatening the conquest of more and
more Russian land, is at first chiefly occupied with the Tartars and
the Teutonic Order—as in 1399, when Vitovt disastrously defies
Timur, or in 1410, when Yagielo and Vitovt crush the German
Knights at Tannenberg.

With Vitovt, the last great *Litva* conqueror (1392–1430), ends the
brief hope that Lithuanian conversion might profit the Eastern

Church. " For Prince Vitovt," the Novgorod Annalist bemoans in 1399, "had previously been a Christian . . . but he renounced the Orthodox Faith and adopted the Polish, and perverted the holy churches to service hateful to God. He thought," continues the Chronicler, " that he would conquer . . . the *Rus* land and Novgorod, but he thought not of the Lord's saying, A thousand shall flee at the rebuke of one." After his ill-starred conflict with Timur, he concludes peace with Novgorod " on the old terms " (1400).

Yet in the fifteenth century Lithuanian aggressions are again alarming. But for their preoccupation with the *Nemtsy*, the *Litva* might have attempted the conquest of all Russia. In 1404 Vitovt gains Smolensk; and in 1415 " by the sufferance of God," he reorganizes the Church in Little Russia, under a Latin Metropolitan. Again, in 1444, Vitovt's successor, Casimir, calls upon Novgorod to submit. The Republic " did not fall in with this," but the famine of 1445 aided his efforts; in their distress some of the Novgorod folk " fled to *Litva*," or " passed over to *Latinism*." More and more this is the danger at the end of the Middle Ages—leading to the conclusion, when Moscow destroys the Republic to keep it from " lapsing into *Latinism*."[92]

V. NOVGOROD AND THE GERMANS.

The relations of Novgorod with the *Nemtsy* are among the latest in historical order, on the political side—though of respectable antiquity on the mercantile. There is no clear reference in the *Chronicle* to the Teutons of the Continent, as opposed to the Scandinavians, before the time of the Third Crusade (1188). And, in the next century, the stirring events of 1201 and the years following—when the *Knights of the Order of Christ*, better known as the *Brethren* or *Bearers of the Sword*, are called in as temporal helpers by Bishop Albert of Riga; when historic Riga is thus founded; and when the Riga Gulf lands and the country of the old heathen Prussians are conquered by these German Crusaders and by their colleagues of the *Teutonic Order* or *Order of St. Mary*—all pass unnoticed in the *Novgorodskaya Lyetopis*.

But in 1231 the Novgorod Annals notice how " *Nemtsy* from beyond sea " succour the city with corn and flour, after a terrible famine, when " already near its end." And in 1237 the union of the two German Orders, under the *Teutonic* title, is apparently

recorded as a piece of good news. " In this year the *Nemtsy* came
. . . from beyond sea to Riga, and all united here . . . the men of
Pleskov sent aid . . . and they went against the godless *Litva* . . ."

But soon the *Nemtsy* appear among the most dreaded foes of
Novgorod and Russia. In 1242 the Swedish victory of Alexander
Nevsky is followed by Alexander's revenge upon the German Order
on the ice of Lake Chudskoe—" lest they should boast, saying, we
will humble the Slovan race under us—for is not Pskov taken, and
are not its chiefs in prison? " (April 5, 1242).

Much lost ground is thus recovered, and Novgorod is saved from
German dominion, in politics if not in trade. But it is a salvation
which has to be worked out again and again in the next two centuries. Thus in 1268 (after an agreement with the " bishops and
godly nobles " of the Teutonic Order, in which these godly men, in
the Russian view, purposed only deceit) the men of Novgorod fight
a desperate drawn battle with " iron troops " of *Nemtsy* on the
Kegola river, massed at one point in a " great wedge like a forest
to look at. . . . It was as if the whole nation of *Nemtsy* had come
together."[93]

Almost every decade of later Novgorod history gives us some
notice of conflict, negotiation, treaty, or commerce with the *Nemtsy*,
mainly represented by the Teutonic Order and the Hanseatic
League.[94] But though lands and towns near or within the Novgorod
frontiers are in German occupation throughout this period
(*c.* 1200–1450) or great part of it; though the whole Baltic coast, from
Danzig to the Gulf of Finland, is at one time held by the Order;
and though such near neighbours as Pskov fall at intervals into
the German grasp—yet the German peril is kept at arm's length,
and Novgorod is never beleaguered (far less taken) by the
Knights, even if her trade passes in great measure under Hansa
control.

And from the German fear Novgorod is finally delivered by the
union of Poland and Lithuania, and the triumph of the new Slav
power over the Teutonic Order. The Novgorod Annals, which so
constantly neglect decisive events of neighbouring history, do not
forget the battle of Tannenberg, which marks the ebbing of the
German *Drang nach Osten*, so active and of such consequence since
the twelfth century—first apparent in the tenth.

" This year (1410) on July 15th, King Yagailo and Prince Vitovt
fought with the Prussian *Nemtsy*, in Prussia . . . and killed the

Master and the Marshal and the Commanders, and routed the whole *Nemtsy* army."[95]

Thus begins a Slavonic Revival which, under Polish or Russian leadership, lasts till the nineteenth century; and a Germanic depression which continues till the rise of Brandenburg-Prussia under the Great Elector.

NOTES TO THE INTRODUCTION

(¹) The Novgorod empire has two chief parts: (1) the homeland of Novgorod settlement, including various tributary states, e.g. Ladoga; (2) the colonial and trade-dominion. This homeland had five traditional sub-divisions (the " Pyatini," or " Fifths "): I. *Vodskaya*, in the North; II. *Shelonskaya*, in the West; III. *Derevskaya*, in the South; IV. *Obonezhskaya*, in the North-East; V. *Byezhetskaya*, in the East. A similar five-fold division is often assumed in (2)—the " Colonial Empire ": I. The *Trans-Volok* or *Zavoloche*, including the lands between the White Lake (*Beloe Ozero*) and the Mezen, and comprising the Northern Dvina country; II. *Ter, Tri* or *Tre*, including Russian Lapland and extensive regions north of Lake Onega (e.g. *Pomoria*); III. *Permia*, the Upper Kama basin; IV. *Pechora*; V. *Yugra*.

(²) " Mais est la ville fermée de meschans murs, fais de cloyes et terre, combien que les tours sont de pierre," says de Lannoy (Louvain ed., 1878, p. 33).

(³) " . . . La grant Noegarde merveilleusement grant ville. . . ." *Oeuvres de Ghill. de Lannoy*, edited by Ch. Potvin and J. C. Houzeau, Louvain, 1878, p. 32. Lannoy's whole description of Novgorod (pp. 32–5 of this edition) is of capital importance.

(⁴) An excellent general account of Old Novgorod is in Bestuzhev-Ryumin's *History of Russia*, St. Petersburg, 1872, vol. I, Ch. VI, Sections iii-v (German trans., Mitau, 1877, vol. I, pp. 230–74); see also Rambaud, *Histoire de Russie* (Paris, 1893), pp. 103–16.

(⁵) We know the Law of Novgorod principally through a late document, the *Letter of Justice* (*Sudnaya Gramota*) in the text of 1471 (see Rambaud, *Russie*, 1893, p. 111); but it rested on the same principles as the *Ruskaya Pravda* of Yaroslav the Lawgiver in the eleventh century. On the early history of Novgorod (to Yaroslav) see also the *Chronicle of " Nestor,"* ed. F. Miklosich, Vienna, 1860, chs. 30, 35, 38, 43, 46–7, 50–1, 53–4 (A.D. 947, 970, 977, 980, 997, 1014, 1018, 1021, 1024–36).

(⁶) See *Nov. Chron.*, 1125, 1136, 1138, 1141, 1154, 1157-8, 1160–1, 1270.

(⁷) See *Nov. Chron.*, 1240–63, and especially 1240, 1242, 1246, 1250, 1259, 1262–3.

(⁸) *Nov. Chron.* 1240–1.

(⁹) See especially *Nov. Chron.*, 1471, and pp. x, xxii, xxvii of this Introduction.

(¹⁰) See *Nov. Chron.*, under the years mentioned, 1134, 1146, 1167, 1209, etc.

(¹¹) *Nov. Chron.*, 1209.

(¹²) See *Nov. Chron.*, 1135 (arbitration), 1214, 1215, 1264 (military and political leadership).

(¹³) *Nov. Chron.*, 1218–19.

(¹⁴) See the *Chronicle of " Nestor,"* chs. 54, 56, 57 (1034, 1045, 1052); also *Nov. Chron.*, 1130, 1156, 1163, etc. (on later bishops).

(¹⁵) See *Nov. Chron.*, 1210, 1215–16, 1218, 1259.

(¹⁶) See *Nov. Chron.*, 1218, 1220.

(¹⁷) E.g., *Nov. Chron.*, 1153, 1180.

(¹⁸) *Nov. Chron.*, 1181, 1192, 1209, 1210, 1255.

(¹⁹) *Nov. Chron.*, 1211, 1219, 1220.

(²⁰) E.g., *Nov. Chron.*, 1153, 1195–6, 1310.

(²¹) E.g., *Nov. Chron.*, 1138, 1160.

(²²) E.g., *Nov. Chron.*, 1263, 1308, 1330, 1388, 1414.

(²³) See E. Worms, *Histoire commerciale de la Ligue Hanséatique* (Paris, 1864), pp. 16, 81–2.

(²⁴) " Torgovaya Storona," see *Nov. Chron.*, 1134, 1345, 1385, 1387, 1392, 1418.

(²⁵) See Worms, *Ligue Hans.*, pp. 196-7; also V. Thomsen, *Origin of the Ancient Russ*, Oxford, 1877, pp. 126.

(²⁶) Worms, *Ligue Hans.*, pp. 82-3.

(²⁷) Worms, *Ligue Hans.*, 83–4, 190–5.

(²⁸) See *Nov. Chron.*, 1137, 1141–2, 1156, 1195; also 1157, 1178, 1192.

(²⁹) *Nov. Chron.*, 1209, 1215–17, 1234, 1299; see also 1203, 1207 (foreign merchants at Kiev), 1225.

(³⁰) *Nov. Chron.*, 1317, 1332, 1337, 1363–4, 1366–7.

(³¹) *Nov. Chron.*, 1410, 1420; also 1437, 1445, 1446.

(³²) E.g., *Nov. Chron.*, 1209, 1214, 1218.

(33) E.g., *Nov. Chron.*, 1125, 1136, 1138, 1141, 1154, 1270.

(34) E.g., *Nov. Chron.*, 1134, 1146, 1156, 1161, 1167, 1171-2 1175, 1189, 1205, 1209, 1218, 1219, 1230.

(35) E.g., *Nov. Chron.*, 1228, 1299, 1342, 1375, 1385, 1388, 1415, 1421, 1437.

(36) E.g., *Nov. Chron.*, 1291, 1316, 1340, 1346.

(37) See *Nov. Chron.*, 1218, 1228, 1270, 1299, 1342 (places of meeting, St. Sophia or Yaroslav's Court); 1342 (rival *Veches* at both places, ending with an appeal to arms and the mediation of the Archbishop—see also 1384); 1215, 1218, 1230, 1345 (*Veches* convoked or led by the *Knyaz* or *Posadnik*); 1214 (*Veche* convoked by the *Knyaz*, but in vain: the Democracy then calls its own *Veche*).

(38) See above, note (35); and Rambaud, *Russie*, p. 114 (Paris, 1893).

(39) See the *Chronicle of Nikon* (*Russkaya Lyetopis po Nikonovu Spisku*), Imperial Academy, St. Petersburg, 1767, vol. I, p. 132 (A.D. 1032). These Iron Gates, not to be confused with the famous Iron Gates of Derbent in the Caucasus, perhaps lay in the Shchugor valley, in about 64° N. Lat., near Mt. Toll Pos Is, the highest summit of the Urals. But Spruner-Menke, *Hand-Atlas* (1880), map 67, *Russland 966-1114*, places them in the Sysola valley, towards the easternmost part of the Northern Dvina basin.

(40) See the *Chronicle of Novgorod*, A.D. 1079. The *Za-Volochye, Trans-Volok*, or *Country beyond the Portage*, includes all the Northern Dvina basin.

(41) See the *Pervonachalnaya Lyetopis* or *Fundamental Chronicle*, otherwise the *Chronicle of Nestor* (*Chronica Nestoris textum Russo-Slovenicum*), ed. Fr. Miklosich (Vienna, 1860), ch. 81, p. 160.

(42) See *Nov. Chron.*, 1169, 1187, 1193, 1194; the *Chronicle of Nikon* (*Russk. Lyet. p. Nikon. Spisk.*), A.D. 1193-4, vol. II, pp. 259-260; and the *Sophia Chronicle* (*Sophiiskaya Lyetopis*) in the *Complete Collection of Russian Chronicles* (*Polnoe Sobranie Russkikh Lyetopisei*), issued by the Russian Archæographical Commission, vol. V, pp. 1691-70.

(43) See Nicholas Karamzin, *History of the Russian Empire* (*Istoriya Gosudarstva Rossiiskago*), vol. IV, p. 59, in Einerling's ed. (St. Petersburg, 1842); *Knyaz* Yaroslav is hereby debarred from possessing any

villages in the domains of Novgorod, even to Zavoloche, Kola, Perm, Pechora, or Yugra.

(⁴⁴) *Nov. Chron.*, 1323, 1329.

(⁴⁵) *Nov. Chron.*, 1332. Ivan Kalita was Grand Prince (*Veliki Knyaz*) of Moscow, 1328–40.

(⁴⁶) *Nov. Chron.*, 1445.

(⁴⁷) On Ivan III's Siberian expeditions of 1465, 1483 and 1499, see the *Chronicle of Great Ustyug* (*Lyetopis Velik. Ustyuzhskaya*), pp. 35–36, 41–42, 44–45, ed. A. K. Trapeznikov (Moscow, 1888); the *Chronicle of Archangel* (*Arkhangelogorodsk. Lyetopis*), Moscow, 1781, pp. 141, 1601–61; Oksenov, *Political Relations of Moscow with Yugraland* (in Russian, 1891): and Karamzin, *History of Russia*, vol. VI, pp. 176-178, in Einerling's ed. (St. Petersburg, 1842).

(⁴⁸) *Nov. Chron.*, 1337, 1340, 1342, 1366, 1393. See *Early Voyages and Travels to Russia*, etc. (London, Hakluyt Society, 1886), vol. I, p. 23.

(⁴⁹) Before the Moscow Princes seized this country, they sent their falconers thither every year by agreement with Novgorod; see Karamzin, *History of Russia* (1842), vol. V, p. 93 and note 170.

(⁵⁰) See *Nov. Chron.*, 1397; Karamzin, *History of Russia*, vol. V, pp. 136–137 (ed. 1842).

(⁵¹) In 1398, the Republic appears to recover most of its Dvina territories, storming Ustyug and inflicting death and fines upon its enemies and the Moscow merchants in this region. Moscow, however, seems to retain great part of the Vologda valley, in spite of a promise in 1435 to relinquish this. In 1411, the Novgorod governor of the Dvina is ordered to guard against Norwegian raiders. Vyatka marauders and Novgorod outlaws burn Kholmogori in 1417, and capture several Novgorod notables; in 1419 return the Northmen or *Murmani*, ravaging far and wide in the Trans-Volok, and sacking the Michael Monastery on the site of the present city of Archangel. Lastly, in 1445, the Swedes attack the Dvina and are driven off. See the *Chronicle of Novgorod*, 1398, 1401, 1411, 1417, 1419, 1435, 1436, 1445.

(⁵²) See *Nov. Chron.*, 1471; Karamzin, *History of Russia* (ed. 1842), vol. V, pp. 201, 206, and notes 356, 367.

(⁵³) Sigismund von Herberstein, *Rerum Moscoviticarum Commentarii* (London, Hakluyt Society, 1851), vol. II, p. 46.

(⁵⁴) On St. Stephen of Perm, see also *Voskresenskaya Lyetopis* in the *Polnoe Sobranie Rusk. Lyet.*, vol. VII, pp. 69-70; the *Life of St. Stephen* in *Monuments of Ancient Russian Literature (Pamyatniki Star. Rusk. Lit.)*, vol. IV, p. 119; and Klyuchevsky, *Lives of the Saints as Historical Material (Zhitiya Svyatykh kak istoricheskii istochnik)*, p. 92, etc.

(⁵⁵) See Karamzin, *History of Russia* (ed. 1842), vol. V, pp. 64-66, 209-210, and notes 125, 126, 137, 232, 377, 378; *Early Travels in Russia* (London, Hakluyt Society, 1886), vol. II, p. 190; Klyuchevsky, *Lives of the Saints* (as above), pp. 198-203; Stroev, *Lists of Russian Hierarchs (Spiski Ierarkhov)*.

(⁵⁶) See Karamzin, *History of Russia*, vol. IV, p. 59, and notes 115-116 (1842); also *The Collection of Imperial Charters and Treatises (Sobranie Gosudarstvennykh Gramot i Dogovorov)*.

(⁵⁷) See *Antiquités Russes* (Copenhagen, 1850-2), vol. II, pp. 490-494.

(⁵⁸) A title which surely belongs of right to Novgorod.

(⁵⁹) See the *Chronicle of Nestor*, ed. Miklosich, chs. 18, 30, 35.

(⁶⁰) E.g., *Nov. Chron.*, 1113, 1118, 1129, 1134, 1145, 1149, 1154-6, 1233.

(⁶¹) E.g., *Nov. Chron.*, 1145, 1149. In the later Middle Ages we find this restriction less observed in Novgorod. See A.D., 1263.

(⁶²) See A. Rambaud, *Histoire de Russie*, p. 88 (1893).

(⁶³) *Nov. Chron.*, 1203, 1235.

(⁶⁴) See *Nov. Chron.*, 1238, 1283, 1293, 1314.

(⁶⁵) See *Nov. Chron.*, 1325-6, 1332, 1335.

(⁶⁶) See *Nov. Chron.*, 1336-7, 1339, 1340, 1342-3, 1353, 1389, 1392, 1406, 1412, 1437, 1441-2, 1446.

(⁶⁷) *Nov. Chron.*, 1332, 1337.

(⁶⁸) See *Nov. Chron.*, 1346, 1348, 1353, 1360.

(⁶⁹) See *Nov. Chron.*, 1366-7, 1375-6, 1380, 1382, 1386, 1445.

(⁷⁰) See *Nov. Chron.*, 1383, 1388, 1391, 1393, 1395-6, 1401, 1411, 1415, 1437.

(71) *Nov. Chron.*, 1397–8, 1401, 1411, 1435, 1437 (Novgorod yields to fresh tax demands), 1441.

(72) See Vilhelm Thomsen, *Origin of the Ancient Russ*, Oxford, 1877, pp. 80–2, 125–6; *Olaf Tryggveson's Saga*, chs. 6, 7, 21; *St. Olaf's Saga*, ch. 191, etc.; *Harald Hardrada's Saga*, chs. 2, 15–17.

(73) *Chronicle of Nestor* (ed. Miklosich), ch. 15, p. 10.

(74) See *Nestor*, ch. 15, p. 10 (Miklosich); Thietmar, *Chronicon*, in Pertz, *Monumenta Germ. hist.*, *Script.*, vol. III, p. 871; V. Thomsen, *Origin of the Ancient Russ*, pp. 124, 126.

(75) See *Nov. Chron.*, 1142, 1164.

(76) *Nov. Chron.*, 1240. See also Rambaud, *Russie*, p. 134; Bestuzhev-Ryumin, *History of Russia*, St. Petersburg, 1872, vol. I, ch. VI, sections iii–iv (German trans., Mitau, 1877, p. 243),

(77) *Nov. Chron.*, 1256, 1292–3, 1295, 1300–2.

(78) *Nov. Chron.*, 1302, 1323, 1338.

(79) *Nov. Chron.*, 1348–50.

(80) See *Nov. Chron.*, 1395–6, 1411, 1445.

(81) *Nov. Chron.*, 1224.

(82) See *Nov. Chron.*, 1236 (conquest of Bolghar); 1238, etc. (conquest of Russia).

(83) *Nov. Chron.*, 1242, 1247, 1257, 1259, 1262–3.

(84) *Nov. Chron.*, 1258.

(85) *Nov. Chron.*, 1259; see also 1293.

(86) *Nov. Chron.*, 1315–16, 1319, 1322, 1325–7.

(87) *Nov. Chron.*, 1380, 1382, 1398–9; see also 1408, 1445.

(88) See, e.g. *Nov. Chron.*, 1183, 1198, 1200, 1203, 1210, 1213, 1219, 1234, etc.

(89) See *Nov. Chron.*, 1258, 1263, 1266–7, 1285, 1323, 1326, 1331, 1335.

(90) Thus for a few years it is from a foreign and hostile land that the Russian primate sends his disregarded orders to Novgorod.

(91) See *Nov. Chron.*, 1342, 1346, 1370, 1376.

(⁹²) See *Nov. Chron.*, 1377, 1399, 1400, 1404, 1410, 1415, 1436 1440, 1444–5 [1471].

(⁹³) See *Nov. Chron.*, 1231, 1233, 1234, 1237, 1240–1, 1242, 1253, 1268.

(⁹⁴) See *Nov. Chron.*, refs. in last note, and also under the years, 1269, 1298, 1328, 1335, 1342–3, 1350, 1362–3, 1367–8, 1370–1, 1377, 1381, 1390–1, 1406–7, 1409–10, 1412, 1417, 1420, 1444–5.

(⁹⁵) *Nov. Chron.*, 1410.

AN ACCOUNT OF THE TEXT OF THE NOVGOROD CHRONI-CLE BY PROFESSOR A. A. SHAKHMATOV, ST. PETERS-BURG UNIVERSITY.

CHRONICLE-WRITING at Novgorod began very early, certainly by the eleventh century, for the chronicle of Nestor (the monk of Kiev), called *Povest vremennykh let* (*Annals of Contemporary Years*), which appeared in 1110, contains a number of items from the Novgorod Chronicle. Thus we read, in Nestor, that in 1063 the Volkhov flowed backwards for six days foreboding disaster, and four years later Novgorod was burned by the Prince Vseslav of Polovtsk. It is clear that this information could only have reached the Pechersk monastery in Kiev, where the *Annals of Contemporary Years* were composed, through the channel of a Novgorod chronicle. The latter was probably composed and kept in the Bishop's Palace or " Court," a fact to which the following data point: In 1136 and 1137, the entries were made by Kirik, one of the clergy of St. Sophia, well known in the history of early Russian literature, and the author of several works, including one of exceptional interest on chronology. Again, the entries in the Chronicle from the twelth to the fifteenth centuries largely relate to the *Vladyka* or Archbishop of Novgorod and the affairs of the See.

Several considerations, mostly founded on the text of the Novgorod Chronicle in the *Synodal*[1] and other transcripts, point to the fact that in 1167 the archiepiscopal chronicle was rearranged as an historical compilation on a larger scale. The foundation for this was formed by the incorporation in it of the text of the Kiev *Annals of Contemporary Years*, to which were added under their respective dates all the annual entries of events made in Novgorod. This rearrangement was probably made by order of Ilya (Elias), first *Archbishop* of Novgorod. In its original form this rearrangement of the archiepiscopal chronicle has not survived; but we can gain some idea of it, first, from the later historical compilations, which were no longer of local, but of general, Russian character and scope, and comprised the Novgorod Chronicle among their other component parts, and secondly, from the oldest existing transcript of the Novgorod Chronicle itself, viz. the *Synodal Transcript* here translated. The *Synodal Transcript* had, as its foundation, an historical compilation made by a priest of the Novgorod Church of St. James, one Herman Voyata. The compiler speaks of himself in the entry for A.D. 1144, saying that in that year he was appointed priest;

[1] So-called because in the possession of the Synodal Library at Moscow.

under the year 1188 we read of the death of Herman Voyata, forty-five years priest of St. James.[1] Herman Voyata prepared for his church a copy of the compilation of Archbishop Elias, which was, however, very much abbreviated up to the beginning of the twelfth century; in this copy remarkable items of news were sometimes omitted, e.g. the consecration of St. Sophia in 1050, and the misadventures of Bishop Luka in 1055 and 1058.

The entry concerning the death of Herman Voyata suggests that his compilation was continued at St. James's after his death. This conclusion is strengthened by the mention of the sacristan Timothy as transcriber, or compiler, of the chronicle (in 1230), and a happy conjecture has identified this person with Timothy, sacristan of the Church of St. James, who in 1262 transcribed an existing liturgical work.   But the chronicle of St. James was probably not carried on independently: it was most likely a compilation of chronicles founded on the archiepiscopal chronicle, added to from time to time.

The archiepiscopal chronicle was carried on uninterruptedly, being as it were a continuation of the compilation of chronicles made in 1167.   A new rearrangement of the archiepiscopal chronicle, undertaken probably on the initiative of Archbishop Basil, a learned and enlightened man, took place c. 1330–5.   This rearrangement was founded on the compilation of chronicles made at the Church of St. James; possibly because a few years previously the compilation of chronicles made in the year 1167 had, at the demand of the Metropolitan, been dispatched to Vladimir (on the Klyazma). About the year 1310, the Metropolitan Peter planned a pan-Russian compilation of chronicles, in which the chronicle-writing of all Russia should be concentrated, and the local annals be brought together.   This plan is connected with the efforts of the Metropolitan to conserve the unity of the Russian metropolitan province, a unity threatened by serious danger, especially since the beginning of the fourteenth century, when the Metropolitan, abandoning Kiev, which had been devastated by the Tartars, migrated to Vladimir. For this plan, then, the local chronicles must be collected in Vladimir; hence the Novgorod archiepiscopal compilation of 1167 was transferred thither.   The Metropolitan's pan-Russian compilation of chronicles has only survived in a later rearrangement (of the fifteenth century), and, to a certain extent, in the so-called *Lavrentevski* (" Laurentian ") transcript of 1377, which borrowed from it

[1] See *Nov. Chron.*, 1144, 1188.

the part covering the period 1240–1305. The appearance in Novgorod of a copy of this pan-Russian compilation (or of certain parts of it) suggested the creation of a Novgorod compilation of chronicles. Its foundation, I repeat, was formed by the compilation of chronicles of the Church of St. James; it was amplified both by data from the Novgorod archiepiscopal chronicle, by annual entries from it, and also by loans from the pan-Russian compilation. Among these are the capture of Kiev by the sons of Oleg and the Polovtsi in 1203; the crusading capture of Constantinople in 1204; the fratricide of *Knyaz* Gleb of Ryazan in 1218; the battle on the river Kalka in 1224; the conquest of Suzdal by the Tartars in 1238.

The Novgorod compilation of chronicles of Archbishop Basil was brought down to the year 1329. This compilation has not come down to us in the original. But the Synodal transcript, which we possess, is an almost contemporary copy, made, as is believed, for the monastery of St. George, near Novgorod. This copy was amplified by entries under the years 1331–3, 1337, 1345 and 1352. It has not come down to us in its entirety, for it lacks the beginning (to A.D. 1016). Judging by the total number of sheets, 128 are missing. These probably contained the text of the *Annals of Contemporary Years* in a redaction similar to those which have survived (the *Ipatevskvi* and *Hlebnikovski* transcripts), for it is just this redaction of the *Annals of Contemporary Years* that was followed by the historical compilation of Archbishop Elias, which formed the foundation of the historical compilation of the Church of St. James.

The historical compilation of Archbishop Basil underwent fresh rearrangement about 1420–30. It was now considerably enlarged by annual entries made uninterruptedly at the Archbishop's Court. But for some reason that beginning of the compilation which was the result of the labours of Herman Voyata (who in his turn had abbreviated his model, viz., the compilation of Archbishop Elias) came to be considered unsatisfactory. No transcript of the *Annals of Contemporary Years* was to be found in Novgorod, but on the other hand, a transcript, incomplete it is true, of the still older *Kiev* historical compilation, the immediate predecessor of the *Annals of Contemporary Years,* was discovered. This incomplete work ends abruptly in 1074, midway in its account of the death of Theodosius, *igumen* or abbot of the Pechersk monastery at Kiev (the complete work probably went down to 1093); besides this the sheets recording events from 1016 to 1052 were lost. From the year 1075 onwards the composer of the new compilation, called the *Sophia Chronicle*, had to follow the compilation of Archbishop Basil. The *Sophia Chronicle* was probably composed at the instance of Archbishop Euthymus, by one of the clergy of St. Sophia in Novgorod called Matvei (Matthew) Mikhailov Kusov.

In the middle of the fifteenth century, a fresh rearrangement of the pan-Russian historical compilation was made at Moscow, probably at the Court of the Metropolitan. Its basis was the pan-Russian compilation of 1423, which largely repeated that of the Metropolitan Peter, and to it were added the *Kiev Chronicle* and the *Sophia Chronicle* of Novgorod. This Moscow compilation has not survived, but it gave rise to existing reproductions (e.g., the so-called *First Sophia Chronicle* and *Fourth Novgorod Chronicle*, published in vols. IV-VI of the *Complete Collection of Russian Chronicles*). In the fifties of the fifteenth century a fresh rearrangement of the *Sophia Chronicle* was made at Novgorod. The text of this compilation follows both the fourteenth-century compilation of Archbishop Basil, and the Moscow compilation of the mid fifteenth century. This rearrangement of the *Sophia Chronicle*, which in all its manuscripts reaches down to 1443, has been preserved in (*a*) the so-called *Commission Transcript* (belonging to the Imperial Archæographical Commission); (*b*) the *Academy Transcript* (belonging to the Imperial Academy of Sciences); and the *Tolstoi Transcript* (belonging to the Imperial Public Library). From their resemblance to Archbishop Basil's compilation there is a close connexion between these MSS. and the *Synodal Transcript*. In editing the *Synodal Transcript* recourse can be had to the *Commission*, *Academy*, and *Tolstoi Transcripts* as auxiliary transcripts offering different readings. The last edition of the *Synodal Transcript* was issued by the Archæographical Commission (*The Novgorod Chronicle According to the Synodal Parchment Transcript*, St. Petersburg, 1888). The text of the *Commission Transcript* of the fifteenth century is, on pp. 1–82, 84–117, provided with different readings and additions from the *Academy* and *Tolstoi Transcripts*. On pages 83–4 (beginning with the words " *but you are carpenters* ") and in various passages between page 84 and page 117, we have the text of the *Synodal Transcript*, while the readings of the *Commission*, *Academy* and *Tolstoi Transcripts* are given as variants.

In the Russian edition of 1888, the difference between the source is marked by printing the *Synodal* text from the beginning of the line, and the *Commission* text at a distance of four letters from the

beginning of the line.   From page 117 (A.D. 1075) down to page 329
(with some slight intervals) the *Synodal* text appears again, while the
Commission, Academy and *Tolstoi* variants are given in footnotes.
On pages 330–428 (A.D. 1333–1446) we have the *Commission* text
afresh till 1443 (p. 423) provided with *Academy* and *Tolstoi* variants
(at 1441 the *Academy* breaks off).   The addenda to this edition
(pp. 431–90) contain a series of supplementary articles from the
Commission Transcript which are not strictly part of the chronicle
(lists of princes, bishops, *posadniks*, and also juridical matter).

A. A. SHAKHMATOV.

For Bibliographical Note see end of this volume.

ALPHABETICAL LIST OF TITLES, TECHNICAL TERMS,
ETC., WHICH IN THE TEXT HAVE BEEN RETAINED IN
THE ORIGINAL RUSSIAN, TOGETHER WITH THE ENGLISH
EQUIVALENTS, AND THE PAGES WHERE THEY FIRST
OCCUR.

Artug = a Norwegian copper coin (p. 181).
Baskak = Tartar official, tax-collector (p. 103).
Berkovets = 10 *puds*, i.e., 400 Russian lbs. (p. 77.)
Boyar = noble (p. 10).
Denga = a small coin, 216 of which went to the rouble (p. 204).
Detinets-gorod = citadel (p. 7). •
Druzhina = bodyguard (p. 1).
Gorodishche = citadel, fort (p. 7).
Grivna = pound (p. 2; cf. appendix).
Igumen = abbot (p. 5).
Igumena = abbess (p. 26).
Kad, Kadka = barrel (a measure, same as *osminka*, q.v., p. 23).
Knyaginya = Princess (p. 20).
Knyaz = Prince (p. 1).
Knyaz, Veliki = Grand Prince (p. 67).
Korobya = basket (a measure, p. 202).
Kuna = money, cf. appendix (p. 23).
Kurgan = fort (p. 65).
Lyakh = Pole (p. 1).
Lyakhi = Poles, Poland (p. 1).
Nemtsy = Foreigners of Teutonic race (p. 44).
Nogata, cf. appendix (p. 10).
Osminka = 11 pecks (p. 11).
Pochka = a small weight, about one-fifth dram (p. 204).
Poprishche = *verst*, q.v. (p. 215).

Posadnik = burgomaster (p. 9).
Pud = about 36 lbs. (p. 27).
Rezana, cf. appendix (p. 15).
Rouble = ¼ lb. of silver, a unit of money and of weight. (p. 128).
Sazhen = 1½ fathom (p. 128).
Schema = the strictest monastic order (p. 34).
Smerd = common person, common soldier (p. 2).
Sotski = commander of a hundred (*sto* = hundred, p. 10).
Starosta = elder (p. 2).
Svei = Swedes (p. 17).
Tamga = a tax levied by the Tartars; properly a seal on merchandise (see p. 95, n. 1).
Tiun = bailiff (p. 71).
Tsar = King, Emperor (p. 30).
Tsargrad = Constantinople (p. 20).
Tsaritsa = Queen, Empress (p. 95).
Tysyatski = commander of a thousand (p. 35).
Veche (pron. vyétché, with the stress on the first syllable) = council (p. 1).
Veliki Knyaz = Grand Prince (p. 41).
Verst = about two-thirds of a mile (p. 26).
Vladyka = Archbishop (p. 6).
Volok = portage (p. 6).
Voyevoda = general (p. 1).
Zverinets = enclosure for animals, park (p. 5).

ALPHABETICAL LIST OF TITLES, TECHNICAL TERMS,
ETC., WHICH IN THE TEXT HAVE BEEN TRANSLATED,
TOGETHER WITH THE RUSSIAN EQUIVALENTS AND
THE PAGES WHERE THEY FIRST OCCUR.

Adventurers = *molodtsy* (p. 111).
Army = *polk* (p. 51).
Bishop = *episkop* (p. 8).
Body-guard = *gridba* (p. 38).
Charter = *gramota* (p. 72).
Clan = *plemya* (p. 38).
Colony = *sloboda* (p. 169).
Council = *Veche* (p. 1). (Pronounced Vyé-tché).
Council-chamber = *gridnitsa* (p. 73).
Court = *dvor* (p. 1, 14, 62).
Courtier = *dvoryanin* (p. 50).
District = *volost* (p. 32).
Document = *gramota* (p. 104).
Fence = *tyn* (p. 82).
Fines = *vira dikaya* (p. 50).
Fortification = *gorod* (p. 51).
Fortified town = *gorod* (p. 8).
Fortress = *osek* (p. 52).
Fortress, prison = *ostrog* (p. 67).
Fosse = *greblya* (p. 118).
House = *dvor* (strictly speaking, the house with yard or court and fence and gates, p. 51).
Lieutenant = *namestnik* (p. 54).
Lithuanians = *Litva* (p. 32).

Lord = *gospodin* (p. 256).
Noble = *velmozha* (p. 90).
Palace = *polata* (p. 52).
Palace = *terem* (p. 130).
Patrimony = *otchina* (p. 132).
Picture (sacred) = *ikon* (p. 43).
Priest = *pop* (p. 36).
Province = *oblast* (p. 13).
Russia = *Rus* (p. 7).
Russian Land, the = *Russkaya Zemlya* (p. 5).
Serf = *kholop* (p. 65).
Serf = *smerd* (p. 11, 14).
Sire = *gospodin* (p. 142).
Sovereignty = *tsarstvo* (p. 90).
Steward = *stolnik* (p. 90).
Stockade = *ostrog* (p. 82).
Stockade = *gorod* (p. 66).
Throne = *stol* (p. 2).
Town = *gorod* (p. 3).
Town = *posad* (p. 79).
Tribe = *yazyk* (p. 64).
Tribune = *amvon* (p. 47).
Tribute = *vykhod* (p. 133).
Usher = *podvoiski* (p. 42).
Village = *pogost* (p. 86).
Wall = *val* (sc. of earth, p. 64).

THE CHRONICLE OF NOVGOROD
1016-1471

The Chronicle of Novgorod

A.D. 1016. A.M. 6524. [There was a fight at Lyubets, and Yaroslav won; and Svyatopolk fled to the *Lyakhi*.[1] And at that time Yaroslav was keeping many Varangians[2] in Novgorod, fearing war; and the Varangians began to commit violence against the wives of the townsmen. The men of Novgorod said: "We cannot look upon this violence," and they gathered by night, and fell upon and killed the Varangians in Poromon's Court; and that night *Knyaz*[3] Yaroslav was at Rakomo. And having heard this, *Knyaz* Yaroslav was wroth with the townsfolk, and gathered a thousand soldiers in Slavno,[4] and by craft falling on those who had killed the Varangians, he killed them; and others fled out of the town. And the same night Yaroslav's sister, Peredslava, sent word to him from Kiev, saying: "Thy father is dead, and thy brethren slain." And having heard this, Yaroslav the next day gathered a number of the men of Novgorod, and held a *Veche*[5] in the open air, and said to them: "My beloved and honourable *Druzhina*,[6] whom yesterday in my madness I slew, I cannot now buy back even with gold." And thus he said to them: "Brethren! my father Volodimir is dead, and Svyatopolk is *Knyaz* in Kiev; I want to go against him; come with me and help me." And the men of Novgorod said to him: "Yes, *Knyaz*, we will follow thee." And he gathered 4,000 soldiers: there were a thousand Varangians, and 3,000 of the men of Novgorod; and he went against him.

And Svyatopolk having heard this, gathered a countless number of soldiers, and went out against him to Lyubets and encamped there in the open country with a number of soldiers. And Yaroslav having come, halted on the bank of the Dnieper; and they stood there three months, not daring to come together (sc. in conflict). Svyatopolk's *Voyevoda*[7] by name Wolf's Tail,[8] riding along the river-bank,

[1] *Lyakhi* = the Poles, Poland.
[2] sc. Scandinavians.
[3] i.e. Prince. See Introduction, pp. ii-iv.
[4] A quarter of the town.
[5] The popular assembly. See Introduction, pp. ii, viii, ix.
[6] Bodyguard.
[7] General.
[8] *Volchii Khvost*.

B

began to reproach the men of Novgorod: " Wherefore have you come with that builder of wooden houses ?]¹

A.D. 1016. A.M. 6524.   " You are carpenters, and we shall make you build houses for us." And the Dnieper began to freeze. And one of Yaroslav's men was on friendly terms with Svyatopolk. And Yaroslav sent one of his attendants to him by night, and he spoke to him. And this is what he said to him: " What dost thou advise to be done now? There is but little mead brewed, and the *Druzhina* is large." And that man said to him: " Say thus to Yaroslav, if there is little mead, but a large *Druzhina*, then give it in the evening." And Yaroslav understood that he was advising him to fight at night; and that evening Yaroslav with his troops crossed to the other bank of the Dnieper, and they pushed the boats away from the bank, and prepared to make battle that night. And Yaroslav said to his *Druzhina*: " Put a mark on you, wind your heads in kerchiefs." And there was a terrible fight, and before dawn they conquered Svyatopolk, and Svyatopolk fled to the Pecheneg people.²

And Yaroslav went to Kiev, and took his seat on the throne³ of his father Volodimir. And he began to distribute pay to his troops: to the *starostas*⁴ ten *grivnas*⁵ each, to the *smerds*⁶ one *grivna* each, and to all the men of Novgorod ten each, and let them all go to their homes.

A.D. 1017. A.M. 6525.   Yaroslav went to Beresti⁷; and St. Sophia was founded at Kiev.

A.D. 1018. A.M. 6526.

A.D. 1019. A.M. 6527.

A.D. 1020. A.M. 6528.   A son Volodimir was born to Yaroslav.

A.D. 1021. A.M. 6529.   Yaroslav defeated Bryacheslav.

¹ The Synodal MS. of the Novgorod Chronicle begins with the words: " You are carpenters." The portion of the chronicle for the year 1016 here printed in brackets is from another MS. and is given here merely to make intelligible the remainder of the entry for this year.—Ed.
² A nomad people in S. Russia.
³ *Stol.*
⁴ Elders, captains.
⁵ Originally the equivalent of a pound of silver, it was at this time about ½ lb.; cf. Appendix.
⁶ Common soldiers (lit. " evil-smelling ").
⁷ Brest, in Poland, now called *Litevski*, or " Lithuanian."

A.D. 1022. A.M. 6530.

A.D. 1023. A.M. 6531.

A.D. 1024. A.M. 6532.

A.D. 1025. A.M. 6533.

A.D. 1026. A.M. 6534.

A.D. 1027. A.M. 6535.

A.D. 1028. A.M. 6536.   There appeared a sign in the sky like a serpent.

A.D. 1029. A.M. 6537.

A.D. 1030. A.M. 6538.

A.D. 1031. A.M. 6539.

A.D. 1032. A.M. 6540.

A.D. 1033. A.M. 6541.

A.D. 1034. A.M. 6542.

A.D. 1035. A.M. 6543.

A.D. 1036. A.M. 6544.

A.D. 1037. A.M. 6545.   Yaroslav founded the town[1] of Kiev, and the Church of St. Sophia.

A.D. 1038. A.M. 6546.

A.D. 1039. A.M. 6547.   The church of the Holy Mother of God was consecrated by Volodimir.

A.D. 1040. A.M. 6548.

A.D. 1041. A.M. 6549.

A.D. 1042. A.M. 6550.   Volodimir, the son of Yaroslav, went against the Yem[2] people with the men of Novgorod.

A.D. 1043. A.M. 6551.   Volodimir went against the Greeks.

A.D. 1044. A.M. 6552.   Two *Knyazes*, Yaropolk and Oleg, sons of Svyatoslav, were buried, and they christened their bones.

A.D. 1045. A.M. 6553.   St. Sophia was burnt down, on a Saturday, after the early morning service, in the third hour, on March 15.

[1] *Gorod*, sc. fortified town.
[2] A Finnish tribe.

The same year St. Sophia at Novgorod was founded by *Knyaz* Volodimir.

A.D. 1046. A.M. 6554.

A.D. 1047. A.M. 6555.

A.D. 1048. A.M. 6556.

A.D. 1049. A.M. 6557.

A.D. 1050. A.M. 6558. Svyatopolk was born.

A.D. 1051. A.M. 6559. Yaroslav appointed Larion the Russian to be Metropolitan.

A.D. 1052. A.M. 6560. Volodimir, son of Yaroslav, died at Novgorod, on October 4; and Izyaslav took his seat on the throne in Kiev.

A.D. 1053. A.M. 6561.

A.D. 1054. A.M. 6562. Yaroslav died.

A.D. 1055. A.M. 6563.

A.D. 1056. A.M. 6564.

A.D. 1057. A.M. 6565.

A.D. 1058. A.M. 6566.

A.D. 1059. A.M. 6567. They [Izyaslav, Svyatoslav and Vsevolod] released [*Knyaz*] Sudislav [their uncle] from prison [having sat there twenty-four years; and they made him take the oath and he became a monk].[1]

A.D. 1060. A.M. 6568. Igor, son of Yaroslav died.

A.D. 1061. A.M. 6569. The Polovets[2] people came on February 1 and defeated Vsevolod on the 2nd.

A.D. 1062. A.M. 6570.

A.D. 1063. A.M. 6571.

A.D. 1064. A.M. 6572.

A.D. 1065. A.M. 6573. Vseslav began to make war; and in the west there appeared a great star.

[1] Words in brackets supplied from another text.
[2] Usually known as *Polovtsy*, i.e. the Kumans, a nomad people of Southern Russia, not Slavs, who in the centuries preceding the Tartar invasion periodically ravaged the country round Kiev.

A.D. 1066. A.M. 6574. Vseslav came and took Novgorod, with the women and children; and he took down the bells from St. Sophia—Oh great was the distress at that time!— and he took down the church lustres.

A.D. 1067. A.M. 6575. They defeated Vseslav at Nemiza. The same year they captured him in *Russia* [*Rus.*][1]

A.D. 1068. A.M. 6576. The wrath of God came on us; the Polovets people came and conquered the Russian[2] Land. The same year the men of Kiev rescued[3] Vseslav from prison. The same year Svyatoslav defeated the Polovets people near Snovsk, and Izyaslav fled to the *Lyakhi*.

A.D. 1069. A.M. 6577. Izyaslav came from the *Lyakhi*, and Vseslav fled to Polotsk.

The same year, in the autumn, on October 23, the day of the Lord's brother, St. James, a Friday, at the sixth hour of the day, Vse . . . again came to Novgorod; and the men of Novgorod drew up their forces against them, near the *Zverinets*[4] on the Kzeml[5]; and God helped *Knyaz* Gleb with the men of Novgorod.

Oh! great was the slaughter among the Vod[6] people, and a countless number of them fell; but the *Knyaz* himself they let go for the sake of God; and the next day the honourable cross of Volodimir was found at St. Sophia's in Novgorod, Fedor[7] being then Bishop.

A.D. 1070. A.M. 6578. [A son] was born [to Vsevolod, and they called him] Rostislav; and the monastery church of St. Michael was founded at Kiev.

A.D. 1071. A.M. 6579.

A.D. 1072. A.M. 6580. Boris and Gleb[8] were transferred from the Lto [river] to Vyshegorod.

A.D. 1073. A.M. 6581. The Pechersk Church was founded by the *Igumen*[9] Feodos.[10] The same year Svyatoslav and Vsevolod drove Izyaslav away to the *Lyakhi*.

[1] Here the Kiev region. See Introduction, p. xvi.
[2] *Russkaya Zemlya*.
[3] *Vysyekosha*=(lit.) cut him out.
[4] An enclosure to keep wild animals (*zver*).
[5] Kzeml, or Gzen, a stream near Novgorod.
[6] A Finnish tribe.
[7] Theodore. A colloquial form of Feodor.
[8] sc. their remains.
[9] Abbot, Superior, Head of a Monastery, from ἡγούμενος.
[10] Theodosius.

A.D. 1074. A.M. 6582. Fedos, *Igumen* of Pechersk, died on May 3.

A.D. 1075. A.M. 6583.

A.D. 1076. A.M. 6584.

A.D. 1077. A.M. 6585. Fedor, *Vladyka*[1] of Novgorod, died.

A.D. 1078. A.M. 6586. Oleg fled to Tmutorokan, and brought back
the Polovets people, and defeated Vsevolod
on the Sozh [river].   The same year there was a fight at Chernigov,
and two *Knyazes*, Izyaslav and Boris, were killed.

A.D. 1079. A.M. 6587. They killed *Knyaz* Gleb beyond the *Volok*[2]
on May 30.   The same year the Polovets
people killed Roman.

A.D. 1080. A.M. 6588.

A.D. 1081. A.M. 6589.

A.D. 1082. A.M. 6590.

A.D. 1083. A.M. 6591.

A.D. 1084. A.M. 6592.

A.D. 1085. A.M. 6593.

A.D. 1086. A.M. 6594.

A.D. 1087. A.M. 6595.

A.D. 1088. A.M. 6596. The Church of St. Mikhail was consecrated.

A.D. 1089. A.M. 6597. The Pechersk Church was consecrated by
the Metropolitan Ioan.[3]
The same year (Vsevolod's daughter) died.

A.D. 1090. A.M. 6598. He fetched Yanek[3] the Eunuch Metropolitan. The same year the Church of Saint
Mikhail at Pereyaslavl was consecrated.

A.D. 1091. A.M. 6599. They transferred the *Igumen* Fedos[4] of Pechersk into the monastery from Pechera.[5] The
same year the Eunuch Metropolitan Ioan died.

[1] Archbishop—lit. ruler.

[2] *Volok*=Portage, the watershed between two river basins, across which
the boats are drawn; " beyond the *Volok*," *za volokom*, or *zavoloche*, is specially the *Dvinskaya Zemlya*, the land of the Dvina, the basin of the Northern
Dvina.   See Introduction, pp. ix, x, xi, etc.

[3] i.e. John.

[4] sc. the remains of.

[5] lit. the cave.

A.D. 1092. A.M. 6600. A panic came over the people of Polotsk,
so that it was impossible to walk in the
streets, because it was as if there was a quantity of soldiers and as
if one could see horses' hoofs; and if anyone went out of his house,
he would be suddenly and unaccountably killed.

A.D. 1093. A.M. 6601. Vsevolod died; and Svyatopolk took his
seat in Kiev. The same summer the
Polovets people defeated Svyatopolk and Mstislav at Trepol.

A.D. 1094. A.M. 6602.

A.D. 1095. A.M. 6603. Svyatopolk and Volodimir went against
David to Smolensk,[1] and gave Novgorod to
David. The same year locusts came to Russia on August 28.

A.D. 1096. A.M. 6604.

A.D. 1097. A.M. 6605. Vasilko was blinded. The same year, in the
winter, Mstislav with the men of Novgorod
defeated Oleg at the Kulatsk[2] during the great fast. The same
year in the spring, the other side[3] was burnt and two days later the
Detinets-gorod[4] was burnt down; and they killed the *Knyaz's*
servants.

A.D. 1098. A.M. 6606.

A.D. 1099. A.M. 6607.

A.D. 1100. A.M. 6608.

A.D. 1101. A.M. 6609. Vseslav, *Knyaz* of Polotsk, died.

A.D. 1102. A.M. 6610.

A.D. 1103. A.M. 6611. All the brethren *Knyazes* of the Russian
Land went against the Polovets people to the
Suten, and defeated them, and captured the belongings of their
Knyaz. The same year the Mordva[5] people defeated Yaroslav at
Murom. The same year *Knyaz* Mstislav founded the Church of
the Annunciation in the *Gorodishche*.[6]

A.D. 1104. A.M. 6612. Nikifor, Metropolitan of Russia, came.

---

[1] " Pitch(town)."
[2] sc. the river Kalaksha.
[3] sc. that part of Novgorod east of the river Volkhov.
[4] The citadel.
[5] A Finnish tribe.
[6] " Citadel," or " fort," on the outskirts of Novgorod, 2 versts away.

A.D. 1105. A.M. 6613. Lazor, Mina, and Amfilokhi were appointed Bishops. The same year they made war against Ladoga; and all the houses from the Stream, past Slavno,[1] up to Saint Ilya were burnt.

A.D. 1106. A.M. 6614. They defeated the Polovets people on the Dunai. The same year *Knyaz* Svyatosha, son of David at Chernigov, father-in-law of Vsevolod, was shorn.

A.D. 1107. A.M. 6615. The earth trembled on February 5.

A.D. 1108. A.M. 6616. Nikita, *Vladyka* of Novgorod, died on January 30; and in the spring they began to paint[2] St. Sophia, by the efforts of the holy *Vladyka*.

A.D. 1109. A.M. 6617. The water was high in the Dnieper, the Desna and the Pripet. And they finished the refectory in the Pechersk monastery. The same year a church was founded at Kiev by *Knyaz* Svyatopolk.

A.D. 1110. A.M. 6618. *Vladyka* Ioan came to Novgorod on December 20.

A.D. 1111. A.M. 6619. Svyatopolk, Volodimir and David and the whole Russian Land to a man went against the Polovets people and defeated them and took their children, and rebuilt the fortified towns of Surtov and Sharukan.

At the same time the Lower town[3] at Kiev was burnt, as well as Chernigov, Smolensk and Novgorod. The same year Ioan, Bishop of Chernigov, died. The same year Mstislav went against Ochela.[4]

A.D. 1112. A.M. 6620.

A.D. 1113. A.M. 6621. Yaroslav, son of Svyatopolk, went out against the Yatvyag people,[5] and having come back from the war he took [to wife] the daughter of Mstislav. In the same year Svyatopolk died, and Volodimir took his seat on the throne in Kiev. David Igorovits died this same year. In this same year Mstislav defeated the Chud[6] people at Bor. That same year was founded in Novgorod the Church of St. Nicholas. That

[1] A quarter of the town, sometimes called the Slavenski End.
[2] sc. to decorate with paintings or frescoes.
[3] *Podole.*
[4] In the Chud country.
[5] A race in W. Russia, closely allied to the Lithuanians.
[6] Finnish.

same year the whole of the outer town on this side[1] was burned down, from a fire at Luka's.

A.D. 1114. A.M. 6622. Svyatoslav died in Pereyaslavl. In the same year Feoktist was installed Bishop of Chernigov.

A.D. 1115. A.M. 6623. The brothers Volodimir, Oleg and David assembled in Vyshegorod, together with the whole Russian Land, and they consecrated the stone church on May 1, and on the 2nd, the 8th of the Induction [the remains of] Boris and Gleb were transferred. The same year there was a sign in the sun, as though it had perished, and in the autumn, on August 1, Oleg, son of Svyatoslav, died. In Novgorod all Mstislav's horses and those of his *Druzhina* died. The same year, on April 28, the foreign merchant, Voi, laid the foundation of a church to St. Theodore of Tyre.

A.D. 1116. A.M. 6624. Mstislav with the men of Novgorod went out against the Chud people and took *Medvezhya Golova*[2] on [the day of] the forty saints. That same year, Mstislav laid the foundations of a larger planned Novgorod (larger than the first). That same year, Paul, *Posadnik*[3] of Ladoga, laid the foundations of the town of Ladoga in stone.

A.D. 1117. A.M. 6625. Mstislav went from Novgorod on March 17 to take the throne at Kiev, and he put his son, Vsevolod, on the throne at Novgorod. On May 14 that same year there was a sign by thunder at ten o'clock during evening service in St. Sophia in Novgorod; one of the chanters, a clerk, was struck by the thunder, and the whole choir with the people fell prone, the people remaining alive; and in the evening there was a sign in the moon. The same year the *Igumen* Anton laid the foundation of the stone church of the monastery of the Holy Mother of God.

The same year, Dobrynya, *Posadnik* of Novgorod, died on December 6.

A.D. 1118. A.M. 6626. Dmitri Zavidits, *Posadnik* of Novgorod, died on July 9, having been sole *Posadnik*

[1] sc. the St. Sophia or Western side of Novgorod.
[2] The Bear's Head; in Finnish: Oden-paa, the modern Odeppe, a village S. of Yurev, or Dorpat, W. of Novgorod.
[3] Burgomaster.

seven months. The same year, Volodimir with Mstislav brought all the *Boyars*[1] of Novgorod to Kiev and led them to the honourable Cross,[2] and then dismissed them to their houses, retaining others by him, being wroth with those because they had plundered Danislav and Nozdrich, and with the *Sotski*[3] Stavro, and he drowned all of them.

A.D. 1119. A.M. 6627. The *Igumen* Kyuryak and *Knyaz* Vsevolod laid the foundation of the monastery church of St. Georgi in Novgorod. The same year died Kosnyatin[4] Moseovits the *Posadnik*. The same year, Anton's Church in the monastery of the Holy Mother of God in Novgorod was completed.

A.D. 1120. A.M. 6628. Boris came to be *Posadnik* in Novgorod.

A.D. 1121. A.M. 6629.

A.D. 1122. A.M. 6630. Mstislav's wife, Christina, died. The same year Mstislav married in Kiev Dmitrovna, daughter of Zavidits of Novgorod.

A.D. 1123. A.M. 6631. Vsevolod, son of Mstislav, married in Novgorod. The same year the Church of St. Mikhail fell in Pereyaslavl, and in the spring, Vsevolod and the men of Novgorod during the Great Fast went against the Yem people and defeated them; but the march was terrible; [a loaf of] bread cost one *nogata*.[5]

A.D. 1124. A.M. 6632. On the 11th day of August before evening service the sun began to decrease and it totally perished; oh, there was great terror and darkness! there were stars and the moon; then it began to re-appear and came out quickly in full; then all the city rejoiced.

A.D. 1125. A.M. 6633. Volodimir the Great, son of Vsevolod, died in Kiev; and they put his son Mstislav on the throne of his father. The same year there was a great storm with thunder and hail; it rent houses and it rent tiles off shrines; it drowned droves of cattle in the Volkhov, and others they hardly

1 Nobles.
2 i.e. made them take the oath of loyalty.
3 Commander of a hundred (*sto*).
4 Constantine.
5 cf. Appendix.

saved alive. The same year they painted the Anton chapel in the monastery (sc. frescoes).

The same year the people of Novgorod put Vsevolod on the throne.

A.D. 1126. A.M. 6634. Vsevolod went to Kiev to his father and he came back to the throne in Novgorod on February 28. The same year they gave the office of *Posadnik* to Miroslav Gyuryatinits.

A.D. 1127. A.M. 6635. Vsevolod founded the stone church of St. Ioan in Novgorod, in the name of his son, in Petryata's Court. The same year a blizzard fell thick over land and water and houses during two nights and four days. The same year the *Igumen* Anton built a refectory of stone in Novgorod. The same year the water was high in the Volkhov and snow lay until James's[1] day. And in the autumn the frost killed all the corn and the winter crop; and there was famine throughout the winter; an *osminka*[2] of rye cost half a *grivna*.[3]

A.D. 1128. A.M. 6636. Kyuryak, *Igumen* of St. Georgi, died. The same year Ioan, son of Vsevolod, grandson of Mstislav, died on April 16. The same year Zavid Dmitrovits was made *Posadnik* in Novgorod. This year it was cruel; one *osminka* of rye cost a *grivna*; the people ate lime tree leaves, birch bark, pounded wood pulp mixed with husks and straw; some ate buttercups, moss, horse flesh; and thus many dropping down from hunger, their corpses were in the streets, in the market place, and on the roads, and everywhere. They hired hirelings to carry the dead out of the town; the serfs could not go out; woe and misery on all! fathers and mothers would put their children into boats in gift to merchants,[4] or else put them to death; and others dispersed over foreign lands. Thus did our country perish on account of our sins. This year, the water was high in the Volkhov, and carried away many houses; and *Knyaz* Boris Vseslavits of Polotsk died; and Zavid Dmitrovits, *Posadnik* of Novgorod, died.

A.D. 1129. A.M. 6637. Daniel came from Kiev to be *Posadnik* in Novgorod.

[1] May 1.
[2] About eleven pecks.
[3] cf. Appendix.
[4] sc. as slaves to the oversea merchants, who came up the river Volkhov from the Baltic to Novgorod in boats.

A.D. 1130. A.M. 6638.   Vsevolod with the men of Novgorod went
against the Chud people in the winter
during the Feast; them he slaughtered, their dwellings he burned,
and their wives and children he brought home. The same year he
went to Kiev to his father. The same year they finished the Church
of St. John. This year coming from beyond sea from the Goths,[1]
seven boats sank; they themselves all sank and their goods; but
some escaped, though naked, and came from Donia[2] in health.

This year *Vladyka* Ioan of Novgorod, resigned, he had sat twenty
years, and they appointed Nifont *Vladyka*, a holy and very God-
fearing man; he came to Novgorod on the 1st day of January, on
St. Basil's day to mid-day service. And they let Petrila be *Posadnik*
over Novgorod.

A.D. 1131. A.M. 6639.   There was a sign in the sun in the evening
time on March 20.   The same year in the
winter, Vsevolod went against the Chud people, and there happened
a great calamity; they did to death many good men of Novgorod at
Klin on Saturday, January 23.   Then also *Vladyka* Nifont made
Anton *Igumen*.

A.D. 1132. A.M. 6640.   Mstislav Volodimirits died in Kiev on
April 14; and Yaropolk, Mstislav's brother,
took his seat on the throne. This year, Vsevolod by order of Yaropolk
went into Russia to Pereyaslavl although he had kissed the Cross
to the people of Novgorod that I wish to die in your midst.   And
Georgi and Andrei said: " Behold our brother Yaropolk, after his
own death wishes to give Kiev to Vsevolod his nephew: " and they
drove him out of Pereyaslavl.   And he came back to Novgorod
and there was a great rising amongst the people.   And the men of
Pleskov[3] and of Ladoga came to Novgorod, and drove out *Knyaz*
Vsevolod from the town; and then again, having taken counsel they
brought him back from the Mouths[4] and they let Miroslav be *Posadnik* in Pleskov and Raguilov in the town of Ladoga.

A.D. 1133. A.M. 6641.   There was a sign in the sun before evening
service.   And the same year they renewed
the bridge across the Volkhov, which had been destroyed, and they

---

[1] sc. Gothland.
[2] i.e. Denmark.
[3] i.e. Pskov.
[4] *Usti*, sc. of the river Volkhov in Lake Ladoga.

built two wooden churches in the market place; to the Holy Mother
of God and to St. George, under *Knyaz* Vsevolod. The same year
in the winter, Vsevolod with the men of Novgorod went against the
Chud people and took the town of Gyurgev[1] on the anniversary of
St. Nikifor, the 9th day of February.

A.D. 1134. A.M. 6642. The people of Novgorod began to talk of a
                        war with Suzhdal,[2] and they killed one of
their own men and threw him from the bridge on Pentecost Saturday.
The same year the business side[3] caught fire, from the Carpenters'
brook to the end of *Kholm*,[4] as it had caught fire before; and ten
honourable churches were destroyed by fire, on August 4. The
same year Vsevolod marched with the men of Novgorod, wishing
to place his brother in Suzhdal, and at the Dubna they turned
back; and during the same journey they took away the *Posadnik*-ship
from Petrila and gave it to Ivanko Pavlovits; and Izyaslav went to
Kiev: and all the Russian Land was rent asunder. The same year
they cut to pieces some men of Novgorod beyond the Sea in Donia[5];
and *Igumen* Isaia went as envoy to Kiev; and he came back with the
Metropolitan Mikhail to Novgorod on December 9. The same year
in the winter, Vsevolod went against Suzhdal with an army and all
the Novgorod province,[6] on December 31; and bad weather set in;
frost and blizzard, very terrible! They fought on Zhdana hill, and
much evil was wrought, and they killed Ivanko, *Posadnik* of Novgorod, a very brave man, on January 26, also Petrila Mikultsits and
many good men, but of the men of Suzhdal yet more; and having
made peace, they came back; and they let the Metropolitan go to
Kiev on February 10 on Sexagesima Sunday, but those who were
going to Suzhdal would not let him go, but he said to them: " Do
not go, God will listen to me."   And having come [back] they gave
the *Posadnik*-ship to Miroslav Gyuryatinits.

A.D. 1135. A.M. 6643. *Posadnik* Miroslav went from Novgorod to
                        make peace between the people of Kiev
and those of Chernigov, and he came [back] without having achieved
anything; for the whole Russian Land was in great disorder; Yaropolk called the men of Novgorod to his side; and the *Knyaz* of

---

[1] i.e. Yurev, or Dorpat.
[2] A town E. of Moscow.
[3] The Eastern side of the town.
[4] A part of Novgorod, lit. " The Mound."
[5] i.e. Denmark.
[6] *Oblast.*

Chernigov to his; and they fought, and God helped the son of Oleg
with the men of Chernigov and he cut up many of the men of Kiev,
and others they captured in the month of August. And this was
not the whole of the evil; the Polovets people and every one began to
muster fighting men. The same year, Vsevolod with *Vladyka* Nifont
founded a stone church of the Holy Mother of God in the market
place. The same year, Irozhnet founded a church to St. Nicholas
in Yakov Street. The same year in the winter, *Vladyka* Nifont
with the best men went into Russia, and found the men of Kiev and
the men of Chernigov ranged against each other, and a quantity of
troops; and by the will of God they were reconciled. And Miroslav
died before the [return of the] *Vladyka* on January 28; the Bishop
came on February 4. And they gave the *Posadnik*-ship in Novgorod
to Kostyantin Mikultsits.

A.D. 1136. A.M. 6644. Of the year of the Indiction 14. The men
of Novgorod summoned the men of Pleskov
and of Ladoga and took counsel how to expel their *Knyaz* Vsevolod,
and they confined him in the Court[1] of the Bishop, together with
wife and children and mother-in-law, on May 28, and guards with
arms guarded him day and night, thirty men daily; and he sat two
months and they let him out of the town on July 15, and they
received his son, Volodimir. And they made these his faults:
I. He has no care for the serfs; II. Why didst thou wish to take thy
seat in Pereyaslavl? III. Thou didst ride away from the troop in
front of all, and besides that much vacillation, ordering us first to
advance against Vsevolodko and then again to retreat; and they did
not let him go till another *Knyaz* came.

Then also the monastery church of the Holy Resurrection was
destroyed by fire. The same year, *Knyaz* Svyatoslav Olgovits
came to Novgorod from Chernigov, from his brother Vsevolodko on
July 19, formerly, the 14th of the Calends of August, the Sunday of
the festival of St. Euphemia, at 3 o'clock of the day, the 19th day of
the moon in the sky.

The same year, already the 15th of the Indiction, they killed Georgi
Zhiroslavits, and threw him from the bridge, in the month of Sep-
tember. The same year they consecrated the Church of St.
Nicholas by a great consecration on December 5. The same year,
Svyatoslav Olgovits married in Novgorod and was wedded by his
own priests in the Church of St. Nicholas; and Nifont did not wed

---

[1] *Dvor.*

him, he did not let priests or monks [go to the wedding] saying: " It behoves him not to take her [to wife]."

The same year the favourites of Vsevolod shot at the *Knyaz*; but he remained alive.

A.D. 1137. A.M. 6645. On March 7, in the 15th year of the Indiction, Kostyantin, *Posadnik* of Novgorod, and some other good men fled to Vsevolod; and they let Yakun Miroslavits be *Posadnik* in Novgorod. The same year Vsevolod Mstislavits came to Pleskov, wishing to take his seat again on his own throne in Novgorod, secretly called on by men of Novgorod and of Pleskov, his friends: " Come, *Knyaz*, they want you again." And when this was heard, that Vsevolod was at Pleskov with his brother Svyatopolk, there was great tumult in Novgorod. The people did not want Vsevolod; and some hurried off to Vsevolod to Pleskov, and took to plundering their houses, Kosnyatin's, Nezhata's, and those of many others, and besides that seeking out those *Boyars* who were friends of Vsevolod, they took one and a half thousand *grivnas* from each and gave it to the merchants to prepare for war; but they also laid hands on the innocent. Then Svyatoslav Olgovits collected the whole Novgorod land and fetched his brother Glebko, [and with] men of Kursk [and] with Polovets people went to Pleskov to drive away Vsevolod; and the men of Pleskov did not submit to them, nor did they drive out the *Knyaz* from them, but they had guarded themselves and barricaded all the ways by felling trees, and *Knyaz* and people having taken counsel on the way, they turned back at Dubrovna, and also having said: " Let us not spill blood with our brothers; rather let God settle by his providence." Then too, Vsevolod Mstislavits died in Pleskov, in the month of February, and the men of Pleskov took sides with his brother Svyatopolk; and there was no peace with them, nor with the men of Suzhdal, nor with those of Smolensk, nor with those of Polotsk, nor with those of Kiev. And all the year a large *osminka* cost seven *rezanas*.[1]

A.D. 1138. A.M. 6646. In the month of March on the 9th day [the day of] the forty Saints, there was great thunder, so that sitting in doors we heard it clearly.

The same year they drove Svyatoslav, the son of Oleg, out of Novgorod, on April 17, on the third Sunday after Easter; having sat two years less three months.

[1] cf. Appendix.

The same year they sent to Suzdhal for Gyurgi Volodimirits; and on the 23rd of that month the people took alarm: for they had falsely said that Svyatoslav was outside the town with the men of Pleskov; and the whole town went out to Silnishche,[1] and it was nothing at all, but Svyatoslav's wife with his best men were taken prisoners in Novgorod, and Svyatoslav himself the men of Smolensk took on the way and kept guard over him in the monastery at Smyadino, likewise his wife in the monastery of St. Barbara in Novgorod, awaiting examination by Yaropolk and Vsevolodko.

The same year *Knyaz* Yaroslav, son of Gyurgi, grandson of Volodimir, came from Suzhdal into Novgorod on to the throne, on May 10; and they made peace with the men of Pleskov. The same year *Knyaz* Yaropolk of Kiev died, and his brother, Vyacheslav, took his seat on the throne.

A.D. 1139. A.M. 6647. *Knyaz* Gyurgi came from Suzhdal to Smo lensk and summoned the men of Novgorod against Kiev against Vsevolod, and they did not listen to him. And then Rostislav fled from Novgorod to Smolensk to his father on September 1, having sat in Novgorod eight years and four months; and Gyurgi was wroth, going back to Suzhdal, he took Novi-torg.[2] The men of Novgorod sent to Kiev for Svyatoslav Olgovits, having given their oath; and there was tumult in Novgorod, and Svyatoslav was away a long time. The same year, Svyatoslav Olgovits entered Novgorod and took his seat on the throne in the month of December on the 25th.

A.D. 1140. A.M. 6648. On March 20 there was a sign in the sun; only so much of it remained as there is in a moon of four days; but it filled out again before setting. The same year they sent Kosnyatin Mikultsits and six others after him to Vsevolod to Kiev; having put in chains Polyud Kosnyatinits, Demyan and some others.

A.D. 1141. A.M. 6649. On April 1 there was a very marvellous sign in the sky; six circles, three close about the sun, and three other large ones outside the sun, and stood nearly all day.
The same year they came from Vsevolod from Kiev for his brother Svyatoslav to take him to Kiev; "and receive my son as your

---

[1] Near Novgorod.
[2] lit., New Market.

Knyaz," he said. And when they sent the Bishop and many best men for his son, they said to Svyatoslav: " Thou wait for thy brother, then thou shalt go; " but he, fearing the men of Novgorod, " whether they are going to deceive me," fled secretly in the night; Yakun fled with him. And they took Yakun on the [river] Plisa, and having brought him hither with his brother Procopi, they nearly did him to death, having stripped him naked, as his mother bore him, and they threw him down from the bridge; but God saved him, he waded to the bank, and they beat him no more, but took from him 1,000 *grivnas,* and from his brother 100 *grivnas,* likewise they took from others; and they exiled Yakun with his brother to the Chud people, having chained their hands to their necks; and afterwards Gyurgi fetched them to him, and their wives from Novgorod, and kept them by him in favour. And Vsevolod was wroth, and he detained all the emissaries and the Bishop and the merchants.

And the people of Novgorod sat without a *Knyaz* nine months: and they summoned Sudila, Nezhata and Strashko from Suzhdal, who had fled from Novgorod on account of Svyatoslav and Yakun; and they gave the *Posadnik*-ship in Novgorod to Sudila; and they sent to Suzhdal for Gyurgi to be *Knyaz,* and he did not go, but sent his son, Rostislav, who had been before.

The same year Rostislav went on to the throne at Novgorod, on November 26.

A.D. 1142. A.M. 6650. They did not let the Bishop and the merchants and the Novgorod emissaries leave Russia, and they did not wish for any other *Knyaz* than Svyatopolk; and he gave them Svyatopolk from his own hands; Gyurgi having broken his oath, by letting his son go back to Novgorod. And they heard in Novgorod that Svyatopolk is coming to them with all their people, and they took Rostislav and put him in the Bishop's Court, having sat (sc. on the throne) four months.

The same year, on April 19, Svyatopolk entered Novgorod; and they let Rostislav go to his father.

The same year came the Yem people, and made war on the Novgorod province; 400 of the men of Ladoga defeated them, and did not let one escape.

The same year a *Knyaz* of the *Svei*[1] with a Bishop in sixty boats attacked merchants who were coming from over sea in three boats;

[1] Swedes.

c

and they fought, they accomplished nothing, and they separated three of their boats, and they killed one hundred and fifty of them.

A.D. 1143. A.M. 6651. All the autumn was rainy, from Our Lady's Birthday[1] to *Korochun*[2] warm, wet; and the water was very high in the Volkhov and everywhere, it carried abroad hay and wood; the lake[3] froze in the night, and the wind broke up [the ice] and carried it into the Volkhov, and it broke the bridge, it carried away four piles, never heard of more.

The same year Svyatopolk married in Novgorod, he brought a wife from Moravia, between Christmas and Epiphany.

The same year the Korel people[4] went against the Yem people and [those] running away, they destroyed two of their vessels.

A.D. 1144. A.M. 6652. They made a whole bridge across the Volkhov by the side of the old one, entirely new.

The same year the whole of *Kholm*[5] was burned, and the church of St. Ilya. The same year they painted fittingly all the porches in the Church of St. Sophia in Novgorod, under *Vladyka* Nifont. Then, too, they gave the *Posadnik*-ship to Nezhata Tverdyatits. The same year they finished the stone church of the Holy Mother of God in the market place in Novgorod. The same year the holy *Vladyka* Nifont appointed me priest.

A.D. 1145. A.M. 6653. There were two whole weeks of great heat, like burning sparks, before harvest; then came rain, so that we saw not a clear day till winter; and a great quantity of corn and hay they were unable to harvest; and that autumn the water was higher than three years before; and in the winter there was not much snow, and no clear day, not till March. The same year, two priests were drowned and the Bishop did not let sing over them. The same year they founded a stone church, Boris and Gleb, at Smyadino by Smolensk. The same year the whole Russian Land went against Galich, they devastated much of their province, but took not one town, and returned, and they went also from Novgorod with *Voyevoda* Nerevin to help the people of Kiev, and returned with love.

1 September 25.
2 The Winter solstice.
3 sc. Lake Ilmen, at the north end of which lies Novgorod.
4 A Finnish tribe.
5 i.e. The Mound, a quarter of the town.

A.D. 1146. A.M. 6654. Vsevolod died in Russia in the month of July, and his brother, Igor, took his seat on the throne and sat two weeks, and the people disliked him; and they sent word to Izyaslav Mstislavich in Pereyaslavl, and he came with soldiers, and they fought; and God helped Izyaslav, and Izyaslav took his seat on the throne; and they took Igor five days after the fight and made him captive; and in the autumn he begged permission to be shorn; and he was shorn.

Then, too, they gave the *Posadnik*-ship to Kostyantin Mikultsits, having taken it away from Nezhata.

The same year they made four churches: to the holy Martyrs Boris and Gleb in the town, to the holy Prophet Ilya, to the holy Apostles Peter and Paul, in the *Kholm* [quarter], and to the Holy Benefactors[1] Kosma and Damyan.

A.D. 1147. A.M. 6655. In the autumn Svyatopolk with the whole Novgorod province went against Gyurgi wishing to go against Suzhdal, and turned back at Novi-torg for the bad roads.

The same year in the winter *Posadnik* Kostyantin died and they gave it again to Sudila Ivankovits.

Then, too, *Igumen* Onton[2] died. The same year they gave the *Igumen*-ship to Andrei in Onton's place.

The same year the people of Kiev killed *Knyaz* Igor Olgovits.

A.D. 1148. A.M. 6656. There was rain with hail on June 27, a Sunday; and thunder set fire to the Church of the Holy Mother of God in the monastery of Zverinets. The same year *Vladyka* Nifont went to Suzhdal, for peace, to Gyurgi; and Gyurgi received him with love, and consecrated the Church of the Holy Mother of God, with great consecration, and released all the men of Novi-torg and all the merchants, untouched, and sent them with honour to Novgorod; but peace he gave not.

The same autumn Izyaslav sent his son, Yaroslav, from Kiev, and the men of Novgorod received him, and he took Svyatopolk away because of his wickedness, and they gave him Volodimir.

The same winter Izyaslav, son of Mstislav, came to Novgorod from Kiev, and went to Rostov against Gyurgi with the men of Novgorod; and they made much war on Gyurgi's people, and took

---

[1] *Bezmezdniki*=ἀνάργυροι; these two saints who were doctors and gave their services gratis, are often so-called.

[2] sc. Anthony.

C 2

six small towns on the Volga, they laid waste as far as Yaroslavl, and took 7,000 heads (captives), and turned back for the bad roads.

A.D. 1149. A.M. 6657. Nifont, *Vladyka* of Novgorod, went into Russia, summoned by Izyaslav and Klim the Metropolitan: for Izyaslav with the Bishops of the Russian province[1] had appointed him, not having sent to *Tzargrad*;[2] and to Nifont he spake thus: " You were not fittingly appointed, for you were neither blessed nor appointed by the great council." And he (Izyaslav) on this account did not hurry to acquit him, but put him in the Pechersk monastery until Gyurgi should come. The same year Gyurgi came against Kiev, summoned by Svyatoslav Olgovits, and they fought at Pereyaslavl, and the men of Pereyaslavl sat on the defensive, at the bidding of Gyurgi; and Gyurgi took his seat in Kiev, and Izyaslav fled to Volodimir. The same year tax gatherers in small number went out; and Gyurgi, aware that they went a small party, sent *Knyaz* Berladski with soldiers, and having fought a little at one point, the men of Novgorod took stand on an island, and the others having taken stand opposite, they began to make a barricade in boats; the men of Novgorod went to them on the third day, and they fought; and many of both were left lying, but of the men of Suzhdal without number. The same winter the Yem people came with armed force against the Vod people, several thousand; and the men of Novgorod having heard, about 500 of them went with the Vod people against them, and did not let a man escape. The same night there was a sign in the moon: the whole of it perished, during early morning service it filled out again, in February.

A.D. 1150. A.M. 6658. *Vladyka* Nifont came from Kiev, released by *Knyaz* Gyurgi; and the people at Novgorod were glad.

A.D. 1151. A.M. 6659. Izyaslav with Vyacheslav defeated Gyurgi at Pereyaslavl on July 17.

The same winter the *Knyaginya*[3] of Izyaslav died.

The same year *Vladyka* Nifont covered St. Sophia all smoothly over with lead and plastered it with lime all about. Then, too, they erected two churches: of St. Vasili and of St. Kostyantin and his mother, Helen.

[1] Kiev and district.
[2] i.e. the Emperor's town, Constantinople.
[3] Princess, sc. wife.

A.D. 1152. A.M. 6660.   On April 23, the Church of St. Michael
                  in the middle of the market place took fire,
and there was much damage; the whole market place was burnt, and
the houses up to the stream, and hitherwards to Slavno, and
eight churches were burnt down, and a ninth, the Varangian one.

A.D. 1153. A.M. 6661.   The God-loving *Vladyka* Nifont went to
                  Ladoga and founded the stone Church of
St. Kliment.

The same year *Igumen* Arkadi built the wooden Church of the
Assumption of the Holy Mother of God, and established for himself
a monastery; and it was a refuge for Christians, a joy to the Angels,
and perdition to the devil.

A.D. 1154. A.M. 6662.   The men of Novgorod drove out *Knyaz*
                  Yaroslav on March 26, and fetched in
Rostislav, son of Mstislav, on April 17.

The same year they built a church to St. Sava.

The same year on November 14, Izyaslav died in Kiev. Then,
too, Rostislav went from Novgorod to [take] the throne in Kiev,
having left his son, David, in Novgorod. And the men of Novgorod were indignant, because he did not make order among them
but tore them more apart; and they showed the road to his son after
him. Then they sent *Vladyka* Nifont with the foremost men to
Gyurgi for his son, and fetched in Mstislav, son of Gyurgi, on January 30. The same winter Vyacheslav died in Kiev.

Then, too, Rostislav went to Chernigov from Kiev, having sat
in Kiev one week, and they defeated him, having deceived [him];
and Izyaslav Davidovits took his seat in Kiev.

A.D. 1155. A.M. 6663.   In Palm week *Knyaz* Gyurgi entered Kiev
                  and took his seat on the throne, and Izyaslav
Davidovits fled to Chernigov; and Gyurgi received his nephews in
peace with love, and distributed proper districts among them; and
there was quiet in the Russian Land.

A.D. 1156. A.M. 6664.   The men of Novgorod drove out Sudila
                  from the *Posadnik*-ship, and he died on the
fifth day after that expulsion; and then they gave the *Posadnik*-ship
to Yakun Miroslavits. The same spring, on April 21, *Vladyka*
Nifont died: he had gone to Kiev against the Metropolitan; many
others, too, said that having plundered St. Sophia, he went to Tsargrad; and they said many things against him, but with sin to them-

selves. About this each one of us should reflect: which bishop ornamented St. Sophia, painted the porches, made an ikon-case, and
ornamented the whole outside; and in Pleskov erected a Church
of the Holy Saviour in stone, and another in Ladoga to St.
Kliment? And I think that God for our sins not wishing to give us
his coffin for our consolation, led him away to Kiev, and there he
died; and they placed him in the Pechersk monastery, in a vault
in the [church of the] Holy Mother of God. The same year the
whole town of people gathered together, and decided to appoint as
Bishop for themselves, Arkadi, a man chosen of God; and the whole
people went and took him out of the monastery of the Holy Mother
of God, both *Knyaz* Mstislav Gyurgevits, and the whole choir of
St. Sophia, and all the town priests, the *Igumens* and the monks,
and they led him in, having entrusted him with the bishopric in
the Court of St. Sophia, till the Metropolitan should come to Russia,
and then you shall go to be appointed. The same year the oversea
merchants put up the Church of the Holy Friday on the market place.

A.D. 1157. A.M. 6665. There was a bad tumult in the people, and
    they rose against *Knyaz* Mstislav Gyurgevits,
and began to drive him out of Novgorod; but the Mercantile¹ Half
stood up in arms for him; and brother quarrelled with brother, they
seized the bridge over the Volkhov, and guards took their stand at
the town gates, and [so did] the others on the other side; and they
were within a little of shedding blood between them.   And then
Svyatoslav Rostislavits and David entered, and that night Mstislav
fled out of the town.   After three days Rostislav himself entered,
and the brothers came together, and there was no harm at all.

The same spring *Knyaz* Gyurgi died at Kiev, and the men of Kiev
set Izyaslav Davidovits on the throne.

The same year Andrei, *Igumen* of the Church of the Holy Mother
of God, died, and they appointed Olksa² in his place.

The same autumn it was very terrible: thunder and lightning, and
hail in size larger than apples, at 5 of the night, on November 7.

A.D. 1158. A.M. 6666. Rostislav went to Smolensk with his
    Knyaginya and he set his son, Svyatoslav,
on the throne in Novgorod, and David in Novi-torg.

The same year there was great mortality in the people, for our
sins, and a quantity of horses died, so that it was not possible to walk

¹ i.e. the Eastern.
² sc. Alexis.

to the market place through the town, nor along the dike, nor out to the fields, for the stench; horned cattle also died.

The same year Arkadi went to Kiev to be appointed Bishop, and he was appointed by the Metropolitan Kostyantin, and came to Novgorod on the 13th day of September, on the eve of the Exaltation [of the Holy Cross].

The same year Mstislav Izyaslavits defeated Izyaslav Davidovits, and drove him away out of Kiev, and summoned Rostislav his uncle to Kiev to the throne.

The same autumn they appointed Dionisi *Igumen* of St. Georgi [in the monastery].

A.D. 1159. A.M. 6667.   Mstislav went to Kiev and took his seat on the throne in Kiev.   The same year Kostyantin, Metropolitan of Russia, died at Chernigov.

A.D. 1160. A.M. 6668.   The men of Novgorod received Svyatoslav Rostislavits and sent him on to Ladoga, and the *Knyaginya* they let enter the monastery of St. Barbara, and his *Druzhina* they put into a dungeon; and they fetched in Mstislav Rostislavits, grandson of Gyurgi, on June 21.

The same winter they gave the *Posadnik*-ship to Nezhata, and took Svyatoslav to Ladoga, and thence he fled to Smolensk.

The same year, in the winter, Rostislav defeated Izyaslav Davidovits at Belgorod,[1] and they killed him himself, and a quantity of Polovets people fell.

A.D. 1161. A.M. 6669.   Rostislav agreed with Andrei about Novgorod, and they fetched away Mstislav, Gyurgi's grandson, having sat one year short of a week, and fetched in Svyatoslav again with his full liberty on September 28.   Then, too, they took the *Posadnik*-ship from Nezhata and gave it to Zakhari.

The same year the sky stood clear all summer and all the corn was scorched, and in the autumn frost killed all the spring corn.

But furthermore for our sins the evil did not stop there, but again in the winter the whole winter stood with heat and rain, and there was thunder; and we bought a little barrel (*kadka*)[2] for seven *kunas*.[3] Oh, there was great distress in the people and want!

A.D. 1162. A.M. 6670.   *Igumen* Olksa of the [monastery of the] Holy Mother of God died, and they ap-

[1] i.e. White-town.
[2] The same as *osminka*, cf. appendix.
[3] i.e. marten-skins, or parts of them, used as money, cf. appendix.

pointed Manuil *Igumen* after him.   The same year they appointed
Sava *Igumen* in the [monastery of the] Descent of the Holy Ghost.

A.D. 1163. A.M. 6671.   Arkadi, Bishop of Novgorod, died on
    September 19; they laid him with great
honour in the porch of St. Sophia.

A.D. 1164. A.M. 6672.   The *Svei*[1] approached Ladoga, and the
    people of Ladoga set fire to their dwellings,
and shut themselves up in the town with *Posadnik* Nezhata, and
sent for the *Knyaz* and for the men of Novgorod.   And they came
right up to the town on a Saturday, and could do nothing to the
town, but took more harm themselves; and they retired to the
river Voronai.   The fifth day after this *Knyaz* Svyatoslav arrived
with the men of Novgorod, and with *Posadnik* Zakhari, and turned
upon them, on May 28, the day of Saint Eulali, on Thursday,
at 5 of the day, and defeated them with God's help, some they
cut down, and others they took.   They had come in 55 boats,
43 boats they took; only a few of them escaped, and those
wounded.

A.D. 1165. A.M. 6673.   Ilya was appointed *Vladyka* of Novgorod by
    the Metropolitan Ioan, under Rostislav,
Knyaz of Russia, on the 28th of March, in Palm week, and he came
to Novgorod on May 11, under Svyatoslav, *Knyaz* of Novgorod,
and *Posadnik* Zakhari.

The same year they put up the Church of the Holy Trinity in
Shetitsinitsa,[2] and *Knyaz* Svyatoslav another to St. Nicholas in the
Gorodishche.

The same year *Igumen* Dionisi went with love to Russia, and the
Vladyka was ordered by the Metropolitan [to assume] the Archbishopric.   The same winter there was severe frost.

A.D. 1166. A.M. 6674.   The Metropolitan Ioan died at Kiev.
    The same year was founded the stone
Church of St. Saviour at the gates of the monastery of St. Georgi.

The same year, in the winter, Rostislav came to Luki from Kiev,
and summoned the men of Novgorod to a council: householders,
guards and principal merchants; and here he fell ill himself, and

---

[1] i.e. Swedes.
[2] sc. Quarter of the Shieldmakers.

turned back, and died on the road; and they carried him to Kiev, and laid him in St. Fedor's.[1]

A.D. 1167. A.M. 6675. Mstislav Izyaslavits took his seat on the throne in Kiev. The same spring Sedko Sitinits founded the stone Church of the Holy Martyrs Boris and Gleb under *Knyaz* Svyatoslav Rostislavits, and *Vladyka* Ilya. The same year Kostyantin came to Russia to be Metropolitan.

The same year *Knyaz* Svyatoslav went out of Novgorod to Luki, and sent to Novgorod, saying thus to them, that: " I do not want to be *Knyaz* among you, it pleases me not." And the men of Novgorod having kissed the picture of the Holy Mother of God, said to themselves that: " We do not want him," and went to drive him away from Luki; and he, having heard that they are coming against him, went to Toropets, and the men of Novgorod sent to Russia to Mstislav for his son. And Svyatoslav went to the Volga, and Andrei gave him help, and he burned Novi-torg, and the men of Novi-torg retired to Novgorod; and he did much damage to their houses, and laid waste their villages. And his brother Roman and Mstislav burned Luki; and the people of Luki took precautions and retired, some into the town, and others to Pleskov. Andrei combined with the men of Smolensk and Polotsk against Novgorod, and they occupied the roads, and seized the Novgorod emissaries everywhere, not letting Mstislav in Kiev know; imposing Svyatoslav on the town by force, and saying this word: " There is no other *Knyaz* for you than Svyatoslav." The men of Novgorod, however, heeded this not, and killed Zakhari the *Posadnik*, and Nerevin, and the herald Nesda, because they thought they gave information to Svyatoslav; and they found for themselves a way to Vyatsko[2] and to Volodar;[3] and Danislav Lazutinits went with a company to Kiev to Mstislav for his son; and Svyatoslav came with the men of Suzhdal, and with his two brothers and with men of Smolensk and Polotsk to Russa[4]; the men of Novgorod with Yakun went against them; but without reaching [them] they turned back: and they accomplished nothing.

They then gave the *Posadnik*-ship to Yakun, and the people of Novgorod sat without *Knyaz* from Simeon's day[5] till Easter under

[1] sc. " Theodore's."
[2] Vyacheslav.
[3] Volodimir.
[4] A town at the S. end of Lake Ilmen, at the N. end of which lies Novgorod.
[5] February 3.

Yakun, awaiting his son from Mstislav. The same winter Mstislav went against the Polovets people and defeated them, and brought booty into the Russian Land in such quantity that there was no number to it. The same year the servant of God Anna, *Igumena*[1] of St. Barbara, died; and they appointed Marmyana in her place.

A.D. 1168. A.M. 6676. *Knyaz* Roman Mstislavits, grandson of Izyaslav, came to the throne in Novgorod on April 14, on the second Sunday after the Great Day,[2] first of the Indiction. And the people of Novgorod were glad at [the fulfilment of] their wishes. The same year the men of Novgorod marched with the men of Pleskov to Polotsk; and having burned the district they turned back at 30 *versts* from the town. In the spring, towards the end of the same year, Roman, with the men of Novgorod, went to Toropets, and they burned their houses, and captured a quantity of prisoners. At the same time the sons of Rostislav with Andreyevits, and with the men of Smolensk and of Polotsk, and of Murom, and of Ryazan, went against Mstislav to Kiev; but he did not fight with them, he retired of his own accord from Kiev.

A.D. 1169. A.M. 6677. Danislav Lazutinits went as tribute collector with a *Druzhina* beyond the *Volok*[3], and Andrei sent his force against him, and they fought with them, there were 400 men of Novgorod, and 7,000 of Suzhdal; and God helped the men of Novgorod, and 1,300 of them fell, and of the men of Novgorod 15 men; and the men of Novgorod retired and having again returned, took the whole tribute, and another one from the serfs of Suzhdal; and they came back all well. The same year in the winter the men of Suzhdal with Andreyevits, Roman and Mstislav with the men of Smolensk, and of Toropets, of Murom and of Ryazan with two *Knyazes*, the *Knyaz* of Polotsk with the men of Polotsk, and the whole Russian Land proper, approached Novgorod. And the men of Novgorod stood firm for *Knyaz* Roman Mstislavits, grandson of Izyaslav, and for *Posadnik* Yakun, and constructed a defence about the town. And they came up to the town on a Sunday to negotiate, and parleyed for three days; and on the fourth day, on Wednesday, they came up in force, and fought all day; and towards evening *Knyaz* Roman with the men of Nov-

[1] Abbess.
[2] sc. Easter.
[3] sc. to the country of the Northern Dvina. cf. p. 6.

gorod defeated them, by the power of the Cross and of the Holy
Mother of God and by the prayers of the faithful *Vladyka* Ilya, on
the 25th of the month of February, the day of the holy Bishop
Tarasi, some they cut down, and others they took, and the rest
of them escaped with difficulty, and they bought men of Suzhdal
at 2 *nogatas*.

A.D. 1170. A.M. 6678. There was dearness in Novgorod; and they
bought a barrel[1] of rye at 4 *grivnas*, and
bread at 2 *nogatas*, honey at 10 *kunas* a *pud*.[2] The men of Novgorod
having taken counsel showed *Knyaz* Roman the road, and themselves
sent to Ondrei[3] for peace with [guarantee of] full liberty. The
same year *Knyaz* Rurik Rostislavits entered Novgorod, on
October 4, on St. Ierofei's. The same year the God-loving
Vladyka Ilya with his brother Gavrilo erected a monastery, the
Church of the Annunciation of the Holy Mother of God. The same
year *Knyaz* Mstislav Izyaslavits, grandson of Volodimir, died.
The same year *Knyaz* Gleb Gyurgevits died at Kiev, and they
fetched in Volodimir Mstislavits.

A.D. 1171. A.M. 6679. *Knyaz* Volodimir died at Kiev, having sat
on the throne three months. The same year
Knyaz Rurik took away the *Posadnik*-ship from Zhiroslav, at Novgorod, and drove him out of the town; he went to Suzhdal to
Ondrei, and they gave the *Posadnik*-ship to Ivanko Zacharinits.
The same year Roman Rostislavits took his seat on the throne in
Kiev. The same year in the winter Rurik went out from Novgorod, and the men of Novgorod sent to Ondrei for a *Knyaz;* and he
sent with his own men Zhiroslav to be *Posadnik*.

A.D. 1172. A.M. 6680. *Knyaz* Gyurgi Andreyevits, Gyurgi's grandson, came to Novgorod. The same year
they founded the stone church of St. Yakov in the Nerev end.[4]
The same year Roman Rostislavits went out from Kiev of his own
accord, and Mikhalko Gyurgevits took his seat in Kiev.

The same year in the winter *Vladyka* Ilya of Novgorod went to
Ondrei, to Volodimir, for full justice.

Then, too, they gave the *Posadnik*-ship to Ivanko Zacharinits.

[1] *Kad.*
[2] About 36 lbs.
[3] i.e. Andrew.
[4] sc. of the town.

A.D. 1173. A.M. 6681. *Knyaz* Gyurgi Andreyevits with the men of Novgorod and of Rostov went to Kiev against the sons of Rostislav, and drove them away out of Kiev; and he stood by Vyshegorod seven weeks, and they came back all well to Novgorod; and Yaroslav Izyaslavits took his seat on the throne in Kiev.

The same year, on the 14th of the month October, Ilya, *Vladyka* of Novgorod, consecrated in Novgorod the stone church of the Holy Martyrs, Boris and Gleb, in the town, and another of stone to the Holy Redeemer at the gates of St. Georgi.

A.D. 1174. A.M. 6682. His own favourites killed *Knyaz* Andrei at Volodimir, on the eve of St. Peter and St. Paul, in the night, when sleeping at Bogolyub's house and there was with him only one young boy; having killed the door-keepers, they came to the vestibule, and the *Kynaz* becoming aware, caught hold of his sword and took his stand in the doorway, struggling with them, but there were many of them, and the *Knyaz* was alone; so they laid on with force and broke the doors, and entered in upon him, and fell on him with pikes, and there he ended his life.   And there was great tumult in that land and great misery, and a quantity of heads fell, so that there was no number [to them]; and then they set on the throne Mstislav Rostislavits with his brother Yaropolk.

The same year Roman Rostislavits, grandson of Mstislav, took his seat in Kiev.

A.D. 1175. A.M. 6683. They led out *Knyaz* Gyurgi Andreyevits from Novgorod, and Mstislav set his son Svyatoslav in Novgorod. The same year he himself entered Novgorod, having fought with his uncle Mikhalko, and took his seat in Novgorod; and Mikhalko took his seat in Volodimir, and set his brother Vsevolod in Pereyaslavl.

The same year a fire broke out from Deigunitsy,[1] and three churches were burnt: St. Michael, St. Yakov, and the Holy Ascension.

The *Posadnik* of Novgorod, Ivanko Zakharinits, died the same year, and they gave it again to Zhiroslav. And towards the end of that year they drove Zhiroslav out of the *Posadnik*-ship and gave it to Zavid Nerevini ts.

t of the town.

A.D. 1176. A.M. 6684. The Volkhov went again into flood for five days. The same spring *Knyaz* Mstislav married in Novgorod and took the daughter of Yakun Miroslavits; and then the men of Rostov summoned him to them and he went to Rostov with his *Druzhina* and left his son in ⁰Novgorod. And he came to Rostov. And at that time Mikhalko had died, and he went with the men of Rostov and with those of Suzhdal to Volodimir; and Vsevolod opposed his forces with the men of Volodimir and Pereyaslavl, and they fought, and a great multitude of both fell, and Vsevolod prevailed. And Mstislav returned to Novgorod, but the men of Novgorod did not receive him, but showed him with his son Svyatoslav the road; and the men of Novgorod took to themselves Yaroslav, the son of Vsevolod.

The same winter Mstislav, with his son-in-law Gleb and with his brother Yaropolk, went against Suzhdal and they fought beyond the Kalaksha; and there the men of Ryazan defeated [them], and took *Knyaz* Gleb with his son, Mstislav, with his brother Yaropolk, and made them captive.

The same winter the whole Chud Land came to Pleskov, and fought with them, and killed Vyacheslav, Mikita Zakharinits, and Stanimir Ivanits, and others, but they killed a quantity of Chud people. The same year Mikhal Stepanits put up a new church of St. Mikhail, and Moisei Domanezhits another of the Decapitation of St. John in Chudinets Street.

A.D. 1177. A.M. 6685. Gleb, *Knyaz* of Ryazan, died in captivity in Volodimir. At the same time *Knyaz* Mstislav was blinded, with his brother Yaropolk, by their uncle Vsevolod, and he let them go into Russia. And the two blind [men], being led with rotting eyes, when they reached Smolensk they came to Smyadino into the Church of the Holy Martyrs Boris and Gleb; and there forthwith the Grace of God and of our Holy Sovereign Lady the Mother of God and of the newly manifested holy Martyrs Boris and Gleb descended on them and there they saw clearly. The same year in the autumn the Nerev end from Ivankovo took fire and five churches were burnt down. And in the winter *Knyaz* Mstislav with his brother Yaropolk came to Novgorod, and the men of Novgorod set Mstislav on the throne, and Yaropolk in Novi-torg, and Yaroslav in Volok-Lamsk, and thus they arranged [things] according to their will.

A.D. 1178. A.M. 6686. Of the Indiction 10. On April 20, *Knyaz* Mstislav, son of Rostislav, and grandson of Gyurgi, died, and they laid him in the porch of St. Sophia; and they set his brother Yaropolk on the throne in Novgorod. Vsevolod seized some merchants of Novgorod, and the men of Novgorod showed Yaropolk the road, and then Vsevolod hastened to Novitorg and took it. Then the men of Novgorod sent for Roman to Smolensk, and he entered the Council on Sunday in Holy Week.

A.D. 1179. A.M. 6687. *Vladyka* Ilya with his brother laid the foundation of a stone church of the Annunciation of the Holy Mother of God, and began to build the church on the 21st of the month of May, on the day of the holy *Tzar* Kostyantin and of Elena, and they finished on August 25, on [the day of] the holy Apostle Tit; and the whole work of building the church [occupied] seventy days; and it was a refuge for Christians.

The same year Elisava, servant of God, *Igumena* of St. Ioan, died, and they appointed Fegnia in her place.

The same year Roman went from Novgorod to Smolensk. And the men of Novgorod then sent into Russia for his brother Mstislav, and Mstislav entered Novgorod on the 1st of the month of November, [the day] of the Holy Benefactors Kosma and Damyan; and in the winter Mstislav went with the men of Novgorod against the Chud people to Ochela, and set fire to their whole land; they themselves fled to the sea, but even there plenty of them fell.

A.D. 1180. A.M. 6688. *Knyaz* Mstislav Rostislavits, grandson of Mstislav, died at Novgorod on the 14th of the month of June, and they laid him in St. Sophia at [the shrine of] the Holy Mother of God. And the men of Novgorod sent to Svyatoslav into Russia for his son, and brought Volodimir to Novgorod, and set him on the throne on August 17. Then, too, they took the *Posadnik*-ship from Zavid and gave it to Mikhal Stepanits. The same year the God-loving *Vladyka* Ilya of Novgorod with his brother Gavrilo founded a stone church in the monastery at the gates by [the church of] the Holy Annunciation. The same year in the winter *Knyaz* Svyatoslav Vsevolodits, Oleg's grandson, went out from Russia against Suzhdal in force against Vsevolod, and his son Volodimir with the men of Novgorod out from Novgorod, and they met on the Volga at the mouth of the Tver,[1] and laid waste all the Volga, and set fire to all the towns, and not having

1 sc. the mouth of the river Tvertsa, where it flows into the Volga at Tver.

reached Pereyaslavl by 40 versts at the Vlena river, there they turned; for there the men of Suzhdal had come out in force, and they made a defence about themselves and did not dare give battle. And the *Knyaz* with the men of Novgorod kept sending to them asking for battle, but God by his mercy did not shed more Christian blood; for they had come together for a little time, and the men of Novgorod killed about 300 of them, and themselves all returned well; and they took the *Knyaz* himself to Novgorod, and they set Yaropolk in Novi-torg; and the great Svyatoslav Vsevolodits entered Novgorod.

A.D. 1181. A.M. 6689. On the 3rd of the month of June the Varangian church in the market-place was set fire to by thunder at 10 of the day, after evening service, and the church of St. Ioan in Ishkovo was burnt. The same year a fire broke out in Slavno, from Kosnyatin's, and two churches were burnt: that of St. Mikhail and that of the Holy Fathers, and many houses along the bank, even as far as the Stream.

The same year they constructed the wooden church of St. Yakov in Dobrynya Street and of the Holy Benefactors Kosma and Damyan and of St. Sava and of St. Georgi and of St. Ioan at Ishkovo.

The same year the men of Novgorod went to Dryutsk with Svyatoslav, Oleg's grandson; and at that time came Vsevolod with his whole force and with men of Murom and of Ryazan against Novitorg; and the men of Novi-torg shut themselves in the town with *Knyaz* Yaropolk, and they besieged the town, and sat [there] five weeks, and they became exhausted in the town: because there was no food for them, others of them ate even horse-flesh; and they shot at *Knyaz* Yaropolk in the town, and there was great distress among them; and the men of Novi-torg surrendered, and he led away Yaropolk with him, having fettered [him], and all the men of Novitorg with wives and children, and set fire to the town; and the men of Novgorod returned from Dryutsk, having set fire to the town.

Then also in the winter they showed the road to Volodimir Svyatoslavits, and he went to his father into Russia, and the men of Novgorod applied to Vsevolod for a *Knyaz*, and he gave them his brother-in-law.

A.D. 1182. A.M. 6690. *Knyaz* Yaroslav, son of Volodimir, and grandson of the Great Mstislav, came to Novgorod.

The same year *Vladyka* Ilya with his brother finished the church

at the gates of the Holy Epiphany. Then also they put up th
church of the Holy Fathers.

A.D. 1183. A.M. 6691.   Radko and his brother put up the church of
                        St. Eupati in Rogata Street.
The same year Vsevolod with his whole province went against the
Bolgar people, and the Bolgar people killed *Knyaz* Izyaslav Glebo-
vits.
The same winter the men of Pleskov fought with the Lithuanians,[1]
and much evil was done to the men of Pleskov.

A.D. 1184. A.M. 6692.   *Vladyka* Ilya with his brother founded the
                        stone church of St. Ioan on the market
place.
The same year Vsevolod fetched away Yaroslav Volodimirovits
from Novgorod, sending his brother-in-law for him, for the men of
Novgorod were indignant with him: because he had done many
wrongs to the Novgorod district.[2]   And having taken counsel the
men of Novgorod applied to Smolensk to David, asking for his son;
and he gave them Mstislav, and they brought him to Novgorod
and set him on the throne in the month of September.
The same year they built a new wooden church of St. Vlasi.

A.D. 1185. A.M. 6693.   On the 1st day of May, at the 10th hour of
                        the day, at evening bell, the sun grew dark,
for an hour or more, and there were the stars; then it shone out
again, and we were glad.
On the 6th of the same month the people of Luki founded a
stone church to the holy Apostles Peter and Paul in Silnishche.[3]
The same year Miloneg founded the stone church of the Holy Ascension under *Vladyka* Ilya and *Knyaz* Mstislav Davidovits.
And in the winter David went to Polotsk with the men of
Novgorod and of Smolensk, and having made peace returned
through Yemenets.

A.D. 1186. A.M. 6694.   Zavid went to David to Smolensk, and they
                        gave the *Posadnik*-ship to Mikhal Stepanits.
The same year the Greek *Tsar* Aleksa Manuilovits came to Novgorod.   Then also some young men went with Vyshata Vasilevits
against the Yem people and came back again well, having got

---

[1] *Litva*, the collective designation of the Lithuanians.
[2] *Volost.*
[3] Near Novgorod.

booty. The same year Ilya, *Vladyka* of Novgorod, died on the
7th day of the month of September, and was laid in the porch of St.
Sophia. And the men of Novgorod having consulted with *Knyaz*
Mstislav and with the *Igumens* and priests, thought good to appoint
for themselves his, Ilya's, brother (Gavrilo); and they sent a request
to the Metropolitan Nikifor; and the Metropolitan sent for him and
all the Russian *Knyazes*, and accepted him with love. The same
winter they killed Gavrilo Nerevinits and Vacha Svenevits in Novgorod, and cast them from the bridge. At the same time there was
an uprising in Smolensk, between *Knyaz* David and the people of
Smolensk, and many heads fell of the best men.

A.D. 1187. A.M. 6695. Gavrilo was appointed *Vladyka* of Novgorod
on the 29th of the month of March, the day
of St. Varikhis and he came to Novgorod on the 31st of the month of
May, the day of the holy Martyr Ermi; and the men of Novgorod
were glad. The same year *Igumen* Moisei [of the church] of the
Holy Mother of God in the Anthony monastery, died, and they
appointed Volos in his place. The same year there was very terrible
thunder and lightning; [the people] having come with crosses from
St. Sophia to St. Michael's and singing nine hymns, the thunder
and lightning struck and all the people fell, and the church caught
fire, but by the mercy of God and by the prayers of St. Michael,
there was no harm in the church; but two men were dead.

The same year the tax-gatherers in the Pechera and Yugra
country[1] were done to death in Pechera, and others beyond the
Volok and about a hundred men of the notables fell.[2]   The same
year there was a sign in the sun at mid-day; it was like the moon,
and grew dim, but after a little time it filled and shone out again, on
September 9.

The same year the men of Novgorod drove out Mstislav Davidovits
and sent to Vsevolod to Volodimir for Yaroslav Volodimirits. And
he entered Novgorod and took his seat on the throne on November 20.

A.D. 1188. A.M. 6696. Simyun Dibakhevits founded the stone
Church of the Assumption of the Holy
Mother of God in the Arkadi monastery. The same year they
made a new bridge over the Volkhov by the side of the
old one. The same year Herman, called Voyata, servant of
God, priest of St. Yakov's, died, having served 45 years

[1] N.E. of Novgorod, what is now Northern Russia.
[2] cf. p. 6.

D

in St. Yakov's in meekness, humility and fear of God. *Vladyka* Gavrilo took him with him to Pleskov, and having reached Pleskov he fell ill and the *Vladyka* shore him into the *schema*[1] and he died on the 13th of October, the day of the holy martyrs Karp and Papil, and they laid him in the monastery of the Holy Saviour. Give peace, O Lord, to the soul of Thy servant Herman, and forgive him all voluntary and involuntary sins.

The same winter things were dear, they bought bread for two *nogatas*, and one barrel of rye for six *grivnas;* but by God's mercy there were no ill effects among the people. The same year the men of Novgorod were plundered by the Varangians in Gothland and by the *Nemtsy*,[2] in Khoruzhk and in Novi-torg, and in the spring they let no man of their own go beyond sea from Novgorod, and gave no envoy to the Varangians, but they sent them away without peace.

A.D. 1189. A.M. 6697. On the 4th of June, the day of St. Mitrofan, Gavrilo, *Vladyka* of Novgorod, consecrated the church of the Assumption of the Holy Mother of God in the Arkadi monastery. The same year *Vladyka* Gavrilo put up a new church in Zhatun in the name of the three Holy Youths, Anani, Azari and Misail, and Danil the Prophet. The same year, on the day of the Nativity of the Holy Mother of God, a daughter *Knyaginya* was born to Yaroslav in Novgorod. The same year they finished painting the church of the Holy Annunciation. The same year they took the *Posadnik*-ship from Mikhal and gave it to Miroshka Nezdinits.

A.D. 1190. A.M. 6698. A son Mikhail was born to Yaroslav in Novgorod, whose name[3] as *Knyaz* was Izyaslav, and grandson of Volodimir. The same year the men of Pleskov did to death [some] Chud people of the coast; for they had come in seven boats[4] and went over by the portage into the lake[5] round [avoiding] the rapids, and the men of Pleskov struck upon them and did not let a man escape, and the boats they brought into the town of Pleskov.

[1] The strictest monastic order.
[2] Nom. Pl., lit. the "dumb" or "incomprehensible" folk, a term applied by all Slavs to all foreigners of Germanic race, sometimes including Scandinavians.
[3] sc. secular name.
[4] *Shnek*.
[5] sc. Lake Chud or Peipus.

A.D. 1191. A.M. 6699. The men of Novgorod went in sailing vessels[1] with the Korel people against the Yem people, and made war on their land and burned it, and cut to pieces the cattle. The same year *Knyaz* Yaroslav built a wooden church in the *Gorodishche* to St. Nikola, and the *Vladyka* one to the Purification of the Blessed Virgin Mary in his own Court; Vnezd Nezdinits in the same year also one to the Sacred Image; and Kosnyatin with his brother one to the Holy Friday, in the market place. The same year the God-loving *Vladyka* Gavrilo consecrated the church of the Holy Ascension erected by the *Tysyatski*[2] Miloneg.

The same year *Kynaz* Yaroslav went to Luki, summoned by the *Knyazes* and people of Polotsk, and took with him the foremost *Druzhina* of the men of Novgorod, and they met on the border and put love between each other, how in the winter they would all meet either against the Lithuanians or the Chud people. And *Knyaz* Yaroslav came to Novgorod with gifts. Then also was a son born to *Knyaz* Yaroslav. And it was in the winter, *Knyaz* Yaroslav with the men of Novgorod, of Pleskov and of his own province went against the Chud people, took the town of Gyurgev, burned their country, and brought countless plunder; and themselves all came back well to Novgorod.

A.D. 1192. A.M. 6700. *Knyaz* Yaroslav went on St. Peter's Day[3] to Pleskov with a few men of Novgorod; and himself took his seat at Pleskov, having sent his court with the men of Pleskov to make war; and having gone they took the town of Medvezhya Golova, burned it, and came back well.

The same year the monk Varlam, whose secular name was Aleksa Mikhalevits, put up a church below at Khutin in the name of the Transfiguration of the Holy Saviour; and *Vladyka* Gavrilo consecrated it on the [day of that] festival, and named the monastery. The same year they finished the church of the Holy Apostles in Silinishche and *Vladyka* Grigori consecrated it on Peter's Day. The same year *Igumen* Marturi built a wooden church at Russa on the island, in the name of the Holy Transfiguration and made a monastery, and it was a refuge to Christians. The same year the church of the Holy Apostles in *Kholm*[4] was burned down, set afire by thunder. The same year *Igumena* Marya of the Holy Resurrec-

---

[1] *Loiva.*
[2] Commander of a thousand (*tysyacha*=1,000).
[3] June 29.
[4] A part of Novgorod. See p. 18.

tion died, and they appointed Evdokia in her place. The same year they appointed Efrosinia, daughter of Peter the merchant, *Igumena* of the Holy Mother of God in Zverinets.

A.D. 1193. A.M. 6701. Gavrilo *Vladyka* of Novgorod died on May 24, the Day of St. Simon of *Divna Gora*,[1] and he was laid in the porch of St. Sophia, by the side of his brother, called in monkhood, Grigori. And the men of Novgorod having consulted with *Knyaz* Yaroslav, the *Igumens*, the people of St. Sophia and the priests,[2] decided on Marturi chosen by God, and sent for him and brought him from Russa, and they set him in the Bishopric; and they sent [word] to the Metropolitan and he sent for him with honour; and he went with the foremost men; and *Knyaz* Svyatoslav received him with love, and the Metropolitan; and they appointed him on December 10, the Day of St. Daniel-*Stolpnik*,[3] and he came to Novgorod on January 16, the day of the Falling off of the Fetters of the Holy Apostle Peter. The same year they went from Novgorod with armed force to the Yugra country with the *Voyevoda* Yadrei, and they came to the Yugra country and took a town[4]; and they came to another town[4] and they shut themselves up in the town, and they stood by the town five weeks; and the Yugra people used to send out to them saying with deceit thus, that: " We are gathering silver and sables, and other precious goods; do not ruin your serfs and your tribute," while deceiving them and gathering troops; and when they had gathered troops, they sent out from the town to the *Voyevoda*, saying thus: " Come into the town, having taken with you the bigger men." And the *Voyevoda* went into the town taking with him a priest and Ivanko Legen and other bigger men; and they cut them down on the eve of St. Barbara; and they sent out again and took 30 of the bigger men; and these they cut to pieces, and then 50 [and did the same to these. Then Savko said to the Yugra *Knyaz*: " If thou, *Knyaz*, dost not also kill Yakovets Prokshinits, but lettest him go alive to Novgorod, then he will again bring troops hither to thee, *Knyaz*, and will make waste thy land." And the *Knyaz* having summoned Yakovets Prokshinits he gave order to kill him. And Yakovets said to Savko: " Brother, God and St. Sophia shall judge thee, inasmuch as thou tookest thought against the blood of

---

[1] The Wonderful Hill, near Antioch.
[2] *Popy*.
[3] Stylites.
[4] *Gorod*—fortified town, but often was merely a fortified post.

thy brothers; thou shalt stand with us before God and shalt answer for our blood." Having said this he was killed: for this Savko had held secret intercourse with the Yugra *Knyaz.*] And when they were exhausted by hunger, for they had stood six weeks listening to their deceit, on the Festival of St. Nicholas, having issued from the town they cut them all up. And there was woe and misery to those who remained alive; for there were 80 men left. And through all the winter there was no word of them in Novgorod, neither of the living nor of the dead. And *Knyaz* and *Vladyka* in Novgorod and all Novgorod grieved. The same year a son, named Rostislav, was born to Yaroslav in Novgorod. The same year they built a wooden church [called] Zhivoglozha to the Holy Apostles in *Kholm*, and one to St. Ioan the Merciful at the gates of the Resurrection.

A.D. 1194. A.M. 6702. A fire broke out in Novgorod on All Saints' Sunday during Fast, on going to early morning service; it started in Savko's Court in Yaryshev Street, and the fire was bad, three churches were burned: St. Vasili, Holy Trinity, and the Holy Exaltation; and many good houses; and they subdued it at Luka's Street. And for our sins evil did not stop here; but on the next day it started in Cheglov Lane, and about ten houses took fire. And then more arose; on Friday in the same week during market, it started from Khrevkov Street as far as the Stream in the Nerev end, and seven churches were burnt and large houses. Thence the evil grew: every day it would start unseen at six and more places, and people dared not feed in their houses, but lived a-field; and then the *Gorodishche*[1] took fire. The same year Ladoga took fire before Novgorod, and then, too, Russa took fire; and in the Lyudin end ten courts took fire; and thus wonders continued from All Saints up to Our Lady's Day.

And then came the rest of the living from the Yugra country. Their own fellow-travellers killed Sbyshko Volosovits and Zavid Negochevits and Moislav Popovits, and others bought themselves off with money[3]; for they thought they had held counsel with the Yugra people against their brothers, but that is for God to judge. The same year they put up the church of the holy apostle Philip in Nutna Street, and *Vladyka* Marturi consecrated it on January 29 on the Translation of the remains of St. Ignati.

---

[1] Near Novgorod; cf. p. 7.
[3] Kunas; cf. appendix.

The same year *Igumen* Dionisi of St. Georgi died, and they appointed Savati in his place. The same winter *Igumen* Gerasim of the Holy Mother of God in the Arkadi monastery, died, and they appointed the priest Pankrati in his place.

A.D. 1195. A.M. 6703. The God-loving *Vladyka* of Novgorod Marturi founded a stone church at the town gate in the name of the Laying Down of the Robe and Girdle of the Holy Mother of God; and they began to make it on May 4, the Day of St. Isaki, and finished on August 2, St. Stephen's Day; and the *Vladyka* himself consecrated it on the Festival of the Holy Mother of God's Laying Down of the Robe and Girdle; and it was a refuge for Christians, and a joy and delight to the faithful. The same autumn *Vladyka* Marturi founded the stone church of the Holy Resurrection in the monastery, and they made it up to about the doors by the autumn. The same year the servant of God, Christina, of St. Barbara, died, and in her place the *Vladyka* and all the Sisters chose and appointed the meek and humble Barbara, daughter of Gyurgi Olekshinits; and the *Vladyka* appointed her on the festival of St. Euphemia. The same year they built a new wooden church for Nozdritsin, to the Holy Exaltation, to St. Vasili and to St. Dmitri.

In the winter of the same year Vsevolod summoned the men of Novgorod against Chernigov, against Yaroslav and against the whole clan[1] of Oleg; and the men of Novgorod did not deny him: householders, body-guards[2] and merchants went with *Knyaz* Yaroslav;[3] and they reached Novi-torg, and Vsevolod sent word and turned them home with honour. And the men of Novgorod sent to him *Posadnik* Miroshka and Boris Zhiroslavits and the *Sotski* Mikifor, asking for his son; being indignant with Yaroslav; and they returned to Novgorod. The same winter the men of Smolensk and of Chernigov fought, and God helped the men of Chernigov and they took *Knyaz* Boris Romanovits, and there was no peace between them. Vsevolod received Miroshka the *Posadnik* and Boris and Ivanko and Foma,[4] and did not let them [return] to Novgorod, while he himself sent to [for] the Polovets people; and Vsevolod and David began to collect forces for themselves, also

[1] *Plemya*.
[2] *Gridba*.
[3] Their own *Knyaz* Yaroslav, against *Knyaz* Yaroslav of Chernigov.
[4] sc. Thomas.

Yaroslav of Chernigov and Igor with their brothers; and there was
no peace between them, but they stirred up war all the more.

A.D. 1196. A.M. 6704. The cousins Kosnyatin and Dmitri founded
the stone church of St. Kyuril[1] in the monas-
tery at Nelezino[2] in Lubyana Street; and they began to make it in
the month of April, and finished it on July 8, the Day of St.
Prokopi, and the *Vladyka* Marturi consecrated it in the winter on
12th of January, the Day of St. Tatyana, with *Igumen* Onisim; and it
was a joy to Christians and eternal remembrance for Kosnyatin and
Dmitri. The same year *Vladyka* Marturi painted the church of the
Holy Mother of God at the gate; the painter was a Greek, Petrovts.
The same year they finished the church of the Holy Resurrection
and the *Vladyka* Marturi consecrated it on September 13, the
Day of St. Kornili, on the eve of the Holy Exaltation, in the presence
of the *Igumen*, the *Vladyka* labouring, burning with heat of the sun
by day, and troubled at night, to finish and see the church completed
and adorned; and he received what he wished, the Kingdom of
Heaven and endless joy, into the ages, Amen.

Towards the end of summer the men of Novgorod applied to
Vsevolod on account of *Posadnik* Miroshka and Ivanko and Foma,
for he had let go Boris and other men with him; but Vsevolod having
gathered his force, and having brought the force of the Polovets
people, went to Chernigov, and led Miroshka the Novgorod *Posadnik*
and Ivanko and Foma with him, and he ordered the men of Novgorod to go to Luki; and they went with Yaroslav, and having sat at
Luki they returned home; and Vsevolod having gone into their land,
God did not allow more bloodshed between them, and they took
peace between each other, and all the *Knyazes* set Novgorod at
liberty: where it pleased them, there they might take to themselves
a *Knyaz*. And Vsevolod having returned, let Foma go to Novgorod, but he did not let go Miroshka nor Ivanko; and incensed the men
of Novgorod; and having taken counsel, the men of Novgorod
showed Yaroslav the road out of Novgorod, and drove him out on
St. Gyurgi's Day, in the Autumn.

Knyaz Yaroslav went to Novi-torg, and the men of Novi-torg
received him with salutations; and the good in Novgorod regretted
him, but the wicked rejoiced. And they sent to Yaroslav to
Chernigov for his son, and sat in Novgorod without *Knyaz* all

[1] Cyril.
[2] Near Novgorod.

winter; and Yaroslav was *Knyaz* in Torzhok[1] in his own district and took tribute along the whole Upper Country[2] and the Msta[3], and he took tribute beyond the *Volok*.[4] And the men of Novgorod having ousted Vsevolod beyond the *Volok*, and in all his land, he detained [their people], not letting them go to Novgorod; but they went about the town of Volodimir at will.

The same winter *Vladyka* Marturi consecrated the church of St. Kyuril at Nelezino.

A.D. 1197. A.M. 6705. *Knyaz* Yaropolk Yaroslavits came from Chernigov to Novgorod in Palm Week, at the beginning of the year in the month of March; and having sat alone from Palm Week to Simon's Day, six months, they drove him out of Novgorod, and sent again for Yaroslav. Yaroslav went from Novi-torg to Volodimir summoned by Vsevolod. The foremost men and the *Sotskis* went from Novgorod and took Yaroslav with all truth and honour; and Yaroslav came in the winter a week after Epiphany and took seat on his throne, and embraced the people, and all was well, and Miroshka the *Posadnik* came, having sat away from Novgorod two years; and all came back unharmed in any way, and all in Novgorod, from small to great, were glad. The same year *Vladyka* Marturi put up a church to St. Nikifor on the island. The same year Polyuzhaya, daughter of Gorodshinits Zhiroshkin, put up the monastery of St. Euphemia in the Carpenter's Quarter.[5]

A.D. 1198. A.M. 6706. The God-loving *Vladyka* Marturi founded a stone church at Russa to the Holy Transfiguration, they began to make it on May 21, the Day of SS. Kostyantin and Elena, and finished on July 31, the Day of Holy St. Ulita, and he consecrated the church on the Assumption of the Holy Mother of God and made an honourable festival, and made a service, and he prayed, saying: " O Lord God! Look down from heaven and see, and visit Thy vineyard, and complete that which Thy right hand has planted; and look down upon this church which Thy servant *Vladyka* Marturi erected, in the name of Thy holy Transfiguration: that whosoever shall pray in this church

---

[1] *Little Market*, the same town as Novi-torg.
[2] Otherwise *Bezhitsy, Bezhitski Verkh*.
[3] A river flowing into Lake Ilmen from the E.
[4] cf. p. 6.
[5] *Plotniki*.

with faith, hear Thou his prayer and remit his sins, by the prayers of the Holy Mother of God and of all Thy Saints, Amen." And the blessed man rejoiced in soul and body, having provided for himself eternal remembrance, and an honourable monastery for all Christians. The same spring Yaroslav's two sons died: Izyaslav had been set to be *Knyaz* in Luki and covered Novgorod from the Lithuanians, and there he died; and Rostislav at Novgorod; and both were laid in the monastery of St. Georgi. The same year the *Veliki Knyaz*[1] Yaroslav, son of Volodimir, grandson of Mstislav, founded the stone church of the Transfiguration of the Holy Saviour in Novgorod on the hill, called Nereditsa[2]; and they began to make it on June 8, on St. Fedor's Day, and finished in the month of September. The same autumn the men of Polotsk with the Lithuanians came against Luki and burned the dwellings, but the people of Luki took warning and escaped out of the town. The same year they founded the stone church of St. Ilya in *Kholm*. The same winter *Knyaz* Yaroslav with the men of Novgorod, of Pleskov, of Novi-torg and of Ladoga and with the whole Novgorod province went to Polotsk, and the men of Polotsk met them with salutation on the Kasopl lake; and having taken peace, they returned to Novgorod: for God did not allow the Christians' bloodshed between each other.

A.D. 1199. A.M. 6707. Vsevolod having sent, he fetched Yaroslav out of Novgorod and brought him to him, and summoned the *Vladyka* and *Posadnik* Miroshka and the bigger men from Novgorod after his son. And when they were on Lake Seregeri the servant of God, *Vladyka* Marturi of Novgorod, died, on August 24, the day of the holy Apostle Barfolomei; and they brought him and laid him in the porch of St. Sophia. People went with the *Posadnik*, and with Mikhalko to Vsevolod; and he. received them with great honour and granted them his son Svyatoslav; and having consulted with the *Posadnik* he sent him to Novgorod with the men of Novgorod, and he put into the Episcopate Mitrofan, a man chosen by God; and all Novgorod having gone they set him with honour, until there should be a summons from the Metropolitan, and then thou shalt go for installation. The same year

---

[1] Grand Prince; in modern Russian the title is used by male blood-relations of the Emperor, and is always translated " Grand Duke," though the title " Knyaz" is otherwise always translated " Prince."
[2] A suburb of Novgorod.

they founded the stone church of the Forty Saints. In the same year Yaroslav's *Knyaginya* put up the church and the monastery of the Birth of the Holy Mother of God in Mikhalitsa Street, and they appointed *Posadnik* Zavid's widow [*Igumena*]. The same year they painted the church of the Holy Transfiguration in the *Gorod-ishche*. The same year they painted the *Vladyka's* church of the Holy Saviour in the monastery in Russa. And *Knyaz* Svyatoslav, son of Vsevolod, grandson of Gyurgi, came to Novgorod on January 1, St. Vasili's Day, and they set him on the throne in St. Sophia, and all Novgorod rejoiced. The same year they walled around the town of Russa.

A.D. 1200. A.M. 7708. The Lithuanians took the Lovot[1] up to [the village of] Nalyuch from Belaya [village] as far as [the villages of] Svinort and Vorch and the men of Novgorod pursued them to [the village of] Tsernyany and fought with them, and killed 80 men of the Lithuanians, and of the men of Novgorod 15 [were killed]: Raguila Prokopinits, with his brother Olksa, Gyurgi Sbyshkinits, Ratimir Nezhatinits, Strashko the silversmith's weight tester, Vnezd Yahinits, young Luka Miroshkin, Mikita[2] Lazorevits, Zhiroshka Ogasovits, Osip[3] the usher[4], Roman Pokt, and four other men; they recovered all the plunder and the rest escaped. The same year Nezdila Pekhtsinits went as *Voyevoda* to Luki; he went with a small *Druzhina* from Luki into Lotygola,[5] and they found them in their bedrooms, killed 40 men of them, took their wives and children, and themselves came all well to Luki; and from those who had not followed them from Molbo-vich with some of the *Druzhina* they took money,[6] having beaten them.

A.D. 1201. A.M. 6709. The men of Novgorod put Mitrofan, chosen by God, into the Episcopate after Marturi, and he went into Russia with men of Novgorod and of Vsevolod, to present himself to the Metropolitan, and he was appointed on July 3, St. Uakinf's[7] Day; and he came to Novgorod on September 14, the Exaltation of the Honourable Cross; and the

---

[1] A river flowing into Lake Ilmen.
[2] Nikita.
[3] Joseph.
[4] *Podvoiski.*
[5] A part of Livonia, lit. " End of the Letts."
[6] *Kunas.*
[7] Hyacinth.

men of Novgorod were glad at their *Vladyka*. On April 15 of the same year the church of St. Nikola in the *Gorodishche*[1] was burnt down by thunder; and the whole summer stood with rain. And they let the Varangians go over sea without peace. The same year they built a wooden defence in Russa; and in the autumn the Varangians came by land for peace; and they gave them peace at all their will.

A.D. 1202. A.M. 6710. They completed the stone church of the Holy Prophet Ilya in *Kholm*, at the Slavno end, and *Vladyka* Mitrofan consecrated it on a festival.

A.D. 1203. A.M. 6711. Rurik with the sons of Oleg and the heathen Polovets people, with Kontsyak and Danila Byakovits captured Kiev, on January 1, St. Vasili's Day; and whomever their hands reached, whether monk or nun, priest or priest's wife, these they led off to the heathen; and all foreign merchants and foreigners of every country shut themselves up in the churches, and they granted them their lives; but their merchandise they divided with them by halves; but everything in the monasteries and in all the churches, all valuables and ornaments and ikons[2] the pagans tore off and carried away into their own land; and they set fire to the town. [Then, too, the Russian *Knyazes* Rurik, Roman, Mstislav and many other *Knyazes* went against the Polovets people. And then the winter was very cruel; and they took much plunder and drove away their herds. The same year Roman sent Vyacheslav ordering him to have Rurik shorn a monk.] The same year the sons of Oleg defeated the Lithuanians, and did to death seven hundred and a thousand of them. The same year Miroshka, *Posadnik* of Novgorod died, he was shorn in St. Georgi's, and then they gave the *Posadnik*-ship to Mikhalko Stepanits. The same year for our sins all the horses died in Novgorod and in the villages so that it was not possible to go anywhere for the stench.

A.D. 1204. A.M. 6712. Oleksa[3] reigning in *Tsargrad*,[4] during the reign of his brother Isak[5] whom having blinded, he himself became *Tsar*, shut up his [Isaac's] son Oleksa in high walls under guard, so that he might not get out.

[1] Near Novgorod, see p. 7.
[2] *Ikony*.
[3] Alexis.
[4] Constantinople; cf. p. 20.
[5] Isaac.

And time having passed, Isak ventured to pray for his son, that he would release him, to come before him from prison, and Isak persuaded his brother, and they took a declaration, he and his son, that they would not take thought against the throne; and he was released from prison, and went about at will. And *Tsar* Oleksa did not trouble about him, trusting his brother Isak and his son, because they had taken the declaration. And then Isak having taken thought, coveted the throne, and instructed his son. secretly sending to him, how that: " I did good to my brother, Oleksa, I ransomed him from the heathen and he has returned me evil, having blinded me, and took my throne." And his son conceived desire, as he instructed him, and they took thought how he should go out of the town into far countries and thence seek the throne. He was led on to a ship and put into a barrel having three false bottoms at one end behind which Isakovits[1] sat, and at the other end was water, where the plug was; for it was impossible otherwise to go out of the town; and so he went out of the Greek land. And the *Tsar* having learnt sent to seek him; and they began to seek him in many places, and entered the ship where he was, and searched all places, and drew the plugs out of the barrels and seeing water running, they went away, and did not find him. And thus, Isakovits went out and came to the Nemetski[2] *Tsar*, Philip, to his brother-in-law and sister. The Nemetski *Tsar* sent to the Pope to Rome, and they informed him thus, not to make war on *Tsargrad*, but as Isakovits said: " The whole town of Kostyantin[3] desires my rule," so setting him on the throne, you will go to the aid of Jerusalem; if they do not want him, bring him back to me, but do no injury to the Greek land.

But the Franks[4] and all their *Voyevodas* conceived lust for the gold and silver, which Isakovits promised them, and forgot the commands of *Tsar* and Pope. First having come to the Sound, they broke the iron locks, and having advanced to the town, they hurled fire into the churches, in four places. Then *Tsar* Oleksa having perceived the flames, did not take up arms against them. Having summoned his brother Isak, whom he had blinded, he set him on the throne and said: " Since thou hast acted thus, brother, forgive

[1] i.e. Isaac's son.
[2] German, cf. p. 34.
[3] Constantinople.
[4] *Fryazi*.

me; this is thy throne "; and fled out of the town. And the town was burnt, and churches of untold beauty, whose number we cannot declare; and the porch of St. Sophia was burnt, where all the patriarchs were painted, and the hippodrome and down to the sea; and hitherwards it burned up to the *Tsar's* palace and to the Sound. And then Isakovits with the Franks pursued *Tsar* Oleksa and did not reach him, and returned to the town, and drove his father off the throne, and became *Tsar* himself and saying thus: " Thou art blind, how canst thou hold the throne? I am *Tsar.*" Then *Tsar* Isak full of regret for his town and throne, for the spoliation of the monasteries, and for the silver and gold promised to the Franks and given them, fell ill, and became a monk, and went away from this world. After Isak's death the populace rose against his son for the burning of the town and the spoliation of the monasteries; and the common people assembled and [drew in] the good men, taking counsel with them whom to appoint *Tsar;* and all wanted Radinos; but he did not want the throne, and hid himself from them, disguising himself in monk's vestments; but having taken his wife they led [her] into St. Sophia, and pressed her much: " Tell us where is thy husband? " And she did not tell about her husband. Then they took a man by name Nikola, a soldier, and put the crown on him without the Patriarch, and remained there with him in St. Sophia six days and six nights.

And *Tsar* Isakovits was in Lakherna,[1] and he wanted to bring the Franks into the town without the knowledge of the *Boyars;* but the *Boyars* having learned, appeased the *Tsar* and did not allow him to let loose the Franks, saying: " We are with thee." Then the *Boyars* fearing the introduction of the Franks, having consulted with Murchufl,[2] took *Tsar* Isakovits, and put the crown on Murchufl. Now Isakovits had taken Murchufl out of prison and he [Murchufl] had taken declaration not to seek the throne from under Isakovits, but keep it under him. And Murchufl sent to Nikola and to the people to St. Sophia: " I have taken your enemy Isakovits; I am your *Tsar.* And I grant Nikola to be first among *Boyars;* put off the crown from thee."

And all the people did not let him put off the crown, but swore the more: " Whosoever shall turn away from Nikola, let him be accursed." The same day having waited for the night they all dispersed and took Nikola and Murchufl and took his wife and put her

[1] sc. Vlakherna, ' Blachernae' in Constantinople (a suburb till Heraclius I, 610–641).
[2] Alexis V, Mourtzouphlos.

into prison and made fast Oleksa Isakovits in walls, and Murchufl himself became *Tsar* on February 5 hoping to destroy the Franks. But the Franks, having learned that Isakovits was taken, made war on the district round the town, asking Murchufl: " Give us Isakovits, that we may go to the *Tsar* of the *Nemtsy*[1] whence we were sent; and have thou his throne." But Murchufl and all the *Boyars* refused to give him alive, and having done Isakovits to death, said to the Franks: " He is dead; come and see him." Then the Franks were troubled for their disobedience; for not thus had the *Tsar* of the *Nemtsy*[1] and the Pope of Rome directed them, and they had done this harm to *Tsargrad*. And they all said themselves: " Since we have not Isakovits, with whom we came, it is better for us to die at *Tsargrad*, than to go away with shame." Therefore, they began to take up the offensive against the town. They bethought them as before, with yards on the masts of their ships, on other ships they constructed battering rams and ladders, and on others they bethought them to hang down barrels packed with pitch over the town, and having lit shavings, they dropped on to the houses, as they fired the town before.

And they advanced to the town on April 9, on Friday of the fifth week of the Fast, but achieved nothing against the town; but they killed nearly 100 men of the Franks. And the Franks stood there three days; and on Monday in Palm week they advanced to the town at sunrise, opposite St. Saviour's called Vergetis,[2] opposite Ispigas,[3] and they took stand as far as Lakherna. And they advanced on forty large ships; and they were lashed between each other, and in them men on horses, dressed in armour, their horses too; and other of their ships and galleys stood back fearing to catch fire, as the Greeks before also had directed ten ships with fire on to them; and having awaited a favourable wind under sail at midnight on St. Vasili's Day, they achieved nothing against the Frank ships: for Isakovits had given them word, and ordered the Greeks to attack them and their ships; in this way the Franks did not take fire.

And thus was the taking of *Tsargrad* the Great: the wind drew the ships up to the town wall; the ladders were high, overlooking the town, and the lower ladders were level with the ramparts; the Greeks fought from the high ladders over the town and the Varangians with stones and arrows and javelins, while from the lower ladders the men climbed down into the town; and thus they took the town.

[1] Germans.
[2] i.e. Εὐεργέτης.
[3] i.e. εἰς πηγάς

And *Tsar* Murchufl kept encouraging the *Boyars* and all the people, wishing there to make a fight with the Franks, and they did not listen to him and they all ran from him; and the *Tsar* ran from them and overtook them in the horse market, and complained much against the *Boyars* and all the people. Then the *Tsar* fled out of the town, and the Patriarch and all the *Boyars*, and all the Franks entered the town on April 12, Monday, Day of St. Vasili the Confessor, and halted where the Greek *Tsar* had stood at St. Saviour's, and halted there for the night. And in the morning at sunrise they entered St. Sophia, and tore down and cut in pieces the doors and the ambo[1] all worked with silver, they cut in pieces the twelve silver pillars and the four [pillars] of the ikon-case, and the ikon bracket, and the twelve crosses which were over the altar, like trees bigger than a man, and the bosses between them, and the altar rail between the pillars, and these were all of silver; they stripped the beautiful altar of its precious stones and large pearl, and it is not known where they put it itself; and they took the forty large cups which were before the altar and the censers and silver lamps, so many that we cannot tell their number, with priceless vessels used on feast-days; they stripped the service copy of the Gospels and the Honourable Crosses, and priceless ikons, and under the altar cloth they found hidden forty barrels of pure gold; and in the chambers, walls, and repositories of vessels no knowing how much gold and silver, beyond number, and priceless vessels. All this I have mentioned [was] in St. Sophia alone; while the [church of the] Holy Mother of God which is in Vlakherna, where the Holy Spirit used to descend every Friday, that they also stripped; and [the number] of other churches no man can tell, because they were beyond number. The wonderful *Digitria*[2] of the Holy Mother of God which used to go through the town was, however, preserved by God with [the help of] good people, and exists to-day and is our hope. The other churches in the town and outside the town and monasteries in the town and outside the town they plundered all—we cannot tell their number, nor their beauty. They robbed the monks and nuns and priests and some of them they beat to death; and the Greeks and the Varangians, who had remained they drove out of the town.

These are the names of their *Voyevodas:*—I. *Markos* of Rome,[3]

[1] *Amvon.*
[2] Ὀδηγήτρια.
[3] i.e. Boniface, *Marquess* of Monferrat.

in the town of Bern where the pagan and wicked Dedrik[1] had dwelled; II. *Kondoflandr*;[2] III. the blind *Duzh*[3] from St. Mark's island, Venedik. *Tsar* Manuel blinded this *Duzh*; for many philosophers had begged the *Tsar*: " If thou lettest this *Duzh* go whole, then he will do much harm to thy empire." And the *Tsar* not wishing to kill him, he ordered his eyes to be blinded with glass; and his eyes were as if uninjured, but he saw nothing. This *Duzh* had planned many attacks on the town and all used to obey him; his ships from off which they took the town were large. The Franks stood before *Tsargrad* from December to April, until they took the town. And on May 9 they appointed *Tsar* their own Latin *Kondoflandr* with their own bishops, and divided the power amongst themselves: [they gave] to the *Tsar* the town, to *Markos* the Sound, and to the *Duzh* the *Desyatina*.[4]

And so perished the empire of the God-protected *Kostyantingrad* and the Greek land in the quarrel of *Tsars;* and the Franks rule it.

A.D. 1205. A.M. 6713. The Moon shone eight nights. The same year the *Veliki Knyaz* Vsevolod sent to Novgorod, saying thus: " Troops are marching to war in your land; your *Knyaz* my son Svyatoslav, is young; I give you my eldest son Kostyantin." Then they took the *Posadnik*-ship from Mikhalko and gave it to Dmitri Miroshkinits. The same year *Knyaz* Kostyantin Vsevolodits, grandson of Gyurgi, came to Novgorod on March 20, St. Gerasim's Day, and the whole town was glad at [the fulfilment of] its desire. Vsevolod's *Knyaginya* died the same year.

A.D. 1206. A.M. 6714. God's servant, Mitrofan, whose secular name was Mikhalko, *Posadnik* of Novgorod, died on May 18; he had had himself shorn at the Church of the Holy Mother of God in the Arkadi monastery. The same year Tverdislav Mikhalkovits put up a church to St. Simon Stylites of the Wonderful Hill[5] over the gates of the Arkadi monastery.

A.D. 1207. A.M. 6715. The Volodarevitsi and Nosovitsi[6] put up the Church of St. Luke in Lubyana Street,

---

[1] Theodoric the Ostrogoth, whose *Bern* is Verona.
[2] i.e. Baldwin, *Count of Flanders*.
[3] i.e. *Doge* Dandolo.
[4] Tenth part.
[5] Near Antioch.
[6] Families.

having transferred it from Koleno. The same year merchants from oversea completed the Church of the Holy Friday on August 30. The same year Fedor Pineshchinits completed the Church of St. Panteleimon. The same year God's servant, Parfuri, whose secular name was Proksha Malishevits, died; he had had himself shorn at the Holy Saviour's [Monastery] at Khutin, under *Igumen* Varlam. God grant peace to his soul.

A.D. 1208. A.M. 6716. Lazor, Vsevolod's man, came from Volo dimir, and Boris Miroshkinits ordered Oleks Sbyslavits to be killed in Yaroslav's court; and they killed him guiltless, on Saturday, March 17, St. Alexis' Day. And the next morning the Holy Mother of God wept in the Church of St. Yakov in the Nerev end.

A.D. 1209. A.M. 6717. The men of Novgorod went with *Knyaz* Kostyantin against Chernigov, summoned by Vsevolod; and they came to the river Oka and there all the troops assembled, and the *Knyaz* of Ryazan stood on the further side of the Oka, come to help Vsevolod; and Vsevolod summoned them to eat; six *Knyazes* sat down in a tent, and Gleb and Oleg and the men of Novgorod sat in Vsevolod's tent. And there the Volodimiritsi[1] accused their brothers falsely: " Have no faith in our brothers, *Knyaz*: they have taken counsel against you with the *Knyazes* of Chernigov." Thus they denounced the *Knyazes* of Ryazan. And Vsevolod took them all and their men, and having fettered them sent them to Volodimir; and himself went with the men of Novgorod and with the two calumniators to the district of Ryazan, and he came to Pronsk, and said: " Surrender yourselves to me." And they were with *Knyaz* Izyaslav, the third Volodimirits; and *Knyaz* Mikhail ran on ahead from Pronsk; and took away their water, and they surrendered. And he took *Knyaz* Mikhail's *Knyaginya*, and countless merchandise; and took peace with Izyaslav and they went away well. From Kolomno he let the men of Novgorod go to Novgorod having made them presents without number, and he gave them all their will and the decrees of their former *Knyazes*, all that the men of Novgorod had wished for, and he said to them: " Who of you is good, him love, but punish the bad," and took his son Kostyantin with him, and *Posadnik* Dmitri who was wounded near Pronsk, and seven foremost men. Having come to Novgorod

---

[1] sc. Gleb and Oleg, sons of Volodimir, *Knyazes* of Ryazan.

E

the men of Novgorod held a Veche over *Posadnik* Dmitri and his brethren, because they had ordered the levying of silver on the people of Novgorod, for collecting money[1] throughout the district, fines[2] from the merchants, for enforcing the collection of taxes at fixed times and everything bad. And they went to plunder their courts, and set fire to Miroshkin's court and Dmitri's, appropriating their effects, sold all their villages and servants, sought out their treasures, and took of them without number, and the rest they divided so that each got some,[3] at three *grivnas* throughout the whole town, and took everything. God alone knows how much any took secretly, and many grew rich from this; and what was on the boards[4] that they left to the *Knyaz*. The same year they brought Dmitri Miroshkinits dead from Volodimir and buried him in the monastery of St. Georgi along side his father; the people of Novgorod wanted to throw him from the bridge, but *Vladyka* Mitrofan forbade them. Vsevolod sent his son Svyatoslav to Novgorod on Sexagesima Sunday. Then they gave the *Posadnik*-ship to Tverdislav Mikhalkovits, and Dmitri's written documents they gave to Svyatoslav; there was a countless [quantity] of them. And the men of Novgorod kissed the honourable Cross, that we will not keep Dmitri's children by us, neither Volodislav nor Boris, nor Tverdislav Stanilovits, nor Ovstrat Domazhirovits; so the *Knyaz* sent them away to their father, and on some they levied a countless [quantity] of silver.

A.D. 1210. A.M. 6718. The men of Novgorod with *Knyaz* Volodimir and *Posadnik* Tverdislav, having pursued and found the Lithuanians in Khodynitsy, killed them.

The same year Vsevolod went against Ryazan and said to them: " Come to me and my son Yaroslav over the Oka to deliberate." And they went over to him and there he seized them all; and sent troops; and took a l their wives and children, and set fire to their town; and thus he distributed them about the towns. The same winter *Knyaz* Mstislav Mstislavits came against Torzhok, and seized Svyatoslav's courtiers[5] and put the *Posadnik* in chains and whoever could lay hands on their goods [took them]; and he sent to Novgorod: " I bow down to St. Sophia and to the tomb of my father and to all the men of Novgorod; I have come to you having heard of the

---

[1] *Kuny.*
[2] *Vira dikaya.*
[3] *Po zubu*—per **tooth.**
[4] sc. rafts.
[5] *Dvoryane.*

violence [done you] by the *Knyaz;* and I am sorry for my patrimony." Having heard this the men of Novgorod sent for him with
great honour: " Come, *Knyaz,* to the throne." And they set
Svyatoslav with his men in the *Vladyka's* court until the settlement
with his father.   Mstislav came to Novgorod and they set him on
his father's throne, and the men of Novgorod were glad; and
Mstislav went with the whole army[1] against Vsevolod, and they were
at Ploskeya and Vsevolod sent to him: " Thou art son to me and I
father to thee; let go Svyatoslav with his men; and all that thou hast
confiscated, make good, and I will let go the merchants and merchandise." And Mstislav released Svyatoslav and his men and Vsevolod
released the merchants and their merchandise; they both of them
kissed the Cross and took peace, and Mstislav came to Novgorod.

A.D. 1211. A.M. 6719. Dmitri Yakunits came from Russia, and
Tverdislav of his own will relinquished the
Posadnik-ship to a senior, and then they gave the *Posadnik*-ship to
Dmitri Yakunits. And *Knyaz* Mstislav sent Dmitri Yakunits to
Luki with the men of Novgorod to build a fortification,[2] and himself
went to Torzhok to inspect the districts; from Torzhok he went to
Toropets, from Toropets he went to Luki and came together with
the men of Novgorod; and to the people of Luki he gave Volodimir
of Pleskov[3] as *Knyaz* of Luki.   The same year by the will of God
Vyacheslav Proshinits, grandson of Malishev, completed the stone
Church of the Forty Saints; and God grant him salvation through
the prayers of the Forty Saints.   The same year in the absence
of the *Knyaz* and of the men of Novgorod there was a great fire in
Novgorod; it broke out in Radyatin Street, and 4,300
houses[4] were burnt down, and fifteen churches.   The same year,
in the winter, on January 22, St. Kliment's Day, the evil-doer who
from the first wished no good [to man] put envy in the people with
Knyaz Mstislav against *Vladyka* Mitrofan; and they did not allow
him to clear himself, and led him to Toropets; but he took this gladly,
like Ioan Zlatoust[5] and Gregory of Akragas; he accepted a like wrong
glorifying God.   At the same time, before the expulsion of *Vladyka*
Mitrofan, Dobrynya Yadreikovits had come from *Tsargrad* and
brought with him the [measure of the] Lord's tomb, and had himself

---

[1] *Polk.*
[2] *Gorod.*
[3] i.e. Pskov.
[4] *Dvory.*
[5] St. John Chrysostom.

shorn at Khutin at the Holy Saviour's [monastery]; and by the will of God *Knyaz* Mstislav and all the people of Novgorod came to love him, and they sent him to Russia to get himself appointed; and he came appointed as *Vladyka* Antoni, and he made the palace[1] of Mitrofan a church in the name of St. Antony.

A.D. 1212. A.M. 6720. Mstislav went with the men of Novgorod against the Chud people called Torma, and made many captives and brought back countless cattle. Later, in the winter, *Knyaz* Mstislav went with the men of Novgorod against the Chud town called Medvezhya Golova, and ruined their villages; and they came up to the town and the Chud people bowed down to the *Knyaz*, and he took tribute from them; and all came [back] well.

A.D. 1213. A.M. 6721. In Peter's Fast, the godless Lithuanians came out against Pleskov, and set fire to it; for the people of Pleskov at that time had driven out *Knyaz* Volodimir from amongst them, and were on the lake[2]; they did much harm and went away.

A.D. 1214. A.M. 6722. On February 1, on Quinquagesima Sunday, there was thunder after morning service, and all heard it; and then at the same time they saw a flying snake.[3] On the same day *Knyaz* Mstislav marched with the men of Novgorod against the Chud people to Ereva,[4] through the land of the Chud people towards the sea, he ruined their villages and captured their forest fortresses.[5] And he stayed with the men of Novgorod by the town of Vorobino,[6] and the Chud people bowed down to him, and *Knyaz* Mstislav took tribute from them; and gave two parts of the tribute to the men of Novgorod, and the third part to the courtiers. There were present also *Knyaz* Vsevolod Borisovits of Pleskov with the men of Pleskov, and *Knyaz* David of Toropets, Volodimir's brother; and all returned well with a quantity of plunder. The same year Vsevolod the Red, son of Svyatoslav, great-grandson of Oleg, drove the grandsons of Rostislav out of Russia, saying thus: " You hanged two of my brothers, *Knyazes*, in Galich[7] as malefactors

1 *Polata.*
2 Lake Chud.
3 Or dragon.
4 Or Narova.
5 *Oseki.*
6 Sparrow-town.
7 Galicia.

and you put shame on all; and there is no portion for you in the Russian Land." The same year the grandsons of Rostislav sent to Mstislav Mstislavich to Novgorod, " Behold Vsevolod Svyatoslavich makes us no portion in the Russian Land; come let us claim our patrimony." And Mstislav summoned a *Veche* in Yaroslav's Court, and began to summon the men of Novgorod to go to Kiev against Vsevolod the Red. The men of Novgorod said to him: " Whither, *Knyaz*, thou shalt look with thy eyes, there will we lay down our heads." And Mstislav went to Kiev with the men of Novgorod in the month of June, the 18th, St. Fedor's Day; and they reached Smolensk and there arose a dispute between the men of Novgorod and the men of Smolensk, and the men of Novgorod killed a man of Smolensk and would not go after their *Knyaz*. *Knyaz* Mstislav began to summon a *Veche*, but they would not come to it. The *Knyaz* having kissed all, and saluted them, went; but the men of Novgorod having made a *Veche* of their own began to deliberate. And *Posadnik* Tverdislav said: " Brothers! as our fathers and grandfathers laboured for the Russian Land, we, too, will go after our *Knyaz*." And so they went from Smolensk and having overtaken the *Knyaz* they began to make war on the towns of Chernigov along the Dnieper; they took Rechitsa by storm and many other towns of Chernigov; and they came up to Vyshegorod and began to fight. And Mstislav with his brothers and the men of Novgorod prevailed and took two *Knyazes:* Rostislav Yaroslavits and his brother Yaropolk, grandsons of Oleg. And the people of Vyshegorod bowed down to him and opened their gates. And Vsevolod fled from Kiev across the Dnieper, and Mstislav with his brothers and the men of Novgorod entered Kiev, and the people of Kiev bowed down to him, and set Mstislav Romanovits, grandson of Rostislav, in Kiev. From Kiev they went to Chernigov, and having stayed twelve days, they took peace and having taken gifts came all well to Novgorod.

A.D. 1215. A.M. 6723. *Knyaz* Mstislav went to Kiev of his own free will, and made a *Veche* in Yaroslav's Court, and said to the men of Novgorod: " I have arms [to work my will] in Russia, and you are free to choose your *Knyaz*." The same year the men of Novgorod, having deliberated much, sent *Posadnik* Gyurgi Ivankovits and the *Tysyatski* Yakun, with ten senior merchant men for Yaroslav Vsevolodits, Gyurgi's grandson, and *Knyaz* Yaroslav entered Novgorod, and *Vladyka* Anton with the men of

Novgorod met him. The same year *Knyaz* Yaroslav seized Yakun Zubolomits and sent for Foma Dobroshchinits *Posadnik* of Novitorg; and having put him in chains imprisoned him in Tver. And for our sins Fedor Lazurtinits and Ivor of Novi-torg informed against the *Tysyatski* Yakun Namnezhits. And *Knyaz* Yaroslav made a *Veche* in Yaroslav's Court; they went to Yakun's Court and plundered it and seized his wife. And Yakun went the next morning to the *Knyaz* with the *Posadnik*, and the *Knyaz* ordered to be seized his son Khristofor on May 21. And then the Prussians killed Ovostrat on a festival day, also his son Lugota, and threw them dead into a pit. The *Knyaz* complained to the men of Novgorod of this. The same year *Knyaz* Yaroslav went to Torzhok taking with him Tverdislav Mikhalkovits, Mikifor, Polyud, Sbyslav, Semen, Olksa and many *Boyars*, and having given them gifts, sent them to Novgorod, and himself settled in Torzhok. The same autumn much harm was done; frost killed the corn crops throughout the district; but at Torzhok all remained whole. The *Knyaz* seized all the corn in Torzhok, and would not let one cart-load into the city; and they sent Semen Borisovits, Vyacheslav Klimyatits, for Zubets Yakun to fetch the *Knyaz* and he detained them; and he detained whomever you sent. And in Novgorod it was very bad, they bought one barrel[1] of rye for ten *grivnas*, one of oats for three *grivnas*, a load of turnips for two *grivnas;* people ate pine bark and lime tree leaves and moss. O brothers, then was the trouble; they gave their children into slavery. They dug a public grave and filled it full. O, there was trouble! corpses in the market-place, corpses in the street, corpses in the fields; the dogs could not eat up the men! The Vod people all died; the rest were scattered. And thus for our sins our power and our town went asunder.

And the rest of the men of Novgorod sent *Posadnik* Gyurgi Ivanovits and Stepan Tverdislavits and others to fetch the *Knyaz*, and those he detained; and having sent Ivor and Chaponos to Novgorod he had his *Knyaginya* Mstislav's daughter brought to him from there. And then they (sc. the men of Novgorod) sent Manuil Yagolchevich with the final message: " Come to thy patrimony, to St. Sophia; if thou wilt not come, then tell us." These Yaroslav likewise would not let go, and he detained all the Novgorod merchants; and there was sorrow and wailing in Novgorod. And then Mstislav Mstislavits having heard of this evil, arrived at Novgorod on February 11, seized Yaroslav's lieutenant,[2] Knota Grigorevits,

[1] *Kad.*
[2] *Namestnik.*

and put all the nobles in chains; and he rode out to Yaroslav's Court and kissed the honourable Cross, and the men of Novgorod [did likewise] to him to be with him in life and death: " I shall either recover the Novgorod men and the districts, or lay down my head for Novgorod." Yaroslav had this news at Torzhok and they erected a stockade and blockaded the road from Novgorod and the river Tvertsa; and he sent 100 of the men of Novgorod to Novgorod to conduct Mstislav out of Novgorod; and they did not undertake this; but they were all of one mind, also those 100 men. And *Knyaz* Mstislav with the men of Novgorod sent the priest Gyurgi of St. Ioan's in the market-place to Yaroslav to Torzhok, with some of his own men: " Son, I greet you; release my men and the merchants; and yourself go from Torzhok, and have love with me." But *Knyaz* Yaroslav not liking this, let go the priest without peace, and summoned the men of Novgorod to a field outside Torzhok on Saturday before Sexagesima, and having seized all the men and merchants and put them in chains sent them to his various towns, and distributed their merchandise and horses; and there were of all the men of Novgorod over 2,000. And the news came to Novgorod; and there were few of the men of Novgorod [left]; the biggest men were captured abroad; and the lesser had been scattered and others had died from famine. And *Knyaz* Mstislav made a *Veche* in Yaroslav's Court: "Let us go," he said, " and recover our men, your brothers, and our districts. Novi-torg shall not be Novgorod, nor shall Novgorod be Torzhok. But where St. Sophia is there is Novgorod. God is in the many; but God and justice are also in the few."

A.D. 1216. A.M. 6724. On March 1 on the Tuesday after Pure Sunday, Mstislav went against his son-in-law, Yaroslav with the men of Novgorod, and on the Thursday the transgressors of oath to the Cross fled to Yaroslav; for they had kissed the honourable Cross to Mstislav with all the men of Novgorod, to be all at one, Volodislav Zavidits, Gavrilo Igorevits, Gyurgi Olksinits and Gavrilo Milyatinits with their wives and children. And Mstislav went by the Seregeri lake, and entered his own district, and said to the men of Novgorod: " Go out foraging, but take no heads." They went, and took their fill of food both they and their horses, and they were at the head of the Volga. Svyatoslav invested Rzhevka, one of Mstislav's towns, with a force of 10,000. But Mstislav with Volodimir of Pleskov went rapidly with 500, for only such was the number of all their men; and he pursued them and they fled. And Yarun had shut himself up in the town with 100 men and beat them off. And Mstislav went and took Zubchev, and they were on the Vozuga; and thither came Volodimir Ruriko-vits with men of Smolensk. They were coming along the Volga, making war, and said to him: " *Knyaz*, go to Torzhok." But Mstislav and Volodimir said: " Let us go to Pereyaslavl; we have a third friend." And there was no news where Yaroslav was, whe-ther at Torzhok or in Tver. And Yaroslav's guards attacked Yarun behind Tver, and God helped Yarun and they killed many, others they captured, and others escaped to Tver. And these got news of Yaroslav and they went along the Volga making war, and they burned [along the river] Shesha and also [the towns of] Dubna and Kosnyatin and all the country along the Volga. And Eremei [coming] from *Knyaz* Kostyantin met them with love and with greeting; and they went making war to Pereyaslavl and were at *Gorodishche*[1] on the river Sarra, at the Church of Saint Marina on April 9 on Great Saturday. *Knyaz* Kostyantin with the men of Rostov came and kissed the Cross.

And Yaroslav went to Torzhok having taken with him the elder men of Novgorod, and young men by selection, and all the men of Novi-torg. And he came to Pereyaslavl and assembled all his district and Gyurgi his, Volodimir and Svyatoslav likewise. And he went out from Pereyaslavl with his forces and those of Novgorod and of Novi-torg. How terrible, wonderful and strange, brothers! Sons went against father, brother against brother, slave against master, master against slave. And Yaroslav and Gyurgi, with their brothers took stand on the Khza river. And Mstislav and Kostyantin, the two Volodimirs, with the men of Novgorod, took stand on the Lipitsa river, and they beheld the forces standing, and sent the *Sotski* Larion to Gyurgi: " We greet thee; we have no quarrel with thee, our quarrel is with Yaroslav." And *Knyaz* Gyurgi having answered: " I am one with my brother, Yaroslav," they sent to Yaroslav, saying: " Let go the men of Novgorod and of Novi-torg that are mine; and all that thou hast occupied of my Novgorod districts and the *Volok* give back; take peace with us, and kiss the Cross to us, and let us not shed blood." But they ans-wered: " We do not want peace, and I have men: you have gone far, and are come out like fish on to dry land." And Larion told this speech to Mstislav and to the men of Novgorod, and the men of

¹ sc. Radilov, q.v.

Novgorod said: " *Knyaz*, we do not want to die on horse-back, but as our fathers fought at the [river] Kalaksha on foot." And *Knyaz* Mstislav was glad at this; and the men of Novgorod having dismounted from their horses, and thrown off their breeches ran forward barefoot, having thrown off their boots. And Mstislav rode after them on horse-back; and the forces of Novgorod came together with the forces of Yaroslav. And so with the power of God and with the aid of St. Sophia Mstislav prevailed and Yaroslav and his forces turned shoulder. And Gyurgi made resistance to Kostyantin, but seeing Yaroslav's forces in flight, he also turned shoulder, on April 21, the day of SS. Timofei and Fedor and the *Tsaritsa* Alexandra. O great was the victory, countless the number, my brethren; numberless the number of killed so that the mind of man cannot imagine it. And Yaroslav having fled into Pereyaslavl, ordered the captives to be cast into a pit, all those who were of Novgorod; others into prison, and there they expired in numbers. And Mstislav and Kostyantin and the two Volodimirs with their forces went in pursuit of Gyurgi to Volodimir, and having come they halted before the town, and that night the town and the *Knyaz's* court took fire. And the men of Novgorod wanted to go right up to the town, but *Knyaz* Mstislav did not let them. And it happened the next morning, *Knyaz* Gyurgi sent out with greeting to the *Knyazes:* " Do nothing against me to-day; and to-morrow I shall go out from the town." And Gyurgi went from Volodimir to the little town Radilov; and the men of Novgorod set Kostyantin on his father's throne in Volodimir. And Kostyantin rewarded the *Knyazes* with honour, and numbers of the men of Novgorod. And Mstislav went with the men of Novgorod to Pereyaslavl, and not going up to the town, levied gifts. He sent and took away his daughter, the wife of Yaroslav, and all the surviving men of Novgorod, and all that were in the army with Yaroslav, and all returned well to Novgorod. O, great, my brethren, is the Providence of God! on that place of defeat of Gyurgi and Yaroslav there fell numberless soldiers. The men of Novgorod killed in the conflict were: Dmitri of Pleskov, Onton, kettle maker, Ivanka Pribyshinits, cloak maker; and in the pursuit: Ivanko, the priest's son, Simeon Petrilovits, and a tax gatherer of Tver. Mstislav came to Novgorod and the *Vladyka* and all the men of Novgorod were glad. They then took the *Posadnik*-ship from Gyurgi Ivankovits and gave it to Tverdislav Mikhalkovits.

A.D. 1217. A.M. 6725. Mstislav went away to Kiev, leaving the
Knyaginya and his son Vasili in Novgorod;
and he took with him Gyurgi Ivankovits, Sbyslav Stepanits, and
Olksa Putilovits. Then, too, Volodimir went to Novgorod on
his own business, and the Lithuanians made war in Shelon. The
men of Novgorod went in pursuit of them but did not reach them;
and they went with Knyaz Volodimir and Posadnik Tverdislav to
Medvezhya-Golova, and halted before the town. And the Chud
people began to send greeting deceitfully, but sent for the Nemtsy.[1]
And the men of Novgorod began to deliberate with the men of
Pleskov about the message of the Chud people; going far away
from their baggage, and the night guards had come in and the day
guards had not gone out, and they [the Chud people] unexpectedly
attacked the baggage, and the men of Novgorod ran from their
Veche to the baggage, and having taken up their arms, beat them
off the baggage. And the Nemtsy fled to the town, and the men of
Novgorod killed two Voyevodas and took a third with their hands;
and they took 700 horses, and returned all well. And Knyaz
Mstislav came to Novgorod without them;[2] and took Stanimir
Dirnovits with his son, Nezdila, and having put them in fetters,
imprisoned them; and seized countless quantity of goods and let
them go again. The same spring, on May 31, a bakery caught fire
in the middle of the morning, at Ivan Yarishevits's; by midday the
whole side was burnt as far as the fishery, not a house was left;
and all who had fled into the stone churches with their goods were
all burnt there themselves together with their goods. And in the
Varangian church all the countless Varangian merchandise was
burnt; fifteen churches were burnt; and the tops[3] and the porches
of the stone churches were burned.

A.D. 1218. A.M. 6726. Knyaz Mstislav came to Torzhok and took
Borislav Nekurishinits, and after taking
much merchandise released him. Then, too, the young Knyaz
Vasili Mstislavich fell ill in Torzhok, and they brought him dead
into Novgorod; and they laid him in St. Sophia at the head of his
grandfather at [the image of] the Holy Mother of God. The same
year Vladyka Anton laid the foundation of the stone Church of the
St. Barbara monastery. Mstislav summoned a Veche in Yaroslav's

---

[1] Germans, cf. p. 34.
[2] sc. while they were away.
[3] Cupolas.

Court, and said: " I make greeting to St. Sophia and my father's tomb, and to you; I wish to go and claim Galich,[1] but I shall not forget you. God grant that I may lie by my father in St. Sophia." And the men of Novgorod begged him much: " Do not go, *Knyaz*," but they could not restrain him; and bidding them farewell, he went away. In the same year, *Vladyka* Mitrofan came from Volodimir; and the men of Novgorod conducted him to [the church of] the Annunciation of the Holy Mother of God. Mstislav went to Russia, and the men of Novgorod sent to Smolensk for Svyatoslav Rostislavits and he came to Novgorod on the first day of August. The same year, Gleb Volodimirich, *Knyaz* of Ryazan, being instigated by Satan to murder, having taken thought in his cursed imagination, having as accomplice his brother, Kostyantin, and with him the devil who seduced them and put the idea to them, they saying that: " Let us kill these, and ourselves take over all the power." And thou dost not know, accursed one, the Providence of God; he gives power to whom he pleases. The Almighty appoints both *Tsar* and *Knyaz*. What did Cain obtain from God after killing his brother, Abel? Was it not a curse and a trembling? or your kinsman the accursed Svyatopolk after killing all his brethren? they received the crown of empire, he eternal torment. And this accursed Gleb, having conceived Svyatopolk's same idea, hid it in his heart, with his brother. And all assembed at a landing place for deliberation: Izyaslav, Mikhail, Rostislav, Svyatoslav, Gleb, Roman; Ingvor could not arrive in time; his time had not yet come. And Gleb Volodimirits with his brother summoned them to them as to the honour of a feast, into their tent; and they not knowing his evil thought and deceit, all six *Knyazes*, each with his *Boyars* and courtiers came into their tent. And this Gleb before their arrival having furnished his nobles and his brothers and a large quantity of pagan Polovets people with arms, hid them in the sleeping tent close to the tent in which they were to drink, no one knowing they were there except those two evil-minded *Knyazes* and their accursed confederates. When they began to drink and make merry, then immediately the cursed Gleb and his brother having drawn their swords, began to slaughter first the *Knyazes*, then the *Boyars* and a quantity of the courtiers; with their own courtiers and with the Polovets people [they slew] six *Knyazes* alone and many *Boyars* and courtiers. These righteous *Knyazes* of Ryazan met their end on July 20, the day of the holy prophet, Ilya, and received crowns

[1] sc. Galicia.

from the Lord God, with their *Druzhina,* like innocent
lambs they gave up their souls to God. And this accursed
Gleb and his brother, Kostyantin, prepared the heavenly kingdom for them, but eternal torment for themselves with their
confederates.

And it happened in the winter, Matei Dushiltsevits fled, having
bound the crier informer Moiseits. And the men of Novgorod having
gone in pursuit caught him and brought him to the *Gorodishche;* and
a lie entered the town that Tverdislav had given up Matei to the
Knyaz; and the people on the other side [of the river] rang the bell
at St. Nicholas throughout the night, and those of the Nerev end at
the church of the Forty Saints likewise assembling people against
Tverdislav. And it happened the next morning, the *Knyaz*
released Matei, having learnt of the uproar and tumult in the town.
And the people on the other side, even the children, went out in
armour as for battle, and the Nerev people likewise, but those of the
outskirts stood up neither for those nor for these, paying no
attention. And Tverdislav looked towards St. Sophia, and said:
" If I be guilty, may I die here; if I be innocent justify thou me,
Lord," and he went with the Lyudin end and with the Prussians.
There was a slaughter at the town gates; and they fled to the other
side, and others to the [Lyudin] quarter; and they raised the bridge
and the men of the other side crossed in boats and came up in force.
O, brethren, the accursed devil wrought a great wonder! When
there should have been war against the pagans, then they began to
fight each other. And they killed a Prussian man, and another man
of the people of the [Lyudin] end, and of those of the other side
[they killed] Ivan Dushiltsevits, Matei's brother, and Kosnyatin
Prokopinits, of the Nerev quarter, and six others, and many of
both sides were wounded. This was on January 27, the day of St.
Ioan Zlatoust[1]; and then there were *Veches* all through the week.
But the devil was crushed by God and St. Sophia; the cross was exalted, and brethren came together with one accord, and kissed the
Cross. And *Knyaz* Svyatoslav sent his *Tysyatski* to the *Veche,* and said:
" I cannot be with Tverdislav; and I take away the *Posadnik*-ship
from him." But the men of Novgorod said: " Is the fault his? "
And he answered: " No." Tverdislav said: " I am glad, that I am
not to blame; and you, brethren, are free to choose *Posadnik* and
Knyaz." And the men of Novgorod answered: " *Knyaz!* as he is

---

[1] St. John Chrysostom.

without blame, and thou didst kiss the Cross to us not to deprive a man without blame, therefore, we bow down to thee, but this is our *Posadnik*, and we will not give in to this." And there was peace.

A.D. 1219. A.M. 6727. The *Veliki Knyaz* Mstislav Romanovits sent his son Vsevolod from Kiev, saying: " Receive to yourselves *Knyaz* Vsevolod, and let the older Svyatoslav return to me." And the men of Novgorod did his will. The same winter, Simeon Emin went with 400 men against [the district of] Toimokary, but neither Gyurgi nor Yaroslav let them through their land; and they came to Novgorod in boats¹ and set up their tents on the fields, with evil intent. Tverdislav and the *Tysyatski* Yakun took thought and sent to Gyurgi not to let them go there, and they stirred up the town. Then they took the *Posadnik* ship from Tverdislav and gave it to Simeon Borisovits, and took the office of *Tysyatski* from Yakun and gave it to Simeon Emin. Then, too, they finished the stone Church of St. Barbara. The same year Tverdislav and Fedor laid the foundation of a stone Church to St. Michael, and another small one to the Three Holy Youths by its side, they completed it in four days. *Knyazes* Mstislav and Volodimir went from Kiev to Galich against the King's son²; and the men of Galich came out against them and *Chekhi* and *Lyakhi*,³ Moravians and Hungarians,⁴ and the forces came together. And God helped Mstislav, and he entered the town of Galich and they took with their hands the King's son and his wife; and he took peace with the King, and let go his son, and himself took his seat in Galich and Volodimir Rurikovits in Kiev. The same year, *Knyaz* Vsevolod went with the men of Novgorod to Pertuyev, and they met outposts of the *Nemtsy*,⁵ Lithuanians and Livonians,⁶ and they fought; and God helped the men of Novgorod; they went up to the town and stood there two weeks; they did not take the town, and returned all well. The same year Anton, *Vladyka* of Novgorod, went to Torzhok. And the men of Novgorod fetched *Vladyka* Mitrofan into the Bishop's court and on to the throne again, and sent to Onton⁷: "Go where thou wilt." And Anton went to Novgorod to the Holy Redeemer's on the Nereditsa. And *Knyaz* and men of

¹ *Lodya.*
² *Korolevich.*
³ Bohemians and Poles.
⁴ *Ugry.*
⁵ cf. p. 34.
⁶ *Lib.*   ⁷ i.e. Anton.

Novgorod said to Mitrofan and to Anton: " Go to the Metropolitan; that whom he send us, that one be our *Vladyka*." And they let go with them the monk Vasyan the priest, and another priest, Boris. And having returned from Pertuev they gave the *Posadnik*-ship to Tverdislav, and to Yakun the office of *Tysyatski* again.

A.D. 1220. A.M. 6728. *Vladyka* Mitrofan came to Novgorod on March 17, having righted himself through God and St. Sophia; and Anton the Metropolitan kept by him in honour and gave him the Bishopric of Peremyshl. The same year, *Knyaz* Vsevolod went to Smolensk on his own business. And in the same winter *Knyaz* Vsevolod came from Smolensk to Torzhok. And the devil wishing no good to the Christian race, and wicked men neither, put sin into the heart of the *Knyaz* and anger against Tverdislav, though without fault. And he came to Novgorod and stirred up the whole town, wishing to kill Tverdislav, and Tverdislav was ill. And *Knyaz* Vsevolod went out from the *Gorodishche* with all his Court[1] in armour as for battle and came to Yaroslav's Court. And the men of Novgorod met him in arms and took stand in battle order in the *Knyaz's* Court. And Tverdislav was sick and they drove him out on a sledge to [the church of] Boris and Gleb and the Prussians and people of the Lyudin end, and from the out-skirts, gathered round him and took stand round him in battle order forming themselves in five troops. And the *Knyaz* perceiving their formation and that they would fight hard for their lives, did not ride out, but sent *Vladyka* Mitrofan with all good messages and the *Vladyka* brought them together in love, and both *Knyaz* and Tver-dislav kissed the Cross. Through God and St. Sophia the Cross was exalted, and the devil was crushed, and all brethren were to-gether. And Tverdislav having come together with the *Knyaz* in love was deprived of the *Posadnik*-ship, for he was ill, and they gave the *Posadnik*-ship to Ivanko Dmitrovits. He continued in that illness seven weeks, and greater illness took hold of him, and he went to [the church of] the Holy Mother of God in the Arkadi mon-astery in secret from his wife and children and from all the brethren, and had himself shorn on February 8. His wife then had herself shorn in another monastery, at St. Barbara's.

A.D. 1221. A.M. 6729. The men of Novgorod showed *Knyaz* Vsevolod the road. " We do not want thee, go whither thou wilt." He went to his father, into Russia.

---

[1] *Dvor.*

A.D. 1222. A.M. 6730. They sent *Vladyka* Mitrofan and *Posadnik* Ivanko with the elder men to Gyurgi Vsevolodits in Volodimir for his son, and he gave them Vsevolod with guarantee of all the liberties of Novgorod. *Knyaz* Vsevolod came to Novgorod, and the *Vladyka* and all the men [came back] with countless gifts; and the men of Novgorod were glad, and there was peace. The same year, *Knyaz* Gyurgi sent his brother Svyatoslav to help the men of Novgorod. The men of Novgorod went with Svyatoslav to Kes,[1] and the Lithuanians also came to their help; and they made much war, but did not take the town. And Yaroslav's men from Smolensk took Poltesk[2] on January 17, under *Knyaz* Boris and Gleb. The same winter, *Knyaz* Vsevolod fled by night secretly out of Novgorod with all his Court. And the men of Novgorod were grieved at this. Then the men of Novgorod sent the elder men to Gyurgi: " If it does not please thee to hold Novgorod through thy son, then give us thy brother." And he gave them his brother Yaroslav.

A.D. 1223. A.M. 6731. *Knyaz* Yaroslav came to Novgorod and all the men of Novgorod were glad. The Lithuanians made war round Toropets, and Yaroslav with the men of Novgorod went in pursuit of them as far as [lake] Vosvyat, but did not catch them. The same year, Mitrofan, *Vladyka* of Novgorod, died on July 3, St. Vakint's[3] Day, on the dawn of Monday, and was laid in the porch of St. Sophia; may God grant through his holy prayers many years to the *Knyaz* and to all the men of Novgorod. The same day they led the monk Arseni from Khutin into the [Bishop's] Court; a good and very God-fearing man. *Knyaz* Yaroslav came from his brother and went with all the province to Kolyvan,[4] and conquered the whole Chud land, and brought back countless plunder, but did not take the town; they took much gold, and returned all well. *Knyaz* Yaroslav with the *Knyaginya* and his children went to Pereyaslavl; and the men of Novgorod made greeting to him: " Do not go, *Knyaz* "; but he went according to his will. And the men of Novgorod sent to Gyurgi for his son, and he again gave them his son Vsevolod.

A.D. 1224. A.M. 6732. *Knyaz* Vsevolod Gyurgevits came to Novgorod. The same year the *Nemtsy* killed

1 Wenden.
2 Polotsk.
3 Hyacinth.
4 Revel.

Knyaz Vyachko in Gyurgev[1] and took the town. The same year,
for our sins, this was not [all] the evil that happened: *Posadnik*
Fedor rode out with the men of Russa and fought with the Lithuanians; and they drove the men of Russa from their horses and took
many horses, and killed Domazhir Torlinits and his son and of the
men of Russa Bogsha and many others, and the rest they drove
asunder in the forest. The same year, for our sins, unknown tribes[2]
came, whom no one exactly knows, who they are, nor whence they
came out, nor what their language is, nor of what race they are, nor
what their faith is; but they call them Tartars,[3] and others say
Taurmen, and others Pecheneg people, and others say that they are
those of whom Bishop Mefodi of Patmos bore witness, that they
came out from the Etrian desert which is between East and North.
For thus Mefodi says, that, at the end of time, those are to appear
whom Gideon scattered, and they shall subdue the whole land from
the East to the Efrant,[4] and from the Tigris to the Pontus sea except
Ethiopia. God alone knows who they are and whence they came
out. Very wise men know them exactly, who understand books;
but we do not know who they are, but have written of them here for
the sake of the memory of the Russian *Knyazes* and of the misfor-
tune which came to them from them. For we have heard that they
have captured many countries, slaughtered a quantity of the godless Yas, Obez, Kasog and Polovets peoples, and scattered others,
who all died, killed thus by the wrath of God and of His immaculate
Mother, for those cursed Polovets people had wrought much evil
to the Russian Land. Therefore the all-merciful God wished to
destroy the Kuman people[5], godless sons of Ishmael, that they [might]
atone for the blood of Christians which was upon them, lawless ones;
for those Taurmen people passed through the whole Kuman country,
and came close to Russia where it is called the Polovets Wall.[6]
And the cursed Polovets people, the survivors of those who were
killed, escaped [to Russia], Kotyan with other *Knyazes*, while Danil
Kobyakovits and Gyurgi were killed, and with them a quantity of
the Polovets people. And this Kotyan was father-in-law to Mstislav
of Galich. And he came with the Polovets *Knyazes* with greeting
to his son-in-law Mstislav in Galich, and to all the Russian *Knyazes*,

[1] Yurev or Dorpat.
[2] *Yazyk*, lit. " tongue."
[3] *Tatary*.
[4] Euphrates.
[5] The Polovtsi.
[6] *Val.*

and brought many gifts: horses and camels, buffaloes and girls; and they gave gifts [of these] to the Russian *Knyazes*, saying thus: " Our land they have taken away to-day; and yours will be taken to-morrow," and Kotyan appealed to his son-in-law, and Mstislav began to appeal to the Russian *Knyazes*, his brethren, saying thus: " If we, brothers, do not help these, then they will certainly surrender to them,[1] then the strength of those will be greater." And thus having deliberated much among themselves, they made themselves ready for the journey because of both the greeting and the appeal of the Polovets *Knyazes*. And they began to organize their forces, each his own province, and they went, having collected the whole Russian Land against the Tartars, and were on the Dnieper at Zarub. Then the Tartars having learned that the Russian *Knyazes* were coming against them sent envoys to the Russian *Knyazes:* " Behold, we hear that you are coming against us, having listened to the Polovets men; but we have not occupied your land, nor your towns, nor your villages, nor is it against you we have come. But we have come sent by God against our serfs,[2] and our horse-herds, the pagan Polovets men, and do you take peace with us. If they escape to you, drive them off thence, and take to yourselves their goods. For we have heard that to you also they have done much harm; and it is for that reason also we are fighting them." But the Russian *Knyazes* did not listen to this, but killed all the envoys and themselves went against them, and took stand on the Dnieper, this side of Oleshe. And the Tartars sent to them envoys a second time, saying thus: " Since you have listened to the Polovets men, and have killed all our envoys, and are coming against us, come then, but we have not touched you, let God judge all." And they let go free their envoys. And then Mstislav having forded the Dnieper went across with 1,000 men, against the Tartar outposts, and defeated them, and the remainder of them fled with their *Voyevoda* Gemya-Beg to the Polovets *kurgan*[3] and there they could not hold out, and they buried their *Voyevoda* Gemya-Beg alive in the earth, wishing to preserve his life; and there the Polovets men, having begged permission of Mstislav, found him, and killed him. And having heard of this the Russian *Knyazes* passed over the Dnieper in a body and went all together, and went after them for nine days, and passed over the Kalka river, sent Yarun with the

[1] sc. the Tartars.
[2] *Kholopy.*
[3] Burial-mound, fort.

F

Polovets men forward as outposts, and themselves took up position there as an advance. And then Yarun came together with them, wishing to fight, but the Polovets men ran away back, having accomplished nothing, and in their flight they trampled the camp of the Russian *Knyazes*, for they had not had time to form into order against them[1]; and they were all thrown into confusion, and there was a terrible and savage slaughter. And Mstislav, *Knyaz* of Kiev, seeing this evil, never moved at all from his position; for he had taken stand on a hill above the river Kalka, and the place was stony, and there he set up a stockade[2] of posts about him and fought with them from out of this stockade for three days. And other Tartars went after the Russian *Knyazes* fighting them up to the Dnieper, but two *Voyevodas* Tsigirkan and Teshukan stopped at that stockade [fighting] against Mstislav and his son-in-law, Andrei and Olexander of Dubrovits; for these two *Knyazes* were with Mstislav. And there were there men in armour with the Tartars and *Voyevoda* Ploskyna; and this accursed *Voyevoda*, having kissed the honourable Cross to Mstislav and to both the *Knyazes* not to kill them, but to let them go on ransom, lied, accursed one; he delivered them bound to the Tartars, and they took the stockade and slaughtered the people, and there they fell dead. And having taken the *Knyazes* they suffocated them having put them under boards, and themselves took seat on the top to have dinner. And thus they ended their lives. And pursuing the other *Knyazes* to the Dnieper they killed six: Svyatoslav of Yanev, Izyaslav Ingvorovits, Svyatoslav Shumski, Mstislav of Chernigov with his son, and Gyurgi of Nesvezh. And then Mstislav Mstislavits having previously escaped across the Dnieper, cut loose the boats from the bank so the Tartars should not go after them, and himself barely escaped. And of the rest of the troops every tenth returned to his home; some the Polovets men killed for their horses, and others for their clothes. And thus, for our sins God put misunderstanding into us, and a countless number of people perished, and there was lamentation and weeping and grief throughout towns and villages. This evil happened on May 31, on Saint Eremei's[3] Day. And the Tartars turned back from the river Dnieper, and we know not whence they came, nor where they hid themselves again; God knows whence he fetched them against us for our sins.

The same year, Tverdislav and Fedor completed the stone

1 The Tartars.
2 *Gorod.*   3 Jeremiah.

Church of St. Mikhail. In the same year, there was terrible thunder on May 20, the Day of St. Falalei; the Church of the Holy Trinity was burnt down, and two men fell dead. The same year, Simeon Borisovich built a stone church to St. Paul and St. Simeon the Accepted of God, and to SS. Kostyantin and Elena,[1] and they consecrated it on November 6, St. Paul's Day. The same year, they consecrated the Church of St. Mikhail, on a feast day. The same year, *Knyaz* Vsevolod went a second time from Novgorod secretly by night with all his Court, and having arrived took his seat in Torzhok; and his father Gyurgi came to him with troops, and his brother Yaroslav and Vasilko Kostyantinovits with the men of Rostov, and Mikhail with those of Chernigov. And the men of Novgorod sent two men to Gyurgi at Torzhok; " *Knyaz*, let come to us thy child, and thyself go from Torzhok." And Gyurgi said to the envoys: " Give up to me Yakim Ivankovits, Mikifor Tudorovits, Ivanko Timoshkinits, Sdila Svanits, Vyachek, Ivats, and Radko; and if you do not give them up, I have watered my horses in the Tvertsa and I will water them in the Volkhov too." And the men of Novgorod collected all their district and raised a wall[2] around the town, and sent Polyud, Vyacheslav Prokshinits, and Ivanko Yaryshevits to Gyurgi: " We greet thee, *Knyaz*, but we do not give up our own brothers, and do not thou shed blood; otherwise, thine is the sword, but ours are the heads." And the men of Novgorod placed outposts on the roads and fashioned forts, they wanted to die for St. Sophia in the cause of *Posadnik* Ivanko Dmitrovits. And *Knyaz* Gyurgi sent his man the *Tysyatski* Roman with our own men and with those of Mikhail: " Receive from me my brother-in-law Mikhail." And the men of Novgorod sent their men for Mikhail, and Gyurgi with the *Knyazes* went from Torzhok, having done them much damage and he took from them another 7,000 [*grivnas*].

A.D. 1225. A.M. 6733. *Knyaz* Mikhail, son of Vsevolod, grandson of Oleg, came to Novgorod, and it was easy throughout the district of Novgorod. And the same year, *Knyaz* Mikhail went to Gyurgi taking with him some men of Novgorod to confiscate the goods which he (Gyurgi) had seized in Torzhok and throughout his district.

The same year having recovered the goods from Gyurgi, *Knyaz* Mikhail came [back] and took stand in Yaroslav's Court, and said to the men of Novgorod: " I do not want to be *Knyaz* amongst you;

---

[1] Constantine and Helen. [2] *Ostrog*.

I am going to Chernigov; let merchants come to me; and as your land is so is my land."[1]   And the men of Novgorod entreated him much and begged him, but could not persuade him, and so they escorted him out with honour.   And the men of Novgorod sent to Yaroslav at Pereyaslavl.   *Vladyka* Anton came from Peremyshl to Novgorod, and took his seat on his own throne; and the men of Novgorod were glad of their *Vladyka*.   The same winter the Lithuanians came and wrought countless havoc around Torzhok; but they did not come to Torzhok by three *versts;* there were 7,000 of them, and they killed many merchants and they occupied the whole district of Toropets; and *Knyaz* Yaroslav and Volodimir with his son and with the men of Novi-torg, the *Knyaz's* Court, some men of Novgorod, and the men of Toropets with their *Knyaz* David, went after them, and they sent for the men of Novgorod, but they having come as far as Russa turned back.   And *Knyaz* Yaroslav overtook them[2] on [lake] Vosvyat and turned on them; and thus with the help of God and St. Sophia they recovered all the plunder and killed 2,000 of them[2] themselves, and the rest of them fled asunder.   And there they killed *Knyaz* David of Toropets and Vasili, Yaroslav's sword-bearer.

A.D. 1226. A.M. 6734.   *Knyaz* Yaroslav came [back] to Novgorod and did not make it a cause of anger that they had not followed him.   Then they put up the Church of the Holy Nativity of Christ.   The same year *Igumen* Savati of St. Georgi, Archimandrite of Novgorod, died on April 16, on Great Thursday.   Before his death Savati summoned *Vladyka* Anton, and *Posadnik* Ivanko, and all the men of Novgorod, and he requested all his brethren and all the men of Novgorod: " Choose for yourselves an *Igumen*."   And they said: " Whom dost thou bless ? " And he said: " Bring in the Greek, the priest of SS. Konstantin and Elena."   And they brought in the Greek, a good and very God-fearing man, and they shore him the same day, March 2, St. Fedot's[3] Day, and they appointed him *Igumen* on March 8, the Day of St. Feofilakt[4] in congregation.   And the same year they founded the Church of St. Yakov[5] in stone, in the Nerev end.

A.D. 1227. A.M. 6735.   *Knyaz* Yaroslav went with the men of Novgorod against the Yem people; and ravaged

[1] sc. they are one.
[2] sc. the Lithuanians.
[3] Theodosius.
[4] Theophylact.   [5] James.

the whole land and brought back countless plunder.   And the same
year they burned four sorcerers, they thought they were practising
sorcery, but God knows, and they burned them in Yaroslav's
Court.   The same year Vyacheslav, Malishev's grandson, painted the
Church of the Forty Saints; and God grant him salvation.

A.D. 1228. A.M. 6736.   Anton, *Vladyka* of Novgorod, went of his
                        own free will to Khutin, to the [church of
the] Holy Saviour.   The same year the Yem people came into lake
Ladoga in boats,[1] to make war, and the news reached Novgorod on
the Saviour's Day.   And the men of Novgorod having taken seat
in their boats, rowed to Ladoga with *Knyaz* Yaroslav.   And Volodislav, *Posadnik* of Ladoga with the men of Ladoga, not waiting for
the men of Novgorod, went after them in pursuit in boats
where they were making war, and came up with them, and fought
with them.   And night came on, and they retired to a small island,
and the Yem people [remained] on the shore with their plunder;
for they had been making war at the landings and at Olonets.
And that same night having sued for peace, the *Posadnik* and the
men of Ladoga did not grant it; and they[2] having slaughtered all
their captives, themselves fled into the forest on foot having cast
the boats adrift.   Many of them fell there, and they burned their
boats.   The men of Novgorod remaining several days on the Neva
held a council; and they tried to kill Sudimir, but the *Knyaz* hid
him in his boat.   Thence the men of Novgorod, without waiting
for the men of Ladoga, returned to Novgorod.   And the Izhora
people who had stayed behind, met them as they fled, and there
killed a great many of them.   And the rest fled asunder; but these
the Korel people, whichever way they went, whether by the woods,
or by the fields, or to their tents, discovered and killed.   It is
thought that 2,000 or more of them had come; God knows, and
few of them escaped to their own country; all the rest perished.
   The same year, before this war, *Knyaz* Yaroslav went to Pleskov
with *Posadnik* Ivanko and the *Tysyatski* Vyacheslav.   The people
of Pleskov hearing that the *Knyaz* was coming to them, shut themselves up in the town and would not let him come to them.   And the
Knyaz having stayed a little at Dubrovna, returned to Novgorod.
For the report had got abroad in Pleskov that he was bringing
fetters, intending to put their biggest men into fetters.   And having

---
[1] *Lodka.*
[2] sc. the Yem people.

returned he called a *Veche* in the *Vladyka's* Court, and said: " I had not planned any harm to the people of Pleskov; but I took presents to them in chests, stuffs and fruit; and they have dishonoured me." And he put a great complaint against them. And then he brought up troops from Pereyaslavl, saying: " I want to go against Riga." And tents stood around the *Gorodishche*, and others about the courts[1] in Slavno. And they made all dearer in the market, bread and meat and fish; and thence forward the dearness remained, they bought bread at two *kunas*, a *kad* of rye at three *grivnas*, of wheat five *grivnas*, millet seven *grivnas;* and thus it remained for three years. And the people of Pleskov having heard that Yaroslav was bringing up troops, became afraid and took peace with the men of Riga independently of Novgorod saying: " You be by yourselves and the men of Novgorod by themselves, we will have nothing to do with either; but if they come against us, then you help us." And they said: " Be it so." And they took of them forty men as hostages. And the men of Novgorod having learnt, said: " The *Knyaz* calls upon us to go against Riga, but he wanted to go against Pleskov." Then the *Knyaz* sent Misha to Pleskov, saying: " Come on the march with me; I have not planned any evil against you. But give over to me those who have calumniated me to you." And the men of Pleskov said, sending a Greek: " We greet thee, *Knyaz*, and our brothers the men of Novgorod. We will not go on the march and will not give up our brethren; and with the people of Riga we have taken peace. You marched to Kolyvan, took silver, and then you went back to Novgorod and you did not do justice, and did not take the town. Then, too, at Kes, and thus at Medvezhya-Golova; and for that they killed our brethren at the lake, and others were captured, and you having embroiled [us] there, went off. If you have planned against us, then we shall resist you with the Holy Mother of God and with our greeting. Then better cut us to pieces and take to yourselves our wives and children, no better than the pagans. This is our greeting to you." And the men of Novgorod said to the *Knyaz;* "Without our brethren the men of Pleskov we will not go against Riga, and we bow down to thee, *Knyaz*." And the *Knyaz* urged them much, but they would not go on the march, and then *Knyaz* Yaroslav sent home his troops. The men of Pleskov had brought up the *Nemtsy*,[2] Chud people, Letts,[3] and Livonians,[4] and then let them go again, and those who had bounty

---

[1] Houses.   [2] cf. p. 34.
[3] *Lotygola.*   [4] *Lib.*

from Yaroslav they drove out of Pleskov: "Go after your own *Knyaz*, you are no brothers to us." Yaroslav then went from Novgorod to Pereyaslavl with his *Knyaginya*, and left his two sons Feodor and Alexander in Novgorod with Fedor Danilovits and the *Tiun*[1] Yakim. The same autumn, great rain came down day and night, on our Lady's Day,[2] and till St. Nicholas Day,[3] we saw not the light of day; the people could not get the hay nor do the fields.

Then the accursed devil, who from the beginning desired no good to man, and jealous of him because he drove him away by nightly vigils, singing, and prayer, stirred up a great tumult amongst the common people against Arseni, a modest and gentle man; and they made a *Veche* in Yaroslav's Court and went to the *Vladyka's* Court, saying: " It is warm so long because he took away *Vladyka* Anton to Khutin and himself took his seat, having given reward to the *Knyaz*." And pushing him through the gates, they drove him out like a miscreant, God barely saved him from death; he shut himself in St. Sophia and then went to Khutin. And the next day they fetched in *Vladyka* Anton again, and put with him two men, Yakun Moisevits and Mikifor the guard. And that was not enough evil, there was more than that: the whole town rose in tumult, and they went from the *Veche* in arms against the *Tysyatski* Vyacheslav, and plundered his Court and those of his brother Boguslav, of Andrei the *Vladyka's* steward, of Davidko Sophiski, and of Sudimir. And against Dushilits, elder of Lipna, they also sent to plunder, and were going to hang him, but he escaped on horseback to Yaroslav. But they took his wife saying that: " These people urge the *Knyaz* to evil," and the tumult in the town was great. The same autumn there was great water in the Volkhov; around the lake and along the Volkhov it carried away the hay. Then the lake[4] having frozen and stood for three days, a south wind drove it up and having broken [the ice] carried it into the Volkhov, tore away nine stays of the great bridge, and carried down eight by night to the Pitba stream on St. Nicholas Day, and the ninth it carried away on December 8, St. Potapi Day. For God wished not to see bloodshed among brothers, nor to give joy to the devil: for the accursed one rejoices in bloodshed among brothers, but the good God so willed it.

[1] Bailiff.
[2] The Assumption.
[3] December 19.
[4] Lake Ilmen.

They then took the office of *Tysyatski* from Vyacheslav and gave it to Boris Negovich, and they sent a message to *Knyaz* Yaroslav about it: " Come to us; lay down an oath not to send judges about the district. On condition of our whole liberty and of all the charters[1] of Yaroslav be thou our *Knyaz*. Or be thou to thyself, and we to ourselves."

The same winter, Fedor Danilovits fled with the *Tiun* Yakim by night on Tuesday in Quinquagesima week, taking with them the two young *Knyazes* Fedor and Alexander. Then the men of Novgorod said: " They must have planned some harm to St. Sophia and have run away; we did not drive them out; but have executed our own brothers, and we have done the *Knyaz* no wrong. May God and the Honourable Cross judge them; and we will provide us a *Knyaz*," and they kissed the [ikon of the] Holy Mother of God that they would all be united, and they sent Khota Stanimirovits and Gavrilo of Lyubyanitsa [Street] for Mikhail to Chernigov. And they came to Smolensk and the *Knyaz* of Smolensk at the instance of Yaroslav would not let them go, and occupied all the roads. But if God be with us, who is against us? And Mikhail having learnt that the emissaries of Novgorod were kept in Smolensk, for he was then at Bryn with his son, went in haste to Torzhok and came to Torzhok in Palm week; and all the people were glad.

A.D. 1229. A.M. 6737. *Knyaz* Mikhail came from Chernigov to Novgorod on Holy Day, at the close of St. Thomas's Week, and the men of Novgorod were glad at their choice; and he kissed the Cross on the whole liberty of Novgorod and on all the charters of Yaroslav, and he granted the serfs freedom not to pay taxes for five years, who ever had fled to other folk's land, and those who live here he ordered to pay taxes as former *Knyazes* had fixed. And the men of Novgorod took much money[2] from Yaroslav's favourites and the people of *Gorodishche ;* they did not plunder their houses but made them give towards the building of the great bridge. The same year they began the foundation of a great bridge above the old bridge. They then took the *Posadnik*-ship from Ivanko Dmitrovits and gave it to Vnezd Vodovik; and they gave Torzhok to Ivanko; he went to Torzhok but the Novi-torg people would not receive him, and thence he went to Yaroslav.

The same year, *Knyaz* Mikhail said: " Behold, you have no *Vladyka*, and it is not seemly for this town to be without a *Vladyka*.

[1] *Gramota.*
[2] *Kuny.*

And since God has laid his punishment on Anton, do you elect a fitting man, whether from amongst priests, *Igumens*, or monks." And some said to the *Knyaz;* "There is a monk, a deacon at St. Georgi's by name Spiridon, he is worthy of it!" And others named Osaf, Bishop of Volodimir in Volynia, and yet others a Greek. "Whomever the Metropolitan shall give, that one shall be our father." And *Knyaz* Mikhail said: "Let us cast three lots, whom God will give us." And having written out the names they laid them on the holy table and sent out the young *Knyaz* Rostislav from the *Vladyka's* council chamber.[1] God chose him a servant and shepherd of the speaking sheep in Novgorod and in all its province, and Spiridon was drawn; and they sent for him to the monastery and having brought him, they set him in the court, until he should go to Kiev to be appointed.

The same year, *Knyaz* Mikhail went to Chernigov to his brothers, taking with him the Novgorod men, Boguslav Gorislavits, Sbyslav Yakunkovits, Domash Tverdislavits, Gleb, son of the *Posadnik*, Mikhail Mikiforovits, and Mikhail Prikupov; and his son Rostislav he left in Novgorod. "God grant me," he said, "that I obtain justice for Novgorod, that then I may take my son from you." And he sent Nezdilo Prokshinits and Ivanko Tudorkovits to Yaroslav, saying: "Give up the *Volok*[2] and all thou hast that belongs to Novgorod, which thou hast occupied by force, and kiss the Cross." And Yaroslav said: "I will not give up that, and do not kiss the Cross; you for yourself and I for myself." And he detained the emissaries all the summer. The same year Spiridon went to Kiev for confirmation by the Metropolitan, to be appointed on December 17. The same winter, the Lithuanians came and ravaged [the towns and districts of] Lyubno, Moreva, and Serigeri, the men of Novgorod pursued them and having overtaken them, beat them, and took away all their captives, in the month of January.

A.D. 1230. A.M. 6738.   The earth quaked on a Friday in the fifth week after Easter during dinner, and some had already dined. And this, brethren, was not for good, but for evil; God shows us his signs because of our sins, that we repent us of our sins. What great mortality God brought on us that spring! And yet seeing this we understood not our ruin; but were more prone to evil. The same year, on May 14, St. Sidor[3] Day, on Tues-

[1] *Gridnitsa.*
[2] Volok Lamsk.
[3] Isidore.

day, in the middle of the morning the sun grew dark and became
like a moon of the fifth night; and it filled out again and we godless
ones were glad. On the 19th of the same month on [the day of]
the *Veche* of the 318 holy Fathers, *Vladyka* Spiridon came
to Novgorod, appointed by the Metropolitan Kuril[1]; he was
appointed priest in Quinquagesima week, and *Vladyka* after Holy
Week on *Veche* [Day].   The same year, *Knyaz* Mikhail had his
son Rostislav shorn in St. Sophia in Novgorod, and *Vladyka* Spiridon
took off his hair; and he set him on the throne, but himself went to
Chernigov.   The same year, Stepan Tverdislavits quarrelled with
Vodovik, Ivanko Timoshkinits siding with Stepan, and the *Posadnik's* servants beat Ivanko; this happened in the *Gorodishche.*
And the next morning he called a *Veche* in Yaroslav's Court
against the *Posadnik,* and went against his Court, and they
plundered it.   The *Posadnik* and Simon Borisovich again roused up
the whole town against Ivanko and Yakim Vlunkovits and Proksha
Lashnev; they went from the *Veche* and plundered many houses
and they killed Volos Blutkinits at the *Veche.* The *Posadnik*
said: " Thou didst try to set fire to my Court."[2]   Proksha's Court
they set fire to, and Yakim fled to Yaroslav, while others hid
themselves, but they made these take oath and then let them go.
And Vodovik having caught Ivanko, later killed him, casting him
into the Volkhov.   And God seeing our lawlessness and our hatred
of our brothers, and our rebelliousness against each other, jealousy,
and false swearings by the Cross which the angels cannot look on
and turn their many-eyed wings from, we holding it in our hands kiss
with foul lips, therefore, God brought the pagans upon us and they
laid waste our land.   Ourselves not watching at all, we [without
mercy] lost our power, and so it became empty: and thus did the
Lord God reward us according to our deeds.

On [the Day of] the Exaltation[3] of the Honourable Cross, a frost
killed the crops throughout our district and from that there arose
great misery.   We began to buy bread at eight *kunas,* a barrel of
rye at twenty *grivnas,* or at twenty-five in the courts, wheat at
forty *grivnas,* millet at eight, and oats at thirteen *grivnas;* our town
and our country went asunder and other towns and countries became full of our own brothers and sisters; and the rest began to die.
And who would not weep at this, seeing the dead lying in the
streets, and the little ones devoured by dogs?   And God put into

---

[1] Cyril.
[2] House.   [3] September 26.

the heart of *Vladyka* Spiridon to do good. He put a common grave by the Church of the Holy Apostles in Prussian Street and engaged a good and gentle man by name Stanila to carry the dead on horses wherever he went about the town and so continuously he dragged them every day; and he filled it up to the top; there were 3,030 in it. The same winter, the young *Knyaz* Rostislav went with *Posadnik* Vnezd to Torzhok, on December 8, on a Sunday. And the next morning, the 9th, they killed Semen Borisovits and plundered his whole house and his villages, took his wife, and himself they buried at the Church of St. Gyurgi[1] in the monastery. Similarly the house and villages of Vodovik and of his brother Mikhail, of Danislav, of Boris the *Tysyatski*, and of Tvorimirits and the houses of many others. And Vodovik having heard this evil fled from Torzhok with his brothers, and the *Tysyatski* Boris with the men of Novitorg fled to Mikhail to Chernigov.

They gave the *Posadnik*-ship to Stepan Tverdislavich, and to Mikita Petrilovits the office of *Tysyatski*, and Semen's and Vodovik's property they distributed among a hundred. They laboured collecting, and these got the fruit of their labours; for of such the Holy Spirit said: " He collecteth, and knoweth not for whom he collecteth."

And they showed young *Knyaz* Rostislav the road from Torzhok and [sent him] to his father in Chernigov: " As thy father said he would mount his horse for war on Exaltation Day,[2] and kissed the Cross; behold, it is now St. Michael's Day,[3] the kissing of the Cross has fallen from us,[4] go thou away, and we will provide a *Knyaz* for ourselves." And they sent for Yaroslav, with [reservation of] all the liberties of Novgorod. And Yaroslav came quickly to Novgorod on December 30, and made a *Veche* and kissed [the ikon of] the Holy Mother of God in [confirmation of] all the charters[5] of Yaroslav. And having sat two weeks he returned to Pereyaslavl, taking some of the younger men of Novgorod with him, and he set his two sons Fedor and Alexander in Novgorod.

The same winter, Yaroslav, *Vladyka* Spiridon and the whole of Novgorod led in *Igumen* Arseni, a mild and gentle man, from the Church of Saint Saviour in Khutin and made him *Igumen* of

---

[1] George.
[2] September 26.
[3] November 21.
[4] sc. our oath is annulled.
[5] *Gramota.*

St. Georgi. And they deprived Sava of it, and confined him in a cell, and being taken ill, he lay six weeks, and died on March 15, on Saturday, before morning, and so he was buried by *Igumen* Arseni and the entire brotherhood. God grant [the fulfilment of] his prayers to all Christians and to me the sinful Timofei, sacristan; for he was a good man, mild, gentle and without anger. May God give peace to his soul with all the righteous in the kingdom of Heaven! And we will turn to the preceding, to the bitter and sad memory of that spring. For what is there to say, or what to speak of the punishment that came to us from God? How that some of the common people killed the living and ate them; others cutting up dead flesh and corpses ate them; others ate horseflesh, dogs and cats; but to those found in such acts they did thus—some they burned with fire, others they cut to pieces, and others they hanged. Some fed on moss, snails, pine-bark, lime-bark, lime and elm-tree leaves, and whatever each could think of. And again other wicked men began to burn the good people's houses, where they suspected that there was rye; and so they plundered their property. Instead of repentance for our wickedness, we became more prone to wickedness than before, though seeing before our eyes the wrath of God: the dead in the streets and in the market-place, and on the great bridge, being devoured by dogs, so that they could not bury them. They put another pit outside at the end of Chudinets Street, and that became full, and there is no counting [the number of bodies in it]. And they put a third at Koleno beyond the Church of the Holy Nativity, and that likewise became full, there was no counting the bodies. And seeing all this before our eyes we should have become better; but we became worse. Brother had no sympathy with brother, nor father with son, nor mother with daughter, nor would neighbour break bread with neighbour. There was no kindness among us, but misery and unhappiness; in the streets unkindness one to another, at home anguish, seeing children crying for bread and others dying. And we were buying a loaf for a *grivna* and more, and a fourth of a barrel of rye for one silver *grivna*. Fathers and mothers gave away their children into servitude to merchants for bread. This distress was not in our land alone; but over the whole Russian province except Kiev alone. And so has God rewarded us according to our deeds.

A.D. 1231. A.M. 6739. A fire broke out, starting from the house of Matvei Vyshkovits and the whole of the

Slavenski quarter[1] nearly to the *Kholm* quarter beyond St. Ilya[2] was burned. But God watched over the holy churches, although the fire was so fierce that it seemed to burn on the water, passing over the Volkhov in the sight of all; and several people were drowned in the Volkhov. The same year, God showed His mercy towards us sinners. He did His mercy quickly. The *Nemtsy*[3] came from beyond sea with corn and with flour, and they did much good, for this town was already near its end.

The same autumn, Yaroslav marched with an army to the Chernigov district, with the men of Novgorod and with all his force against Mikhail, and burned Sherensk; and after camping near Mosalsk he turned back again, having destroyed many crops. And there, too, near the town they shot the commander [of the troops] Oldan, and they went away without peace. The same year the *Posadnik* of Novgorod, Vodovik Vnezd died in Chernigov.

A.D. 1232. A.M. 6740. Boris Negotsevich, Mikhal with his brother Peter Vodovikovits, Gleb the brother of Smen, Misha Borisovich with the *Knyaz* Svyatoslav [Trubetskoi, came in mid-Lent from Chernigov, and reached the village of Buitsa, the village of St. Georgi, and thence they turned back again] into Russia, on finding that these men had lied to them. And they pushed on to Pleskov, seized Vyacheslav, and after beating him, put him in chains. Meantime, in Novgorod, there was a great tumult, for *Knyaz* Yaroslav was not there, he was then in Pereyaslavl. And on his arrival from Pereyaslavl he seized the men of Pleskov and imprisoned them in the *Veche* chamber in the *Gorodishche* and he sent to Pleskov, saying: " Let my men go and show those the road, whence they came." They, however, stood · staunchly for them, but said: " Send their wives and goods to them, ' then we will let go Vyacheslav; otherwise we to ourselves and you to yourselves." And so all the year they were without peace; and the *Knyaz* did not let merchants go to them; and they were buying salt at seven *grivnas* a *berkovets*[4]; and they let go Vyacheslav. And the *Knyaz* let the wives of Boris, Gleb and Misha go to them; but he did not take peace. And it happened in the winter the men of Pleskov came to the *Knyaz* and did obeisance to him: " Thou art our *Knyaz*," and they asked Yaroslav for his son Fedor, but he did not give them his son, and said: " Lo, I give you my brother-

---

[1] Slavno.
[2] Elias.
[3] cf. p. 34. [4] Ten *puds*.

in-law, Gyurgi, that is your *Knyaz.*" They took him and led him
to Pleskov, and they showed the road to the sons of Boris, with
their wives; and they went to Medvezhya Golova.

The same year, Svyatoslav Mstislavich, grandson of Roman,
took Smolensk by assault with the men of Polotsk, on Boris Day,
cut to pieces the people of Smolensk, and took his seat on the throne.
Vladyka Anton died on October 8 of the same year. This blessed
Vladyka Anton before his exile had sat on the Bishop's chair eight
years after Mitrofan, and [was] in exile six years; he then came from
Peremyshl to Novgorod and sat two years, and became dumb on St.
Olex Day; he was in that illness six years and seven months and
nine days; and so he died, and they laid him in the porch of St.
Sophia in the presence of *Knyaz* Yaroslav Vsevolodits and of
Vladyka Spiridon.

A.D. 1233. A.M. 6741. The people of Izborsk drove out the children
of Boris together with *Knyaz* Yaroslav
Volodimirits and the *Nemtsy.*[1] But the men of Pleskov surrounded Izborsk, captured the *Knyaz* and killed the *Nemets*[2] Danila,
and the rest fled; and they delivered them to the great Yaroslav
who imprisoned them in Pereyaslavl.

The same year *Knyaz* Fedor, the eldest son of Yaroslav, died,
on June 10, and he was laid in the monastery of St. Georgi; he was
still young. And who would not pity him? The wedding was
arranged; the mead was brewed, the bride was brought, the *Knyazes*
invited. And in place of merriment there was weeping and grieving
for our sins. But O, Lord, glory to Thee, heavenly ruler; since this
was Thy will! But rest be to him with all the righteous!

The same year the Church of St. Fedor at the gates of the Nerev
quarter was founded.

The same year died the blessed Metropolitan of Kiev and of all
Russia, by name Kyuril, he was by birth a Greek, and had been
brought from Nikeya.[3]

The same year, the *Nemtsy* drove out Kyuril Sinkinits from Tesov
and led him to Medvezhya Golova and he sat in chains from
our Lady's Day until Lent, *Knyaz* Yaroslav not being in Novgorod, but he had gone away to Pereyaslavl. And the *Knyaz*
having come set him free with the aid of God and St. Sophia,

1 cf. p. 34.
2 German.
3 Nicæa.

and he brought his troops in great numbers to Novgorod, intending to go against them.

A.D. 1234. A.M. 6742. *Knyaz* Yaroslav with the men of Novgorod and with the whole district, and with his own forces, went against the *Nemtsy* towards Yurev, and the *Knyaz* halted before he had reached the town with his forces, and he let his people ravage the land. But the *Nemtsy* issued out of the town, some staying to guard Medvezhya Golova, and fought with them right up to the main force. And God helped *Knyaz* Yaroslav with the men of Novgorod; and they drove them down to the river, and several of the best *Nemtsy* fell there; and when the *Nemtsy* were crossing the river Omovyzh[1] they broke through and many were drowned; and some of the wounded escaped to Yurev, others to Medvezhya Golova. And they laid much of their land waste, and destroyed many of their crops about Yurev and Medvezhya Golova. And the *Nemtsy* did obeisance to the *Knyaz*, and Yaroslav took peace with them on his own terms, and the men of Novgorod returned all well, but some men of the Low country[2] fell.

The same year the Church of St. Luke in the Lyudin quarter was burned down from thunder in the evening of June 10.

The same year the Lithuanians drove the men of Russa nearly as far as the market place and the men of Russa halted; and [there was] an ambuscade; and the citizens and body-guard and some of the merchants and traders drove them out of the town[3] again, fighting in the field, and here they killed several of the Lithuanians, and four of the men of Russa: the priest Petrila, Paul Obradits, and two other men. And they pillaged the whole monastery of St. Saviour, and the whole church they stripped, the images and the altar, and four monks they killed, and retired to Klin. Then the news came to Novgorod to *Knyaz* Yaroslav, and the *Knyaz* with the men of Novgorod taking to the boats, and others on horse-back, went after them up the Lovot. And when they came to the village of Moravin the boatmen turned back thence to the town; and the *Knyaz* let them go because they had not enough bread, and he himself with the mounted men went after them and overtook them

[1] Embach.
[2] *Niz, Nizovskaya zemlya*, sc. the basin of the Volga, and the country S.E. of Moscow generally.
[3] *Posad.*

at Dubrovna, a village in the Toropets district, and there he fought with the accursed and godless [Lithuanians]. And there God [helped them] and the Holy Cross and the Holy Sophia, the Mighty Wisdom of God, helped *Knyaz* Yaroslav and the men of Novgorod over the pagans, and they took from them 300 of their horses with their goods and they fled into the woods, having thrown down their arms and shields and lances and everything from themselves; and others fell here dead. And of the men of Novgorod they killed there ten men: Feda Yakunovich the *Tysyatski*, Gavrilo the shield-maker, Negutin from Lubyanitsa, Nezhila the silversmith, Gostilets of Kusma-Demyan Street, Fedor Uma of the *Knyaz's* household, a townsman, and three other men. And may God grant peace to their souls in the kingdom of Heaven, who spilt their blood for St. Sophia and for Christian blood.

A.D. 1235. A.M. 6743. The accursed and all-destroying devil, who from the beginning wished no good to the human race, raised discord among the Russian *Knyazes*, that men might not dwell in peace; for this reason too the evil one rejoices in the shedding of Christian blood. *Knyaz* Volodimir Rurikovich with the men of Kiev, and Danilo Romanovich with the men of Galich went against Mikhail Vsevolodich the Red, to Cherni-gov, and Izyaslav fled to the Polovets people, and laid much waste around Chernigov, and burnt villages. And Mikhail came out from Chernigov and having devastated much around Chernigov went away again. And Mikhail having practised deceit on Danilo killed many of the men of Galich, even without number, and Danilo barely escaped. And Volodimir having come back again, he sat in Kiev. And not even thus was there enough of evil, but Izyaslav with the pagan Polovets people in great strength, and Mikhail with the men of Chernigov came to Kiev, and took Kiev. And the Polovets men having taken Volodimir and his *Knyaginya* led them away to their own country, and did much harm to the people at Kiev. And Mikhail took his seat in Galich, and Izyaslav in Kiev. And then again the Polovets men let Volodimir and his wife go for ransom, and the *Knyazes* took ransom from the *Nemtsy*.

A.D. 1236. A.M. 6744. *Knyaz* Yaroslav went from Novgorod to [take] the throne in Kiev, taking with him some of the best men of Novgorod: Sudimir of Slavno, Yakim Vlunkovich, and Kosta Vyacheslavich, also 100 men from Novi-torg. He set his son Olexander in Novgorod and having arrived in Kiev he took his seat on the throne, and having kept the men of Novgorod and of Novi-torg for one week and having bestowed gifts on them he let them go; and they all returned well.

The same year the godless Tartars having come, they captured all the Bolgar Land¹ and took their great city, and they slew all, both wives and children.

A.D. 1237. A.M. 6745. There was a sign in the sun on August 3, the Day of the commemoration of the Holy Fathers Dalmat, Faust, and Isak, at mid-day. The sign was of this kind: there was a darkness on the western side of the sun; it became like a moon of five nights; and on the eastern side it was light, then again on the eastern side there was darkness, like a moon of five nights, while on the western side it was light; and thus it became full again.

The same year the *Nemtsy* came in great strength from beyond the sea to Riga and all united there; both the men of Riga and all the Chud Land, and the men of Pleskov from themselves sent a help of 200 men, and they went against the godless Lithuanians; and thus for our sins they were defeated by the godless pagans,² and each tenth man came back to his home.

The same year a Metropolitan by name Esif, a Greek, came to Kiev from Nikeya.

A.D. 1238. A.M. 6746. The wife of Semen Borisovich made a monastery at the Church of St. Paul.

That same year foreigners³ called Tartars came in countless numbers, like locusts, into the land of Ryazan, and on first coming they halted at the river Nukhla, and took it, and halted in camp there. And thence they sent their emissaries to the *Knyazes* of Ryazan, a sorceress and two men with her, demanding from them one-tenth of everything: of men and *Knyazes* and horses—of everything one-tenth. And the *Knyazes* of Ryazan, Gyurgi,⁴ Ingvor's brother, Oleg, Roman Ingvorevich, and those of Murom and Pronsk, without letting them into their towns, went out to meet them to Voronazh. And the *Knyazes* said to them: " Only when none of us remain then all will be yours." And thence they let them go to Yuri⁴ in Volodimir, and thence they let the Tartars at

¹ Bulgaria on the Volga, the present Kazan, etc.
² Lithuanians.
³ *Inoplemennitsi.*
⁴ George.

G

Voronazh go back to the Nukhla. And the *Knyazes* of Ryazan sent to Yuri of Volodimir asking for help, or himself to come. But Yuri neither went himself nor listened to the request of the *Knyazes* of Ryazan, but he himself wished to make war separately. But it was too late to oppose the wrath of God, as was said of old by God, to Joshua the son of Nun, when leading them to the promised land, then he said: " I shall before you send upon them perplexity, and thunder, and fear, and trembling." Thus also did God before these men take from us our strength and put into us perplexity and thunder and dread and trembling for our sins. And then the pagan foreigners surrounded Ryazan and fenced it in with a stockade.[1] And *Knyaz* Yuri of Ryazan, shut himself in the town with his people, but *Knyaz* Roman Ingorovich began to fight against them with his own men. Then *Knyaz* Yuri of Volodimir sent Yeremei as *Voyevoda* with a patrol and joined Roman; and the Tartars surrounded them at Kolomno, and they fought hard and drove them to the ramparts. And there they killed Roman and Yeremei and many fell here with the *Knyaz* and with Yeremei. And the men of Moscow ran away having seen nothing. And the Tartars took the town on December 21, and they had advanced against it on the 16th of the same month. They likewise killed the *Knyaz* and *Knyaginya*, and men, women, and children, monks, nuns and priests, some by fire, some by the sword, and violated nuns, priests' wives, good women and girls in the presence of their mothers and sisters. But God saved the Bishop, for he had departed the same moment when the troops invested the town. And who, brethren, would not lament over this, among those of us left alive when they suffered this bitter and violent death? And we, indeed, having seen it, were terrified and wept with sighing day and night over our sins, while we sigh every day and night, taking thought for our possessions and for the hatred of brothers.

But let us return to what lies before us. The pagan and godless Tartars, then, having taken Ryazan, went to Volodimir, a host of shedders of Christian blood. And *Knyaz* Yuri went out from Volodimir and fled to Yaroslavl, while his son Vsevolod with his mother and the *Vladyka*, and the whole of the province shut themselves in Volodimir. And the lawless Ismaelites approached the town and surrounded the town in force, and fenced it all round with a fence.[2] And it was in the morning *Knyaz* Vsevolod and *Vladyka* Mitrofan saw that the town

[1] *Ostrog.*
[2] *Tyn.*

must be taken, and entered the Church of the Holy Mother of God and were all shorn into the monastic order and into the *schema*,[1] the *Knyaz* and the *Knyaginya*, their daughter and daughter-in-law, and good men and women, by *Vladyka* Mitrofan.   And when the lawless ones had already come near and set up battering rams,[2] and took the town and fired it on Friday before Sexagesima Sunday, the *Knyaz* and *Knyaginya* and *Vladyka*, seeing that the town was on fire and that the people were already perishing, some by fire and others by the sword, took refuge in the Church of the Holy Mother of God and shut themselves in the Sacristy.   The pagans breaking down the doors, piled up wood and set fire to the sacred church; and slew all, thus they perished, giving up their souls to God. Others went in pursuit of *Knyaz* Yuri to Yaroslavl.   And *Knyaz* Yuri sent out Dorozh to scout with 3,000 men; and Dorozh came running, and said: " They have, already surrounded us, *Knyaz*." And the *Knyaz* began to muster his forces about him, and behold, the Tartars came up suddenly, and the *Knyaz*, without having been able to do anything, fled.   And it happened when he reached the river Sit they overtook him and there he ended his life.   And God knows how he died; for some say much about him.   And Rostov and Suzhdal went each its own way.   And the accursed ones having come thence took Moscow, Pereyaslavl, Yurev,[3] Dmitrov, *Volok*,[4] and Tver; there also they killed the son of Yaroslav.   And thence the lawless ones came and invested Torzhok on the festival of the first Sunday in Lent.   They fenced it all round with a fence as they had taken other towns, and here the accursed ones fought with battering rams for two weeks.   And the people in the town were exhausted and from Novgorod there was no help for them; but already every man began to be in perplexity and terror.   And so the pagans took the town, and slew all from the male sex even to the female, all the priests and the monks, and all stripped and reviled gave up their souls to the Lord in a bitter and a wretched death, on March 5, the day of the commemoration of the holy Martyr Nikon, on Wednesday in Easter week.   And there, too, were killed Ivanko the *Posadnik* of Novi-torg, Yakim Vlunkovich, Gleb Borisovich, and Mikhailo Moisievich.   And the accursed godless ones then pushed on from Torzhok by the road of Seregeri right up to Ignati's

---

[1] cf. p. 34.
[2] *Porok.*
[3] Yurev Polski, N.E. of Moscow.
[4] Volok Lamsk.

cross, cutting down everybody like grass, to within 100 *versts*[1] of Novgorod. God, however, and the great and sacred apostolic cathedral Church of St. Sophia, and St. Kyuril,[2] and the prayers of the holy and orthodox *Vladyka*, of the faithful *Knyazes*, and of the very reverend monks of the hierarchical *Veche*, protected Novgorod. And who, brothers, fathers, and children, seeing this, God's infliction on the whole Russian Land, does not lament? God let the pagans on us for our sins. God brings foreigners on to the land in his wrath, and thus crushed by them they[3] will be reminded of God. And internecine war comes from the prompting of the devil: for God does not wish evil amongst men, but good; but the devil rejoices at wicked murder and bloodshed. And any land which has sinned God punishes with death or famine, or with infliction of pagans, or with drought, or with heavy rain, or with other punishment, to see whether we will repent and live as God bids; for He tells us by the prophet: " Turn to me with your whole heart, with fasting and weeping." And if we do so we shall be forgiven of all our sins. But we always turn to evil, like swine ever wallowing in the filth of sin, and thus we remain; and for this we receive every kind of punishment from God; and the invasion of armed men, too, we accept at God's command; as punishment for our sins.

A.D. 1239. A.M. 6747. *Knyaz* Olexander,[4] son of Yaroslav, married in Novgorod, he took the daughter of Bryacheslav of Polotsk; and was wedded at Toropets and the feast was held both in Novgorod and in Toropets.

In the same year *Knyaz* Alexander[4] with the men of Novgorod built[5] a town[6] by the Shelon [river].

A.D. 1240. A.M. 6748. The *Svei*[7] came in great strength with the Murman, Sum, and Yem people in very many ships. The *Svei* came with their *Knyaz* and with their bishops, and halted in the Neva at the mouth of the Izhera, wishing to take possession of Ladoga, or in one word, of Novgorod, and of the whole Novgorod province. But again the most kind and merciful God, lover of men, preserved and protected us from the foreigners since they laboured in vain without the command of God. For the news came to Novgorod that the *Svei* were going towards Ladoga, and *Knyaz*

[1] About 66 miles.
[2] Cyril.
[3] sc. the Russian people.
[4] Oleksandr, Aleksandr.
[5] *Srubi*—cut, because made of wood.
[6] Fort.   [7] Swedes.

Olexander with the men of Novgorod and of Ladoga did not delay at all; he went against them and defeated them by the power of St. Sophia and the prayers of our Sovereign Lady the Holy Mother of God and eternally Virgin Mary on the 15th day of July, the Commemoration Day of Saints Kyurik and Ulita, and the Day of the *Veche* of the 630 Holy Fathers of Khalkidon.[1] And there was a great slaughter of *Svei*. Their *Voyevoda*, by name Spiridon, was killed, and some thought that their bishop was also killed there; and a very great number of them fell. And having loaded two vessels[2] with their best men got away first to sea; and the rest of them having dug a pit they threw into it without number; and many others were wounded; and the same night without waiting for the light of Monday they went away in shame. And of the men of Novgorod and Ladoga there fell there Kostyantin Lugotinits, Gyuryata Pineshchinich, Namest, Drochilo son of Nezdilo the tanner, twenty men in all with the men of Ladoga, or less, God knows. And *Knyaz* Alexander with the men of Novgorod and of Ladoga all came back in health to their own country, preserved by God and St. Sophia, and through the prayers of all the saints.

The same year the *Nemtsy*[3] with the men of Medvezhya [Golova], of Yurev, and of Velyad[4] with *Knyaz* Yaroslav Volodimirich took Izborsk. And the news came to Pleskov that the *Nemtsy* had taken Izborsk and all the men of Pleskov went out and fought with them and the *Nemtsy* beat them. And there they killed the *Voyevoda* Gavrilo Gorislavich, and pursuing the men of Pleskov, killed many of them and others they caught with their hands. And having driven them up under the town, they burned the whole place, and there was much damage, churches, honourable ikons, books and Gospels were burnt, and they devastated many villages around Pleskov. And they stayed near the town a week, but they did not take the town. But the children of good men they took as hostages, and went away and so they were without peace. For the men of Pleskov had made treachery with the *Nemtsy*, and Tverdilo Ivankovich with others had got them to come and himself began to rule in Pleskov with the *Nemtsy*, ravaging the Novgorod villages. And some of the people of Pleskov fled to Novgorod with their wives and children.

[1] i.e. The Council of Chalcedon, A.D. 451.
[2] *Korabl.*
[3] cf. p. 34.
[4] Fellin.

In the winter in the same year *Knyaz* Olexander went out from Novgorod with his mother and his wife and all his court, to his father in Pereyaslavl, having quarelled with the men of Novgorod. The same winter the *Nemtsy* came against the Vod people with the Chud people, and ravaged them, and laid tribute upon them, and made a fort in the village[1] of Koporya. Nor was this the only evil: but they also took Tesov and pushed to within thirty *versts* of Novgorod, attacking merchants, and hitherwards to Luga and up to [the village of] Sablya. And the men of Novgorod sent to Yaroslav for a *Knyaz*, and he gave them his son Andrei. And then the men of Novgorod having taken counsel sent the *Vladyka* with others again for Olexander; and the Lithuanians, *Nemtsy* and the Chud people invaded the Novgorod district and seized all the horses and cattle about Luga, and in the villages it was impossible for any one to plough and nothing to do it with, till Yaroslav sent his son Alexander again.

A.D. 1241. A.M. 6749. *Knyaz* Olexander came to Novgorod, and the men of Novgorod rejoiced. The same year *Knyaz* Olexander went with the men of Novgorod, and of Ladoga, and with the Korel and Izhera people against the town of Koporya, against the *Nemtsy*[2]; and took the town and brought some *Nemtsy* to Novgorod and let others go free; but the Vod and Chud traitors he hanged.

A.D. 1242. A.M. 6750. *Knyaz* Olexander with the men of Novgorod and with his brother Andrei and the men of the Lower country went [in the winter in great strength against the land of the Chud people, against the *Nemtsy*, that they might not boast, saying: " We will humble the Sloven race under us," for Pskov was already taken, and its *Tiuns* in prison]. And *Knyaz* Olexander occupied all the roads right up to Pleskov; and he cleared Pleskov, seized the *Nemtsy* and Chud men, and having bound them in chains, sent them to be imprisoned in Novgorod, and himself went against the Chud people. And when they came to their land, he let loose his whole force to provide for themselves. And Domash Tverdislavich and Kerbet were scouring [the country] and the *Nemtsy* and Chud men met them by a bridge; and they fought there, and there they killed Domash, brother of the *Posadnik*, an honest man, and others with him, and others again they took with their

1 *Pogost.*
2 cf. p. 34.

hands, and others escaped to the troops of the *Knyaz*. And the *Knyaz* turned back to the lake and the *Nemtsy* and Chud men went after them. Seeing this, *Knyaz* Olexander and all the men of Novgorod drew up their forces by Lake Chud at Uzmen by the Raven's rock[1]; and the *Nemtsy* and Chud men rode at them driving themselves like a wedge through their army; and there was a great slaughter of *Nemtsy* and Chud men. And God and St. Sophia and the Holy Martyrs Boris and Gleb, for whose sake the men of Novgorod shed their blood, by the great prayers of those Saints, God helped *Knyaz* Alexander. And the *Nemtsy* fell there and the Chud men gave shoulder, and pursuing them fought with them on the ice, seven *versts* short of the Subol shore.[2] And there fell of the Chud men a countless number; and of the *Nemtsy* 400, and fifty they took with their hands and brought to Novgorod. And they fought on April 5, on a Saturday, the Commemoration Day of the Holy Martyr Feodul,[3] to the glory of the Holy Mother of God. The same year the *Nemtsy* sent with greeting, in the absence of the *Knyaz:* " The land of the Vod people, of Luga, Pleskov, and Lotygola, which we invaded with the sword, from all this we withdraw, and those of your men whom we have taken we will exchange, we will let go yours, and you let go ours." And they let go the Pleskov hostages, and made peace.

The same year *Knyaz* Yaroslav Vsevolodich summoned by the Tartar *Tsar* Baty, went to him to the Horde.

A.D. 1243. A.M. 6751. God's servant Varlaam, in the world Vyacheslav Prokshinich, died at Khutin in the monastery of the Holy Redeemer, on May 4; and he was buried on the morrow the fifth, St. Irena's Day, by *Vladyka* Spiridon and *Igumen* Sidor in the presence of *Knyaz* Olexander. On the 18th of the same month, the Day of the Holy Martyr Alexander, there appeared a sign in the monastery Church of St. Ioan in Pleskov, from the image of the Holy Redeemer over the tomb of the *Knyaginya* of Yaroslav Volodimirovich, who was killed by her stepson at Medvezhya Golova; there came ointment from the ikon for twelve days, it filled four wax cups as into a glass vessel, and they brought two to Novgorod to be blessed and they kept two in Pleskov. But, O Lord, Glory to Thee, who gavest us Thy unworthy and sinful servants such a blessing! In Thee, we hope, O Lord Almighty, who loving mankind dost

---

[1] *Voroni Kamen.*
[2] Of Lake Chud.
[3] Theodoulos.

look with Thy abundant mercy upon us poor ones. The same year
on August 16 died God's servant, Stefan Tverdislavich, grandson of
Mikhail, *Posadnik* of Novgorod, on Sunday at 1 o'clock of the night,
and he was buried on Monday the 17th, the Day of SS. Paul and
Uliana, in the porch of St. Sophia where lie *Vladykas* Arkadi and
Marturi, having been *Posadnik* thirteen years less three months.

A.D. 1244. A.M. 6752. The *Knyaginya* of Yaroslav died, having
                  been shorn in the monastery of St. George;
and there she was laid by the side of her son Fedor, on May 4, the
Day of St. Irina; her name was called Efrosinia.

A.D. 1245. A.M. 6753. [*Tsar* Baty killed *Knyaz* Mikhail of Cher-
                  nigov and his *Voyevoda* Fedor in the Horde
on September 18. And the killing of them was like this. There
was an invasion of pagan Tartars into the Russian Land; and
these[1] shut themselves in the towns. And envoys came from
Tsar Baty to Mikhail, who then held Kiev; and he, seeing their
words of deceit, ordered them to be killed and himself fled with his
family to Hungary[2]; and some fled to distant parts; and others hid
in caves and forests, and few of them stayed behind; and these after
some time settled in the towns; and they counted their number and
began to levy tribute upon them. And *Knyaz* Mikhail having
heard this, he brought back the people who had fled on all sides to
strange lands, and they came to their own land. And the Tartars
began to summon them with insistence to go to Baty, saying to
them: " It is not meet for you to live in the land of the *Khan* and of
Baty without doing homage to them." And many having gone
bowed. And Baty had this custom of the *Khan's*: If any one came
to do obeisance, he would not order him to be brought before him,
but wizards used to be ordered to bring them through fire and make
them bow to a bush and to fire; and whatever anyone brought with
him for the *Tsar*, the wizards used to take some of everything and
throw it into the fire, and then they used to let them go before the
Tsar with their gifts. And many *Knyazes* with their *Boyars* passed
through the fire, and bowed to the bush, their idols, for the glory
of this world, and each asked of them power and they used to
give it them without dispute, that they might deceive them with the
glory of this world. And the most reverend *Knyaz* Mikhail being
then in Chernigov, and seeing many deceived by the glory of this

[1] sc. Mikhail and Fedor—Michael and Theodore.
[2] *Ugry.*

world, God sent grace and the gift of the Holy Spirit upon him; He put into his heart to go before *Tsar* Baty and to denounce his deceit with which he deceived Christians. And he came to his spiritual father and told him saying: " I wish to go to *Tsar* Baty." His spiritual father answered him: " Many having gone have done the will of the pagan *Tsar* Baty, deceived by the glory of this world; went through the fire and bowed to the sun and to the bush, and destroyed their souls and bodies. And thou, my son, Mikhail, if thou wilt go, do not thus, as the others; go not through the fire; bow not to their idols, nor eat their food, nor take their drink between thy lips; but confess the Christian faith, for it becometh not Christians to bow to any thing, but only to our Lord Jesus Christ." And Mikhail and his *Voyevoda* said to him: " By thy prayer, father, as God wills so be it; I would like to pour out my blood for Christ and for the Christian faith." His *Voyevoda* Fedor spoke likewise. Their spiritual father said to them: " You two will be fresh holy martyrs in the present generation for the confirmation of faithful people, if you do thus." Mikhail and Fedor his *Voyevoda* promised to do thus and were blessed by their spiritual father. Then their father gave them the holy communion for the journey, calling it pre-sanctified and having blessed them, dismissed them and said to them: " May God give strength to you and may God for whom you are eager to suffer send you help." Then Mikhail came to his house, and took from his goods what he needed. And going through many lands they yet reached *Tsar* Baty. And they told Baty: " The Russian *Veliki Knyaz* Mikhail has come to bow to thee." And *Tsar* Baty ordered them to bring his wizards; and the wizards having come before the *Tsar*, the *Tsar* said to them: " As it is according to our custom, do to *Knyaz* Mikhail, and then bring him before me." And they having gone to Mikhail, saying to him: " The *Tsar* Baty summons thee." And he having taken his *Voyevoda* Fedor, went with him, and having reached the place where fire was laid on both sides, many pagans were going through the fire, and were bowing to the sun and to the idols. And the wizards led Mikhail and his *Voyevoda* Fedor through the fire. Mikhail said to them: " It does not become Christians to go through fire and to bow to the idols, to which these bow; such is the Christian religion, not to bow to any thing nor to idols, but to bow to the Trinity: to the Father, the Son, and the Holy Ghost." And Mikhail said to his *Voyevoda* Fedor: " Better it is for us not to bow to the things to which these bow." And they having left them at

the place to which they had been brought, went to tell *Tsar* Baty:
" Mikhail the *Veliki Knyaz* does not listen to thy command, does
not go through the fire and does not bow to thy gods: he says, it
does not become Christians to go through the fire, nor do they bow
to things, neither to the sun nor to idols, but they bow to the
Father who made all things, to the Son, and to the Holy Ghost."
And *Tsar* Baty grew very angry, he sent one of his nobles,[1] his
steward[2] named Eldega, and he said: " Why hast thou made nought
of my command, and hast not bowed to my gods? but from this
moment choose for thyself life or death; if thou keepest my command
thou shalt both live and shalt receive all thy princedom, but if thou
wilt not go through the fire, nor bow to the bush and to the idols
then thou shalt die by a cruel death." Then Mikhail answered:
" To thee, *Tsar*, I bow, since God hath granted thee the sovereignty[3]
of this world, but to the things to which these bow I shall not bow."
And Eldega, the *Tsar's* steward, said to him: " Mikhail, beware:
thou art dead." And Mikhail answered him: " Indeed, I wish to
suffer for Christ and to shed my blood for the true faith." Then
said Boris, *Knyaz* of Rostov, to Mikhail with much weeping: " My
lord father, do the *Tsar's* will." Then likewise the *Boyars* of Boris
also said: " We will all receive public penance for thee with all our
power." Then Mikhail answered: " Brothers, I do not wish to call
myself a Christian by name only and to do the work of the pagans;
but on the contrary I believe in Christ the only God." When
Mikhail had said this, his *Voyevoda* Fedor began to think in himself
saying: " What if Mikhail should grow weak by the prayer of these
men, remembering the love of his wife and the caresses of his children?" Then remembering the words of his spiritual father, Fedor said
to Mikhail: " Dost thou remember the word of our spiritual father
which he taught us from the holy gospels? The Lord said: ' he
that desireth to save his soul shall destroy it, and he that destroyeth
his soul shall save it.' And again, he said: ' what shall it profit a
man if he receive the sovereignty of all this world and lose his
soul? and what will he get in exchange for his soul? for whosoever
shall suffer shame for me and for my words and shall confess me
before men, I too will confess him before my Father which is in
Heaven, and whosoever shall deny me before men I also will deny
him before my Father who is in Heaven!' " And Mikhail and Fedor

---

[1] *Velmozha.*
[2] *Stolnik.*
[3] *Tsarstvo.*

saying this, they began to pray them urgently, that they would listen to them. And Mikhail said to them: " I will not listen to you, nor will I destroy my soul." Then taking off his mantle Mikhail threw it to them, saying to them: " Receive the glory of this world if you desire it." And Eldega having heard that they were unable to persuade him, then went to inform the *Tsar* of what Mikhail had said; for there was a quantity of Christians and pagans in that place, and they were listening to what Mikhail answered to the *Tsar*. Then the blessed Mikhail and Fedor began to sing, and having finished singing they took holy communion, the body and blood of Christ, which their father had given them who had blessed them for this to suffer for Christ. And those who stood by said: " Mikhail, the executioners are coming from the *Tsar* to kill you; bow, and you will live." And Mikhail and Fedor answered as with one mouth: " We will not bow, and will not listen to you, for the sake of the glory of this world," and began to sing: " Thy martyrs, O Lord, did not deny Thee, nor did they turn away from Thy commandments, but rather suffered for Thy sake, O Christ, and endured many tortures and received perfect crowns in heaven," and so forth. And then the executioners having arrived, and having jumped off their horses, they seized Mikhail, they stretched him out and holding his arms, began to strike him with their hands over the heart, and threw him prone on to the ground and struck him with their heels. And when he had been overpowered a certain man who had been a Christian and then become pagan having denied the Christian faith, and become a pagan transgressor of the law, named Doman, this man cut off the head of the holy *Veliki Knyaz* Mikhail, and hurled it away. And at that minute they said to Fedor: " Bow thou to our gods and thou wilt receive the whole *Knyazdom*[1] of thy *Knyaz*." And Fedor said to them: " I do not desire the *Knyazdom* and do not bow to your gods; but I wish to suffer for Christ like my *Knyaz*." Then again they began to torture Fedor as before they had Mikhail, and then they cut off his honoured head too. Thus, these men thanking the Lord suffered for Christ, and gave over their holy souls to the Lord into the hands of God, new holy martyrs. And their holy bodies were thrown to the dogs to eat, but on the contrary the holy bodies having lain many days were by the grace of God preserved and in no way injured. And our merciful God the Lord who loves mankind glorifying His holy and obedient servants who had suffered for Him and for the Orthodox faith, a pillar of fire

[1] *Knyazhenie*—sovereignty.

appeared from earth to heaven over their honourable bodies, shining with exceeding bright rays for the confirmation of Christians and for the conviction of the faithless who leave God and bow to things, and for the terrifying of the pagans. And their holy and honourable bodies were saved by some God-fearing Christians. The killing of them was on the 20th day of September; through whose prayers and through the supplication of these sufferers of pain and martyrs, Mikhail and Fedor, we shall be worthy to find mercy and remission of our sins at the hands of our Lord Jesus Christ, in this and in the future life, together with the Father, the Son and the Holy Ghost, now and for ever and ever, Amen.]

The Lithuanians made ravages about Torzhok and Bezhitsy, and the men of Novi-torg with *Knyaz* Yaroslav Volodimirovich chased and fought them; and they took the horses from the men of Novi-torg, and beat the men themselves and went away with their plunder. And Yavid and Erbet with the men of Tver and of Dmitrov, and Yaroslav with the men of Novi-torg, pursued them and beat them near Toropets, and the sons of their *Knyaz* took refuge in Toropets.

The next morning Olexander came up with men of Novgorod and took away all the plunder, and slew more than eight of their *Knyaz's* sons. And from there the men of Novgorod turned back; but the *Knyaz* pursued them[1] with his own court[2] and defeated them near [the village of] Zizech, and did not let a single man go, and there he killed the rest of the *Knyaz's* sons. And he himself took his own son from Vitebsk and went with a small company and met another force at lake Vosvyat; and there God helped him, and he destroyed those two and himself returned well and his company also.

A.D. 1246. A.M. 6754. [*Knyaz* Yaroslav Vsevolodits died in the Horde of the Khan.] *Knyaz* Olexander went to the Tartars.

A.D. 1247. A.M. 6755. God's slave Kostyantin Vyacheslavich, whose monastic name was Ankyudin, died, and was honourably laid in [the Church of] Saint Saviour at Khutin.

A.D. 1248. A.M. 6756.

[1] sc. the Lithuanians.
[2] *Dvor.*

A.D. 1249. A.M. 6757. Spiridon, *Vladyka* of Novgorod, died, and was honourably laid in St. Sophia.

A.D. 1250. A.M. 6758. *Knyaz* Olexander returned from the Horde, and there was great joy in Novgorod.

A.D. 1251. A.M. 6759. The Metropolitan Kyuril and the Bishop of Rostov, also named Kyuril, came to Novgorod, and established Dalmat as *Vladyka* of Novgorod.

[At this time also Nevrui came against the land of Suzdal, against *Knyaz* Andrei; and *Knyaz* Andrei Yaroslavich fled beyond sea to the land of the *Svei*, and they killed him.]

Heavy rains came the same year and took away all the ploughed fields and crops and hay; and the water carried away the large bridge over the Volkhov, and in the autumn a frost struck the crops, but a remnant was preserved. For the Lord God sends down on us for our sins at one time famine at another war and all other kinds of punishment; but, oh! His mercy is great! And He is patient with us, awaiting repentance, as He Himself said: " I desire not the death of a sinner, but his conversion to life," and He leaves us remnants for our revival.

A.D. 1252. A.M. 6760. Slavno was burnt down from St. Ilya[1] up to Nutna Street.

A.D. 1253. A.M. 6761. The Lithuanians ravaged the district of Novgorod and went off with captives, and the men of Novgorod with *Knyaz* Vasili overtook them at Toropets; and so Christian blood was avenged on them. And they defeated them and took back the captives from them, and returned well to Novgorod. The same year the *Nemtsy* came to Pleskov and burned the town[2], but the men of Pleskov killed many of them. And the men of Novgorod went out to them in arms from Novgorod, and they ran away; and the men of Novgorod having come to Novgorod, and having armed and prepared themselves, went beyond the Narova and laid waste their district; and the Korel people also did much harm to their districts. And the same year they went with the men of Pleskov to ravage them, and they put out a force against them; and the men of Novgorod with the men of Pleskov defeated them by the power of the honourable cross; for they began it against themselves, the accursed transgressors of right; and they sent to

---

[1] Elias.
[2] *Posad.*

Pleskov and to Novgorod desiring peace on all the terms laid down by Novgorod and Pleskov. And so they made peace.

In the winter of the same year *Knyaz* Yaroslav Yaroslavich fled from out of the Low Country, and they set him in Pleskov.

A.D. 1254. A.M. 6762. It was well with the Christians.

A.D. 1255. A.M. 6763. The men of Novgorod led out Yaroslav Yaroslavich from Pleskov and set him on the throne, and they drove out Vasili. And having heard this, Vasili's father, Olexander, went with an armed force against Novgorod; and Olexander as he was going along with a large force, and with the men of Novi-torg, Ratishka met him with treacherous information: " Advance, *Knyaz*, thy brother Yaroslav has fled." And the men of Novgorod put a force in the quarter [of the church] of the Nativity of Christ; and those who were a-foot, took up a position opposite the *Gorodishche* beyond St. Ilya's; and at a *Veche* at St. Nicholas' the lesser men said: " Brothers, lo, how the *Knyaz* says: " ' surrender me my enemies.' " And the lesser men kissed the cross how that all should stand in life or death for the rights of Novgorod, for their patrimony. And among the greater men there was an evil counsel, how to overcome the lesser and to bring in the *Knyaz* on their own terms. And Mikhalko hastened out of the town to St. Georgi's how he might with his force strike our side and crush the people. And Anani having learned of this, wishing him well, sent Yakun secretly after him. And the common people having learned of this, went in chase of him, and tried to get into his house; and Anani prevented them: " Brothers, if you are going to kill him, kill me first." For he did not know that they had counselled an evil thought about him to seize him himself and to give the *Posadnik*-ship to Mikhalko. And the *Knyaz* sent Boris to the *Veche:* " Deliver *Posadnik* Anani to me; or if you do not, I am not your *Knyaz*, and shall come against the town in arms." And the men of Novgorod sent to the *Knyaz* the *Vladyka* and Klim the *Tysyatski:* " Come, *Knyaz*, to thy throne, and listen not to evil-doers, but forgive thy anger to Anani and to all the men of Novgorod." And the *Knyaz* did not listen to the request of the *Vladyka* and Klim. And the men of Novgorod said: " Brothers, inasmuch as our *Knyaz* has thus taken counsel with our transgressors of the Cross,[1] they have God and St. Sophia; but the *Knyaz* is without sin." And the whole force stood three days for its rights, and on the

1 sc. of the oath.

fourth day the *Knyaz* sent saying thus: " If Anani is deprived of the *Posadnik*-ship I will forgive you my anger." And Anani was deprived of the *Posadnik*-ship, and they took peace on all the terms of Novgorod. And the *Knyaz* entered the town and *Vladyka* Dalmat met him at Prikupovich's Court with all the hierarchy, and with the crosses; and all were filled with joy, and the evil-doers were covered with darkness; because it was joy for Christians, and perdition for the devil, for that there was not great shedding of Christian blood. And *Knyaz* Olexander took his seat on his throne. And the same year they gave the *Posadnik*-ship to Mikhalko Stepanovich.

A.D. 1256. A.M. 6764. There came *Svei* and the Yem and Sum people, and Didman with his province, and a quantity of armed men, and they began to make a town on the Narova. And the *Knyaz* was not then in Novgorod, and the men of Novgorod sent to the Low Country to the *Knyaz* for armed men, and themselves sent throughout their province, thus gathering armed men. And they, accursed ones, having heard, fled beyond the sea. *Knyaz* Olexander arrived in the winter of the same year, and the Metropolitan with him; and the *Knyaz* took the road together with the Metropolitan, and the men of Novgorod did not know where he was going, some thought that he was going against the Chud people. And having reached Koporya, Olexander went against the Yem people; but the Metropolitan returned to Novgorod, and many other men of Novgorod turned back from Koporya. And the *Knyaz* went with his own force and with the men of Novgorod. And the road was bad, so that they saw neither day nor night, and it was perdition to many of those on foot, but God spared the men of Novgorod. And he came to the Yem land; some they killed, and others they captured. And the men of Novgorod with *Knyaz* Olexander returned all well. And then the *Knyaz* went to the Low Country, he took with him the Novgorod envoys, Eleuferi and Mikhail Pinishchinich, and set his son Vasili on the throne.

A.D. 1257. A.M. 6765. Evil news came from Russia, that the Tartars desired the *tamga*[1] and tithe on Novgorod; and the people were agitated the whole year. And at Lady-day *Posadnik* Anani died, and in the winter the men of Novgorod killed *Posadnik* Mikhalko. If any one does good to another, then good would come of it; but digging a pit under another, he falls into it himself.

[1] A Customs-tax: properly, a seal on merchandise.

The same winter Tartar envoys came with Olexander, and Vasili fled to Pleskov; and the envoys began to ask the tithe and the *tamga* and the men of Novgorod did not agree to this, and gave presents to the *Tsar*, and let the envoys go with peace.

And *Knyaz* Olexander drove his son out of Pleskov and sent him to the Low Country, and punished Alexander and his company. He cut off the noses of some, and took out the eyes of others, of those who had led Vasili to evil; for evil every man shall perish evilly! The same winter they killed Misha. The same winter they gave the *Posadnik*-ship to Mikhail Fedorovich, having brought him out of Ladoga, and they gave the post of *Tysyatski* to Zhirokha.

A.D. 1258. A.M. 6766. The Lithuanians with the men of Polotsk came to Smolensk and took [the town of] Voishchina by assault. The same autumn the Lithuanians came to Torzhok, and the men of Novi-torg issued out. For our sins the Lithuanians ambushed them; some they killed, others they took with their hands, and others barely escaped; and there was much evil in Torzhok. The same winter the Tartars took the whole Lithuanian land, and killed the people.

A.D. 1259. A.M. 6767. There was a sign in the moon; such as no sign had ever been. The same winter Mikhail Pineschinich came from the Low Country with a false mission, saying thus: " If you do not number yourselves for tribute there is already a force in the Low Country." And the men of Novgorod did number themselves for tribute. The same winter the accursed raw-eating Tartars, Berkai and Kasachik, came with their wives, and many others, and there was a great tumult in Novgorod, and they did much evil in the province, taking contribution for the accursed Tartars. And the accursed ones began to fear death; they said to Olexander: " Give us guards, lest they kill us." And the *Knyaz* ordered the son of the *Posadnik* and all the sons of the *Boyars* to protect them by night. The Tartars said: " Give us your numbers for tribute or we will run away."[1] And the common people would not give their numbers for tribute but said: " Let us die honourably for St. Sophia and for the angelic houses."[2] Then the people were divided: who was good stood by St. Sophia and by the True Faith; and they made opposition; the greater men bade the lesser be counted for tribute. And the accursed ones wanted to

[1] Presumably " and return in greater strength."
[2] sc. churches.

escape, driven by the Holy Spirit, and they devised an evil counsel how to strike at the town at the other side, and the others at this side by the lake; and Christ's power evidently forbade them, and they durst not. And becoming frightened they began to crowd to one point to St. Sophia, saying: " Let us lay our heads by St. Sophia." And it was on the morrow, the *Knyaz* rode down from the *Gorodishche* and the accursed Tartars with him, and by the counsel of the evil they numbered themselves for tribute; for the *Boyars* thought it would be easy for themselves, but fall hard on the lesser men. And the accursed ones began to ride through the streets, writing down the Christian houses; because for our sins God has brought wild beasts out of the desert to eat the flesh of the strong, and to drink the blood of *Boyars*. And having numbered them for tribute and taken it, the accursed ones went away, and *Knyaz* Olexander followed them, having set his son Dmitri on the throne.

The same year, on the eve of Boris Day, there was a great frost throughout the province; but the Lord did not wish to leave this place of St. Sophia waste. He turned away His wrath from us and looked down on us with the eye of His mercy, pointing us to repentance; but we sinners return like dogs to our vomit, unmindful of God's punishments which come upon us for our sins.

A.D. 1260. A.M. 6768. There was quiet all the year.

A.D. 1261. A.M. 6769. *Vladyka* Dalmat of Novgorod covered the whole roof of St. Sophia with lead. The same year, on November 8, the Feast of St. Michael, the Church of St. Vasili and thirty big houses were burnt down, and on the morrow the Church of St. Dmitri in Slavkov Street was burnt down, and fifty big houses.

A.D. 1262. A.M. 6770. The men of Novgorod built the town afresh, and took peace with the Lithuanians. The same year the Church of the Holy Martyrs, Boris and Gleb, was burnt down from thunder; and it was very large and beautiful. In the autumn of the same year the men of Novgorod with *Knyaz* Dmitri Alexandrovich went in large force to Yurev. And at the same time *Knyaz* Kostyantin, brother-in-law of Alexander, was there, and Yaroslav, Alexander's brother, with their own men, also *Knyaz* Tovtivil of Polotsk with 500 men of Polotsk and of the Lithuanians, and of the Novgorod force a countless number, God alone knows. The town of Yurev was strong, of three walls, and a quan-

H

tity of people in it of all kinds; and they had constructed strong defences, but the power of the Holy Cross and of St. Sophia always overthrows those who are wrong. And so this town, its strength was for nothing, but by the aid of God it was taken by single assault, and many of the people of that town were killed, others were taken alive, and others were burnt by fire, and their wives and children; and they took countless booty and captives, and they shot many good men from the town, and they killed Peter Myasnikovich-And *Knyaz* Dmitri with all the men of Novgorod returned to Nov. gorod with much booty. The same year the monk Vasili built the Church of St. Vasili; but God knows whether he did this with his own [means] or with those of Boris Gavshinich; but the Lord grant them both remission of their sins, and St. Vasili. The same year *Knyaz* Olexander went to the Tartars; and Berka kept him, not letting him back to Russia; and he wintered with the Tartars and fell ill.

A.D. 1263. A.M. 6771. *Knyaz* Olexander came back from the Tartars in very bad health, in the autumn; and he came to Gorodets[1] [monastery] and was shorn on November 14, the day of the holy Apostle Philip; and he died the same night and they took him to Volodimir and laid him in the monastery of the Nativity by the Church of the Holy Mother of God. And the Bishops and *Igumens* having come together with the Metropolitan Kyuril and all the hierarchy and monks and with all the people of Suzdal, they buried him honourably on the 23rd of the same month, Friday, the Day of St. Amfilokhi. Grant him, O merciful Lord, to see Thy face in the future age, for he laboured for Novgorod and for all the Russian land.

The same year there was a tumult amongst the Lithuanians, God sending down his wrath upon them; they rose themselves against themselves and the *Veliki Knyaz* Mindovg[2] was killed by his own relatives, who conspired without anybody's knowledge. The same year the murderers of Mindovg having quarrelled over his goods they killed the good *Knyaz* Tovtivil of Polotsk, and put the *Boyars* of Polotsk in chains and called on the people of Polotsk to kill Tovtivil's son, too; and he escaped to Novgorod with his men. Then the Lithuanians set their own *Knyaz* in Polotsk; and let go the men of Polotsk whom they had taken with their *Knyaz* and took peace.

[1] sc. Radilov, on the Volga.
[2] Mindvog, Grand Prince of Lithuania, 1247–63.

A.D. 1264. A.M. 6772. The men of Novgorod having taken counsel
           with *Posadnik* Mikhail drove out *Knyaz*
Dmitri Alexandrovich, because the *Knyaz* was still young. And
they sent to Tver the son of the *Posadnik* and the better *Boyars*
for Yaroslav the brother of Alexander.

A.D. 1265. A.M. 6773. They set *Knyaz* Yaroslav Yaroslavich on
           the throne in Novgorod on January 27.
The same year there was a great tumult amongst the Lithuanians
by God's infliction on them, for our Lord God could not bear to look
upon the unrighteous and pagan seeing them shedding Christian
blood like water and others scattered by them over strange lands;
then the Lord will repay them according to their works. *Knyaz*
Mindovg of Lithuania had a son named Voishelg; him the Lord chose
as champion of the true faith; for having gone to Mount Sinai,
away from his father and his kindred, and from his pagan faith, he
acknowledged the true Christian religion, and was baptized in the
name of the Father, and Son, and Holy Ghost, and studied the
sacred books, and was shorn into the monastic order on the Holy
Mount; and having remained there three years, he went to his own
country to his father.   And his father being a pagan tried to persuade him to renounce the Christian faith and the monastic order, and
to take up his rule.   But he, armed with the power of the Cross,
would not even listen to his father's persuasion and feared not his
threats, but having gone away from his father built himself a monastery among Christians and remained there, glorifying the Holy
Trinity, the Father, the Son and the Holy Ghost.   But after the
murder of his father, though undesirous to do so, but God inflicting
him on them, the pagan Lithuanians, for the Christian blood, laid
it in his heart, and he taking off from him his gown, vowed himself
to God for three years, when he should resume his gown, and did not
leave the monastic order.   He gathered about him his father's
soldiers and friends, and having prayed to the honourable Cross, he
went against the pagan Lithuanians and defeated them, and stayed
in their country all the year.   Then the Lord repaid the accursed
ones according to their works; for he took the whole of their country
captive by force of arms, and there was joy everywhere throughout
the Christian land.   Then about 300 Lithuanians escaped into
Pleskov with their wives and children, and *Knyaz* Svyatoslav with
the priests and people of Pleskov baptized them; and the men of
Novgorod wanted to slay them, but *Knyaz* Yaroslav would not give
them up, and they were not slain.   H2

A.D. 1266. A.M. 6774. The men of Pleskov set as their *Knyaz*, Dovmont, *Knyaz* of Lithuania. The same year God laid his grace into the heart of Dovmont to fight for St. Sophia and the Holy Trinity, to avenge the Christian blood, and he went with the men of Pleskov against the pagan Lithuanians, and they ravaged much and took Gerden's *Knyaginya* and two young *Knyazes*. And *Knyaz* Gerden collected about him the Lithuanian forces and pursued them. And when the men of Pleskov learned of the pursuit, they sent away their captives and stood firmly against them on this side of the Dvina. And the Lithuanians began to ford over to this side; then the men of Pleskov engaged them, and God helped *Knyaz* Dovmont with the men of Pleskov and they slew a great quantity of them, others they drowned in the river; only *Knyaz* Gerden alone escaped with a small *Druzhina*. And the men of Pleskov returned all well.

In the winter of the same year the men of Pleskov again went against the Lithuanians with *Knyaz* Dovmont.

The same year *Knyaz* Yaroslav came to Novgorod with the forces of the Low Country, wishing to go against Dovmont to Pleskov; but the men of Novgorod forbade him, saying: " Surely thou canst not go against Pleskov, *Knyaz*, after consulting with us." And the *Knyaz* sent away his men.

A.D. 1267. A.M. 6775. For our sins on May 23 a fire broke out in Kuzma-Demyan Street before evening service and the whole of the Nerev quarter was burnt down. Alas, my brothers! the fire was so fierce, that the flames went over the water, and much good merchandise was burnt in the boats on the Volkhov, and several heads[1] were burnt; in a single hour everything was burnt. And many from that grew rich, but many others were made beggars.

The same year the men of Novgorod with Eleferi Sbyslavich and with Dovmont and the men of Pleskov went against the Lithuanians, ravaged much of theirs and returned all well.

A.D. 1268. A.M. 6776. The men of Novgorod consulted with their *Knyaz* Yuri, they wished to go against the Lithuanians, while others [wished to go] against Poltesk[2], and others beyond the Narova. And when they reached the village of Dubrovna there was a quarrel; and they went back and went beyond

---

[1] People.
[2] sc. Polotsk.

the Narova to Rakovor,[1] and made great havoc in their land, but did not take the town; and they shot the good man Fedor Sbyslavich from the town, and six others; and they returned all well.   The same year the men of Novgorod having taken counsel with *Posadnik* Mikhail, called *Knyaz* Dmitri Alexandrovich to come with a force from Pereyaslavl, and they sent envoys from Yaroslav.   And in place of himself Yaroslav sent Svyatoslav with a force.   And they sought out competent men and began to make the battering rams in the *Vladyka's* Court.   And the *Nemtsy* sent their envoys, the men of Riga, Velyad and Yurev, and from other towns with deceit, saying: " We have peace with you; deal with the people of Kolyvan and of Rakovor as you can, we shall not join with them; and we kiss the Cross."   And the envoys kissed the Cross.   And Lazor Moisievich having gone there led them all to the Cross; the Bishops and godly courtiers, not to assist the people of Kolyvan and of Rakovor; and they took into their own hands a good man Simeon from Novgorod, having kissed the Cross.   And all the *Knyazes* having assembled in Novgorod : Dmitri, Svyatoslav, his brother Mikhail, Kostyantin, Yuri, Yaropolk, Dovmont of Pleskov, and some other *Knyazes*, they went to Rakovor on January 23.   And as they entered their country they separated along three roads, and fought a very great number of them.   And there they came upon an impenetrable cave into which a large number of Chud people had clambered, and it was impossible to take them, and they stood (before it) three days.   Then the expert with the ram cunningly turned the water on to them, and the Chud people ran away of themselves, and they slew them, and all their goods the men of Novgorod gave to *Knyaz* Dmitri.   And thence they went on to Rakovor, and when they reached the Kegola river they found there a force of *Nemtsy* in position, and it was like a forest to look at; for the whole land of the *Nemtsy* had come together. But the men of Novgorod without any delay crossed the river to them, and began to range their forces: and the men of Pleskov took stand on the right hand, and Dmitri, and Svyatoslav took stand also on the right higher up; on the left stood Mikhail, and the men of Novgorod stood facing the iron troops opposite to the great wedge; and so they went against each other.   And as they came together there was a terrible battle such as neither fathers nor grandfathers had seen.   And there a great evil befell; they killed *Posadnik* Mikhail and Tverdislav the Red, Nikifor Radyatinich, Tverdislav Moisievich,

[1] Wesenberg.

Mikhail Krivtsevich, Ivach, Boris Ildyatinich, his brother Lazor, Ratsha, Vasili, Voiborzovich, Osip, Zhiroslav, Dorogomilovich, the usher Poroman, Polyud, and many good *Boyars*, and countless other common men; and of others there was nothing known, the *Tysyatski* Kondrat, Ratislav Boldyzhevich, Danil Mozotinich and many others, God knows, and men of Pleskov also, and of Ladoga. And *Knyaz* Yuri turned shoulder, or there was treachery in him, God knows. But as regards that, brothers, God punishes us for our sins and takes from us good men, that we may repent; as the Scripture says: " Wonderful weapons are prayer and fasting," and again: " Charity combined with fasting saves a man from death," and again let us remember the Prophet Isaiah saying: " If ye be willing to listen to me, ye shall eat the blessings of the earth: but if ye be unwilling and do not listen to me, the sword shall devour you, and thus shall one cut down 100 of you, and by 100 shall 1,000 of you perish." Yet we, seeing this terror, not in the least do we repent of our sins, but turned more to evil, brother seeking to devour brother through envy and one man another, kissing the Cross and again transgressing it not knowing what is the power of the Cross, for by the Cross are the enemies and the powers of the devils vanquished; the Cross helps *Knyazes* in battles; protected by the Cross faithful people conquer their foes; for whoever transgresses the Cross receives punishment here, and in the next world eternal torment.

But let us return to the foregoing.

Now that great encounter having taken place and the laying down of the heads of good men with their heads for St. Sophia, the merciful Lord speedily sent His mercy, not wishing utter death to the sinner; punishing us, and again pardoning, He turned away his wrath from us, and regarded us with His merciful eye: by the power of the Honourable Cross and through the prayers of the Holy Mother of God our Sovereign Lady, the Immaculate Mary, and those of all the Saints, God helped *Knyaz* Dmitri and the men of Novgorod on February 18, on the Saturday before Quinquagesima, the Day of the Holy Father Leo; and they pursued them fighting them, as far as the town, for seven *versts* along the three roads, so that not even a horse could make its way for the corpses. And so they turned back from the town, and perceived another large force in the shape of a great wedge which had struck into the Novgorod transport; and the men of Novgorod wished to strike them, but others said: " It is already too near night; how if we fall into confusion and get beaten ourselves." And so they stood near together opposite each other waiting daylight. And they, accursed transgressors of the Cross, fled, not waiting for the light. And the men of Novgorod stood on the field of battle three days, and returned to Novgorod, and brought their dead; and they laid *Posadnik* Mikhail in the Church of St. Sophia. Grant, O most merciful God, lover of mankind, that they may stand in the next world at Thy right hand, together with all the Saints who have pleased Thee in the ages, who shed their blood for St. Sophia, having given their life honourably. And they gave the *Posadnik*-ship to Pavsha Ananinich; and the office of *Tysyatski* they gave to no one, in case Kondrat were alive.

A.D. 1269. A.M. 6777. The *Nemtsy* came in great force to Pleskov in All Saints week and attacked the town and did not effect anything, but suffered great hurt and stood ten days. And the men of Novgorod with *Knyaz* Yuri pursued them, they went off some on horseback and others in boats, in haste; and when the *Nemtsy* learned about the Novgorod force, they fled across the river.[1] And the men of Novgorod reached Pleskov and took peace across the river on all their own terms.

The same year *Knyaz* Yaroslav came to Novgorod and began to complain: "My men and my brothers, and yours also, are killed, and you have engaged in war with the *Nemtsy* for Zhiroslav Davidovich and Mikhail Mishinich and Yuri Sbyslavich, wishing to deprive them[2] of their districts." But the men of Novgorod stood for them; so the *Knyaz* was about to go out from the town. But the men of Novgorod bowed to him: "*Knyaz*, forgive them thy anger, and do not go from us"; for they had not yet made good their peace with the *Nemtsy*. But the *Knyaz* did not listen to that, and went away. And they sent the *Vladyka* and the greater men with request, and brought him back from Broninitsa.[3] Then they gave the office of *Tysyatski* to Ratibor Kluksovich by wish of the *Knyaz*.

In the winter of the same year *Knyaz* Yaroslav having consulted with the men of Novgorod, sent Svyatoslav to the Low Country to collect forces, and he collected all the *Knyazes*, and armed men without number, and brought them to Novgorod. And there was there the great *Baskak*[4] of Vladimir, named Amragan, and they wished to go to Kolyvan. And the *Nemtsy* having learned this, sent envoys

[1] sc. the " Great " river, *reka Velikaya*, on which Pskov is situated.
[2] sc. the Nemtsy.
[3] The village of Bronnitsy, on the river Msta, E. of Novgorod.
[4] Tartar official, tax-gatherer.

with the request: " We bow to all your terms, we withdraw from the whole of the Narova; but do not you shed any blood "; and so the men of Novgorod having taken counsel, took peace on all their own terms. But the *Knyaz* wanted to go against the Korel people, and the men of Novgorod persuaded him not to go against the Korel people, and the *Knyaz* sent his force back.

A.D. 1270. A.M. 6778. Varlam, *Igumen* of St. George's, and Archimandrite of Novgorod, died. In the same year there was a tumult in Novgorod; they set about driving *Knyaz* Yaroslav out of the town, and they summoned a *Veche* in Yaroslav's Court and killed Ivanko, and others escaped into the Church of St. Nikola; and on the morrow the *Tysyatski* Ratibor, Gavrilo Kiyaninov and other of his friends fled to the *Knyaz* to *Gorodishche;* and they took their houses for plunder and divided up their dwellings, and sent to the *Knyaz* in the *Gorodishche* having written out a document[1] with all his faults: " Why hast thou taken up the Volkhov with snarers of wild ducks, and taken up the fields with catchers of hares? Why hast thou taken Olex Mortkinich's homestead? Why hast thou taken silver from Mikifor Manush-kinich and Roman Boldyzhevich and Varfolomei? And another thing, why dost thou send away from us the foreigners who dwell among us? and many faults of this kind. And now, *Knyaz*, we cannot suffer thy violence. Depart from us; and we shall think of a *Knyaz* for ourselves." And the *Knyaz* sent Svyatoslav and Andrei Vorotislavich to the *Veche* with greeting: " I renounce all that, and I kiss the Cross on all your terms." But the men of Novgorod ans-wered: " *Knyaz*, go away, we do not want thee; else we shall come, the whole of Novgorod, to drive thee out." And the *Knyaz* went out of the town against his will. And the men of Novgorod sent for Dmitri Alexandrovich, but Dmitri declined, saying thus: " I do not wish to take the throne before my uncle." And the men of Novgorod were sad. And Yaroslav began to collect forces against Novgorod, and he sent Ratibor to the Tartar *Tsar* asking for help against Novgorod. And *Knyaz* Vasili Yaroslavich having heard this sent envoys to Novgorod saying thus: " I bow to St. Sophia and to the men of Novgorod; I have heard that Yaroslav is going against Novgorod with all his force, and Dmitri with the men of Pereyaslavl, and Gleb with the men of Smolensk; I am sorry for my patrimony," and he himself went to the Tartars, taking with him Petrila Rychag

[1] *Gramota.*

and Mikhail Pineshchinich, and he turned back the Tartar forces,. saying thus to the *Tsar:* " The men of Novgorod are right, and Yaroslav is to blame."

For the *Tsar* had already sent off an army against Novgorod according to Ratibor's false word, for Ratibor said to the *Tsar:* " The men of Novgorod do not listen to thee; we demanded tribute for thee, but they drove us out; and others they killed, and plundered our houses, and dishonoured Yaroslav." And the men of Novgorod raised a stockade[1] about the town on both sides and brought the merchandise into the city. And Yaroslav's scouts pushed almost up to the *Gorodishche*, and the whole town, great and small, went out armed to the *Gorodishche*, the foot soldiers stood two days behind the Zhilotug,[2] and the mounted men behind the *Gorodishche*. Yaroslav having learned this, went by the other side to Russa and halted in Russa, and sent Tvorimir into Novgorod: " I forego all that caused your displeasure with me,. and all the *Knyazes* will stand security for me." But the men of Novgorod sent to him Lazor Moisievich: " *Knyaz*, thou hast taken counsel against St. Sophia; come on, that we may die honourably for St. Sophia. We have no *Knyaz*, but God and the truth and St. Sophia; and we do not want thee." And into Novgorod there were collected the whole Novgorod district, the men of Pleskov, of Ladoga, the Korel, Izhera, and the Vod people, and great and small, all went to Golino, and stood a week at the ford, and Yaroslav's force stood on the opposite side. And the Metropolitan sent a document to Novgorod, saying thus: " God has entrusted me with the Archbishopric in the Russian Land, you are to listen to God and to me; shed no blood; Yaroslav foregoes all anger, and for that I am guarantee; and if you will kiss the Cross, I will do public penance and answer for that before God." And God did not allow the shedding of Christian blood. And Yaroslav sent greeting to the Novgorod army, and they took a peace on all the terms of Novgorod; they set Yaroslav and led him up to the Cross.

In the winter of the same year *Knyaz* Yaroslav went to Volodimir,. and thence he went to the Horde, and left in Novgorod Andrei Vorotislavich, and gave *Knyaz* Aigust to the men of Pleskov.

A.D. 1271. A.M. 6779. The sun grew dark on Wednesday morning in the fifth week of Lent, and then again filled out and we rejoiced.

¹ *Ostrog.*
² Stream.

In the same year Fedor Hotovich erected the Church of St. Sava; they erected another in Kholop Street to the SS. Kosma and Demyan.

A.D. 1272. A.M. 6780. The *Veliki Knyaz* of Novgorod, Yaroslav Yaroslavich died among the Tartars, and they laid him in Tver in the Church of SS. Kosma and Demyan. And *Knyaz* Dmitri sent his envoys to Novgorod with greeting, wishing to take his seat in Novgorod. And Vasili Yaroslavich also sent with greeting, wishing to take his seat on the throne. And both envoys lodged in Yaroslav's Court. And the men of Novgorod with *Posadnik* Pavsha declared for Dmitri, and sent for him. *Knyaz* Dmitri Alexandrovich came the same year to Novgorod and took his seat on the throne on October 9.[1]

[The same year *Knyaz* Vasili came to Torzhok and burned the dwellings and installed his own *Tiun*[2] and went back to Kostroma. And Svyatoslav with the men of Tver began to ravage the Novgorod district: *Volok*, Bezhitsy, and Vologda. Bread was dear in Novgorod, and they seized the merchandise of Low Country merchants.

The same winter *Knyaz* Dmitri with the men of Novgorod and the whole district went to Tver, and they sent Smen Mikhailovich, Lazor Moisievich and Stephen Dushilovich to Vasili: " Give back to us those Novgorod districts which thou hast taken, and take peace with us." And Vasili let go the envoys with honour, but did not give peace. And while the men of Novgorod were at Torzhok the people rose and wished for Vasili. And Dmitri retired from the throne voluntarily and went away with love. And they then took the *Posadnik*-ship from Pavsha, and he fled to Dmitri with Roman, and thence they went to Vasili and bowed to him. And they gave the *Posadnik*-ship to Mikhail Mishinich, and sent for Vasili, and at Torzhok kissed the picture of the Lord that they would all be at one with the *Posadnik* Mikhail.

Knyaz Vasili Yaroslavich took his seat on the throne in Novgorod. And the same year they took the *Posadnik*-ship from Mikhail and gave it again to Pavsha having brought him from Kostroma.[3]

---

[1] From this point there are several missing sheets of the original, and the continuation up to the year 1299, as published, is borrowed from another text.

[2] Bailiff.

[3] No record for 127**3**.

A.D. 1274. A.M. 6782. Dalmat, *Vladyka* of Novgorod, died on Saturday, October 21, at 1 at night, and was honourably buried in the morning of Sunday. God grant compliance with his holy prayers for those kneeling at his tomb!

The same winter Pavsha *Posadnik* of Novgorod died, and *Knyaz* Vasili came to Novgorod, they again gave the *Posadnik*-ship to Mikhail Mishinich. Before the death of Dalmat the *Posadnik* Pavsha with the elder men had beat with their foreheads[1] to Dalmat: " Whom wilt thou bless as our shepherd and teacher in thy place ? " And Dalmat named two *Igumens:* Ioan of St. Georgi and his own spiritual father, Kliment. " I will bless whomever you prefer." The *Posadnik* went to Ioan's house, and called the men of Novgorod together, and told them Dalmat's words. And all preferred Kliment nominated of God, and Dalmat blessed him with his hand; and on the death of Dalmat they sent Kliment to Kiev for confirmation.

A.D. 1275. A.M. 6783. A fire broke out by night in the *Knyaz's* Court next to the court of the *Nemtsy*,[2] and the market place was burnt, hitherwards and up to Slavno and hitherwards as far as Rogatitsa Street: seven wooden churches were burnt down and four stone churches were damaged by fire, and, fifth, the Church of the *Nemtsy*.[2]

A.D. 1276. A.M. 6784. The wall of St. Sophia fell to its foundation, at the Nerev end, at mid-day on May 9.

In the winter of the same year Kliment returned from Kiev to his bishopric and he was established *Vladyka* of Novgorod. And they installed him honourably in St. Sophia, and all Novgorod met him honourably with crosses and chants on Sunday the second day of August.

In the winter of the same year the *Veliki Knyaz* Vasili Yaroslavich died, and he was laid in the Church of St. Fedor in Kostroma. And the men of Novgorod sent for Dmitri Alexandrovich.

A.D. 1277. A.M. 6785. *Knyaz* Dmitri arrived in Novgorod and they set him on the throne on All Saints' Sunday.

A.D. 1278. A.M. 6786. *Knyaz* Dmitri with the men of Novgorod and with the whole of the Low Country, chastised the Korel people and took their country by conquest.

---

[1] i.e. Petitioned.
[2] *Nemetski*, German.

A.D. 1279. A.M. 6787. *Knyaz* Dmitri obtained permission from Novgorod to build a town[1] at Koporya for himself; and having gone, built it himself.

A.D. 1280. A.M. 6788. The *Veliki Knyaz* Dmitri going with *Posadnik* Mikhail and with the greater men encircled the town of Koporya with stone. The same year *Knyaz* Dmitri and the men of Novgorod took away the *Posadnik*-ship from Mikhail Mishinits, and gave it to Smen Mikhailov having brought him from Ladoga. And after three months Mikhail Mishinits died, on November 9, the day of St. Paul the Confessor.

A.D. 1281. A.M. 6789. *Knyaz* Dmitri began to make war on the men of Novgorod; and the men of Novgorod sent the *Vladyka* with entreaty; and he did not listen to him. In the winter of the same year *Knyaz* Dmitri came to Novgorod with an armed force and did much harm to the district of Novgorod and having halted on the Shelon he made peace and withdrew.

The same winter Kyuril, the Metropolitan of all Russia, died in Pereyaslavl on December 6; his remains were taken to Kiev to St. Sophia.

A.D. 1282. A.M. 6790. *Knyaz* Andrei Alexandrovich with Smen Tolignevits beat with their foreheads[2] to the *Tsar* against his brother Dmitri, and raised the Tartar forces and took Pereyaslavl by assault. And *Knyaz* Dmitri rode out with his men and court and passed by Novgorod making for Koporya. And the men of Novgorod went out in full force against him to the Ilmer[3] lake. And the *Knyaz* retired from Koporya and the men of Novgorod showed him the way, and they did not seize him, but his two daughters and his *Boyars* with their wives and children they brought to Novgorod as hostages: " If thy men retire from Koporya, then we will let them go free "; and they went each his own way on January 1. On the same day Domont drove the Ladoga men out of Koporya and they seized all the goods of *Knyaz* Dmitri, and seizing also Ladoga goods they took them into Koporya on Vasili day. And the men of Novgorod sent for *Knyaz* Andrei and themselves went to Koporya. Dmitri's men went out from the town because the men of Novgorod had showed them the road, and they plundered the town. The same winter *Knyaz* Andrei

[1] Or fort, *gorod.*
[2] sc. petitioned.
[3] sc. Ilmen.

Alexandrovich came to Novgorod, and they set him honourably on the throne in Quinquagesima week.   And then *Knyaz* Andrei taking with him the Novgorod men Smen Mikhailovich and other elder men, went out from Novgorod and went to Volodimir and from Volodimir he let the men of Novgorod go back, and himself went to Gorodets.[1] And Smen Mikhailovich came to Torzhok, and he sat in ambush at Torzhok not letting Dmitri's lieutenants enter Torzhok, and he sent all the crops to Novgorod in boats; for in Novgorod bread was dear.

A.D. 1283. A.M. 6791. The men of Novgorod went to Pereyaslavl against Dmitri, as also did Svyatoslav with the men of Tver, and Danilo Alexandrovich with the men of Moscow.   And Dmitri came out against their army with all his forces, and halted at Dmitrov; and the men of Novgorod halted five *versts* short of Dmitrov and they stood five days near each other, sending to each other envoys; and they made peace on all the terms of Novgorod, and withdrew.   The same year the *Nemtsy*[2] came up into lake Ladoga by the Neva with an armed force; they killed the Obonezh[3] merchants of Novgorod; and the men of Ladoga entered the Neva and fought with them.

A.D. 1284. A.M. 6792. *Knyaz* Andrei came to Torzhok, and summoned to him *Posadnik* Smen with all the Elders, and they concluded peace, and the *Knyaz* kissed the Cross, and the men of Novgorod did to him, how Andrei should not withdraw from Novgorod, and the men of Novgorod should not seek another *Knyaz;* in life or in death the men of Novgorod with Andrei. And the *Knyaz* let the men of Novgorod go back, and he himself went to the Low Country, and having gone there he ceded the Novgorod throne to his brother Dmitri.

The same year the *Nemetski Voyevoda* Trunda entered lake Ladoga up the Neva in sailing vessels and boats[4] with an armed force, intending to take tribute from the Korel people.   And the men of Novgorod with *Posadnik* Smen and with the men of Ladoga going out halted at the mouth of the Neva, and having waited, killed them, and the rest ran away, on September 9, the Day of the

---

[1] sc. Radilov, on the Volga.
[2] cf. p. 34.
[3] i.e. from the shores of lake Onega, N.-E. of Novgorod.
[4] *Loiva, shnek.*

Righteous Akim[1] and Anna.   In the winter of the same year *Knyaz* Dmitri came to Novgorod with his brother Andrei with an armed force, and with Tartars and with the whole of the Low Country, and they did much harm and burned the districts; and having come they halted at the [river] Korichka and made peace; and Dmitri took his seat on his throne in Novgorod.

A.D. 1285. A.M. 6793.   The Metropolitan Maxim came to Novgorod. The same winter the Lithuanians ravaged the district.

A.D. 1286. A.M. 6794.   In the winter they took the *Posadnik*-ship from Smen and gave it to Andrei Klimo-vich, and they took the office of *Tysyatski* from Ivan and gave it to Andreyan Olferevich.[2]

A.D. 1287. A.M. 6795.   There was a great tumult in Novgorod against Smen Mikhailovich; all Novgorod rose against him without just cause, they went out against him from all the quarters, like a strong army, every man armed, in great strength, a pitiful sight! and thus they went against his house and took his whole house with uproar.   Semeon fled to the *Vladyka* and the *Vladyka* led him into St. Sophia; and thus God preserved him; and on the morrow they came together in love.   But Semeon in a few days fell ill with an illness, and having lain some days, he died on Monday, July 16, the Day of St. Tikhon.

A.D. 1288. A.M. 6796.

A.D. 1289. A.M. 6797.   *Knyaz* Dmitri went with an armed force to Tver, and summoned the men of Novgorod; the men of Novgorod went with *Posadnik* Andrei, and fired the district and took peace.

A.D. 1290. A.M. 6798.   The men of Novgorod took the *Posadnik*-ship from Andrei Klimovich and gave it to Yuri Mishinich, during the Great Fast, towards the end of the eighth year.
     The same year they gave the *Posadnik*-ship of Ladoga to Matvei Semenovich.   The same fast, in Thanksgiving Week, they killed Samoila Ratshinich in the *Vladyka's* Court after morning service,

[1] Ioachim.
[2] Eleferevich (Eleutherius).

at the entrance to the Church of the Nativity of Christ. And the men of Novgorod rang together a *Veche* at St. Sophia and at St. Nikola, assembled in haste, took the Prussian Street, and plundered their houses and set fire to the whole street, and the Church of the Holy Mother of God was also burnt.

A.D. 1291. A.M. 6799. The water was big in the Volkhov in the spring. The same year the Lord sent His punishment for our sins: the horses all died in Novgorod, and but few were left. The same year a frost attacked the crops throughout the whole of the Novgorod district. Thus God warns us, wishing from us repentance that we might leave from our wickedness. Yet we are not any more mindful of our sins; but the Lord suffers long, awaiting our repentance. The same year rioters plundered the market, and the next day the men of Novgorod held a *Veche* and hurled two rioters from the bridge. The same year there was a tumult among the Tartars; *Tsar* Nogui killed *Tsars* Telebeg and Algui.

A.D. 1292. A.M. 6800. Alexander, son of the *Veliki Knyaz* Dmitri, died among the Tartars. Kliment, *Vladyka* of Novgorod laid the foundations of the stone Church of St. Nikola in [the village of] Lipna. The same year they began to build the Church of St. Fedor which had collapsed. The same year some Novgorod braves[1] with *Voyevodas* of the *Knyaz* went against the country of the Yem people and having ravaged it came back all well. In the same year the *Svei*, 800 of them, came in arms to ravage, 400 went against the Korel, and 400 against the Izhera people; and the Izhera people killed them, and the Korel people killed theirs, and others they took with their hands.

A.D. 1293. A.M. 6801. The *Svei* having come put up a town in the Korel land. The same year *Knyaz* Andrei with other *Knyazes* beat with their foreheads to the Tartar *Tsar* with complaints against *Knyaz* Dmitri, and the *Tsar* sent his brother Duden with a numerous army against Dmitri. Oh, great was the harm done to Christians! they seized unoffending towns; Volodimir, Moscow, Dmitrov, *Volok*,[2] and other towns, they laid waste the whole land. And Dmitri escaped to Pskov. And the men of Novgorod sent presents with Smen Klimovich to *Tsar* Duden to *Volok:* "Turn back the soldiers from *Volok*," and they sent with greetings for

[1] *Molodets*, pl. *molodtsy*.
[2] Volok Lamsk.

Andrei. *Knyaz* Andrei sent back the army and himself came to Novgorod and took his seat on the throne on Quinquagesima Sunday.

The same Lent the *Veliki Knyaz* Andrei sent *Knyaz* Roman Glebovich with Yuri Mishinich and the *Tysyatski* Andreyan and a few men of Novgorod to the *Sveiski* Town; they fought hard on Tuesday in the sixth week of Lent, and they shot the good man Ivan Klekachevich from the town, and many were wounded. The same night for our sins a thaw set in; water covered all the land; round the town was flooded, and there was no fodder for the horses. They retired, and came back all well, except for the wounded; and Ivan Klekachevich after being brought back, died of his wound.

The same Lent *Knyaz* Andrei with *Posadnik* Andrei and with the greater men went to Torzhok to catch Dmitri, but Dmitri escaped from Pleskov to Tver; and sent into Torzhok the *Vladyka* of Tver with Svyatoslav, with greeting to his brother Andrei and to the men of Novgorod, sending envoys to each other they took peace, and *Volok* [was given] back to Novgorod.

A.D. 1294. A.M. 6802. *Knyaz* Andrei sent the *Posadnik* from Torzhok to Novgorod, and himself went against the Low Country. The same year *Knyaz* Dmitri died in *Volok*; he had been shorn, and they took him to Pereyaslavl. The same year Titmanovich secretly put up a fort on this side of the Narova, and the men of Novgorod went and burned it down, and they took and burned down his big village.

The same year they completed the Church of St. Fedor and *Vladyka* Kliment consecrated it on October 18.

A.D. 1295. A.M. 6803. The *Svei* under their leader, Sig, put up a town[1] in the Korel land, but the men of Novgorod went and plundered it, and killed Sig and let no man escape.

A.D. 1296. A.M. 6804. Kliment, *Vladyka* of Novgorod erected a stone Church of the Holy Resurrection over the gates.

A.D. 1297. A.M. 6805. The men of Novgorod put up the town of Koporya. The same year *Igumen* Kiril of St. Georgi erected the stone Church of the Holy Transfiguration over the gates of the Lyudin quarter.

[1] sc. Keksholm.

A.D. 1298. A.M. 6806. In the winter the *Nemtsy* overran the country of Pleskov and did much harm; the town was burnt down, and in the monasteries they slew all the monks.

And the men of Pleskov with *Knyaz* Dovmont, fortified by God and the Holy Mother of God, drove them away, giving them no little hurt.][1]

A.D. 1299. A.M. 6807. On Great Saturday, April 18, a fire broke out at 1 at night, in the Varangian Street, and for our sins a great evil happened; a storm arose with a hurricane, and soon the fire grew so strong that all, taking what little they could, ran out of their houses; all the rest the fire took. The fire leapt from the court of the *Nemtsy* to the Nerev quarter. It broke out in Kholop Street and there still more fiercely; and amongst the Nerev residents on the other side, and the fire took the Great Bridge. And thus there was a great calamity so that only God and the good people on earth stopped it, and evil men fell to plundering. What was in the churches they took all in plunder without fear of God, and knowing God's punishment instead of repentance they did worse evil: at St. Ioan's they killed the warehouse guard, at St. Yakov's the warehouse-guard was burnt. In the market quarter twelve churches were burnt; they had not time to bring out all the pictures, nor books. And in Christ Church several people were burnt, also two priests In the Nerev quarter ten churches were burnt with many embroideries in the churches, and the good man Elferi[2] Lazorevich was burnt. And on the morrow there was grief and lamentation in place of gladness. All this was for our sins; the prophecy of the prophet Isaiah was fulfilled who said: " I shall turn your feasting to tears and your merrymaking into lamentation." For thus, brethren, God punishes us for our sins, showing us the way to repentance, that we might abandon our wickednesses; though we may have sinned, yet do we not despair of Thy mercy; for thine Lord, is the power to punish and then to forgive. Having chastised us, Lord, be Thou merciful.

The same year *Vladyka* Kliment of Novgorod died, at seven in the morning, on the twenty-second day of May, the day of the holy martyr, Vasilisk, Friday in the fourth week after Easter, having occupied the Bishopric twenty-three years, and he was taken from the *Vladyka's* court and laid in the porch of St. Sophia by the

1 Here the original Synodal Text is resumed.
2 Eleutherius.

I

Archimandrite Kyuril and all the *Igumens*, the whole of the hierarchy, *Posadnik* Andrei and all the men of Novgorod.

Dovmont, *Knyaz* of Pleskov died the same year; having borne much for St. Sophia and for the Holy Trinity. On Kliment's death the men of Novgorod after much consultation with *Posadnik* Andrei chose the appointed of God, the good and humble man Feoktist, *Igumen* of the Holy Annunciation, and having rung together a *Veche* at St. Sophia, *Knyaz* Boris Andreyevich with all the men of Novgorod led him in with greeting, and set him in the *Vladyka's* court, until they should learn where the Metropolitan was.

A.D. 1300. A.M. 6808.   The Metropolitan Maxim came to Novgorod, also Semen, Bishop of Rostov, and Andrei, Bishop of Tver; and they established Feoktist as *Vladyka* of Novgorod. The Metropolitan and the Bishops and the most reverend *Igumens* appointed him in the Church of Holy Boris and Gleb, on June 29; in the same month on the day of the Holy Apostles Peter and Paul, they installed him in St. Sophia; and held a great festival; and there was joy in Novgorod at their *Vladyka*.

In the spring of the same year Novi-torg was burnt down.

The same spring they founded the stone Church of St. Mikhail in Mikhail Street. In the same year they erected four wooden churches: those of the Holy Mother of God in the monastery in Zverinets,[1] of St. Lazar, of St. Dmitri in Boyanya Street, and of the Holy Boris and Gleb in the Podol.[2]

The same year the *Svei* came from beyond sea in great strength into the Neva; they brought masters[3] from their own land, and they brought a special master from great Rome from the Pope, and they established a town at the mouth of the river Okhta on the Neva and strengthened it with indescribable strength, and placed battering rams within it. And the accursed ones boasted, calling it the " Crown of the land." For they had a king's lieutenant with them named Maskalka; and having placed special men in it with the *Voyevoda* Sten, they went away, the *Veliki Knyaz* not being then in Novgorod.

A.D. 1301. A.M. 6809.   The *Veliki Knyaz* Andrei came with the forces of the Low Country and went with the men of Novgorod to that town, and came up to the town on May

---

[1] Near Novgorod, lit. an " enclosure for wild animals."
[2] A part of Novgorod—" lower town."
[3] sc. experts.

18, the Day of St. Patriki, on the Friday before the Descent of the Holy Ghost, and they strove mightily. By the power of St. Sophia and by the help of the martyrs Boris and Gleb, that fortress came to nothing, for their pride, because their labours were in vain, without God's command. The town was taken; some they beat to death and slew, and having bound others they led them out of the town, and they fired the town and sacked it. Grant rest, Lord, in Thy kingdom to the souls of those who laid their heads at that town for St. Sophia, and multiply the years, Lord, of the *Veliki Knyaz* Andrei with his men of Novgorod and of Ladoga.

A.D. 1302. A.M. 6810. They founded a stone wall at Novgorod.
          The same year they founded the stone Church of Boris and Gleb, which had collapsed.

The same year they sent envoys beyond sea to the Danish land, and they brought them back having concluded a peace.

The same year the *Veliki Knyaz* Andrei went to the Tartars.

The same year they completed the Church of St. Mikhail in Mikhail Street.   May Saint Mikhail be a help to those who laboured for this church.

A.D. 1303. A.M. 6811. They took the *Posadnik*-ship from Semen Klimovich and gave it to his brother Andrei.

The same year they built four wooden churches: St. Georgi in the market-place, St. Ioan Ishkov, the Holy Kosma and Demyan in Kholop Street, and St. Georgi in Borkov Street.

The winter of the same year was a warm winter; there was no snow all through the winter. The people could not get corn, and prices were very high, great hardship and distress for the people. But we despair not of Thy mercy; correcting, punish us, Lord, but give us not over to death; for though we have sinned, yet have we not drawn away from Thee; having punished us, have mercy on us, O Lord, that lovest mankind not according to our wicked works, but according to Thy great mercy.   Thou art our God, and we know no other God but Thee.

A.D. 1304. A.M. 6812. The *Veliki Knyaz* Andrei Alexandrovich, grandson of the great Yaroslav, died on July 27, on St. Panteleimon's Day; he had been shorn into monk's orders, and was laid in Gorodets[1]; and his *Boyars* went to Tver. The two *Knyazes*, Mikhail Yaroslavich of Tver and Yuri Danilovich

---

[1] sc. Radilov, on the Volga.

of Moscow disputed for the place of *Veliki Knyaz,* and both journeyed
to the Horde. There was great commotion throughout the Suzdal
land in all the towns; the people of Tver sent Mikhail's lieutenants
to Novgorod with a force, but they did not receive them; but the men
of Novgorod went to Torzhok to guard Torzhok, and they united
the whole land against them; and sending envoys to each other they
separated, having made peace till the arrival of the *Knyazes.*

A.D. 1305. A.M. 6813.　Semen Klimovich erected a church at the
gates at the end of Prussian Street. The
same year they made a new bridge over the Volkhov. The same
year the Church of the Holy Martyrs Boris and Gleb was consecrated with the great consecration by Feoktist,[1] *Vladyka* of Novgorod,
on December 29, the Conception of St. Anne, in the reign of the
Christ-loving *Knyaz* Mikhail.

A.D. 1306. A.M. 6814.

A.D. 1307. A.M. 6815.

A.D. 1308. A.M. 6816.　The *Veliki Knyaz* Mikhail Yaroslavich, grandson of the great Yaroslav Vsevolodich, took
his seat on the throne in Novgorod on the Sunday of the *Veche* of
the 630 Holy Fathers held in Khalkidon.[2]

In the winter of the same year *Vladyka* Feoktist[1] went out from the
Vladyka's Court on account of his ill health, having blessed Novgorod, and went into the monastery of the Annunciation of the
Holy Mother of God, having chosen a silent life. And the men
of Novgorod with all the *Igumens* and all the hierarchy chose his
spiritual father David, the elected of God and of St. Sophia, and
they set him with honour in the *Vladyka's* Court, and Feoktist[1]
blessed him in his place, and they sent him to the Metropolitan for
confirmation.

The same year Yakim Stolbovich's wife erected a stone church
in the *Knyaz's* Court, to [the honour of] the 318 Holy Fathers at
Nikia.[3]

A.D. 1309. A.M. 6817.　David, *Vladyka* of Novgorod was con-
firmed in Volodimir by the Metropolitan
Peter on June 5, St. Nikander's Day, and he came to Novgorod on
July 20, on Ilya's Day, being met at the Church of St. Ilya by the

---

[1] Theoktistos.
[2] The Council of Chalcedon, A.D. 451.
[3] i.e. the Council of Nicæa, A.D. 325.

Igumens and priests and all Novgorod with honour and with crosses; and they set him on the throne, and the men of Novgorod were glad at their *Vladyka*.

In the winter of the same year they gave the *Posadnik*-ship to Mikhail Pavshinich.

A.D. 1310. A.M. 6818. The men of Novgorod went in boats and in ships into the lake to the Uzerva river where they put up a new fort of wood by the rapids, having cleared away the old one. The same year the Archimandrite Kyuril built a stone church at Kolomtsy,[1] to the Assumption of the Holy Mother of God, and they erected another of stone to the Intercession of the Holy Mother of God at Dubenka,[2] by the efforts of God's servant the monk Oloni [surnamed Shkila; and the monastery was a refuge to Christians]. The same year in the winter they plundered the villages around Novgorod. The same year Feoktist *Vladyka* of Novgorod, died, on December 23, the Day of the Ten Martyrs in Crete, and he was laid in the church of the monastery of the Annunciation of the Holy Mother of God, honourably, by all the hierarchy.

A.D. 1311. A.M. 6819. The men of Novgorod went in war over sea to the country of the *Nemtsy*,[3] against the Yem people, with *Knyaz* Dmitri Romanovich, and having crossed the sea they first occupied the Kupets river, they burned villages, and captured people and destroyed the cattle. And there Konstantin the son of Ilya Stanimirovich was killed by a column that went in pursuit. They then took the whole of the Black river,[4] and thus following along the Black river they reached the town of Vanai and they took the town and burned it. And the *Nemtsy* fell back into the *Detinets*[5]: for the place was very strong and firm, on a high rock, not having access from any side. And they sent with greeting, asking for peace, but the men of Novgorod did not grant peace, and they stood three days and three nights, wasting the district. They burned the large villages, laid waste all the cornfields, and did not leave a single horn of cattle; and going thence, they took the Kavgola river and the Perna river, and they came out on the sea and returned all well to Novgorod.

1 Kolmovo, near Novgorod.
2 Near Novgorod.
3 *Nemetskaya Zemlya*, here S.-W. Finland.
4 *Chernaya reka*.
5 Citadel.

The same spring, on May 19, a fire broke out at night in Yanev Street, and forty less three houses were burnt and seven people. Then in the night of June 28 Glebov's house in Rozvazha Street caught fire, and the Nerev quarter was burnt, on one side so far as the fosse,[1] and on the other beyond Borkov Street; and the Church of SS. Kosma and Demyan was burnt, also that of St. Sava, and forty churches were damaged by fire and several good houses. Oh, woe, brethren, the conflagration was fierce, with wind and hurricane! And wicked and bad men having no fear of God, seeing peoples' ruin, plundered other men's property. Then on July 16 a fire broke out at night in the Ilya Street, and here likewise was a fierce conflagration with a high wind, and crashing noise; the market place was burnt, and houses up to Rogatitsa Street, and the churches burnt were—seven wooden churches: St. Dmitri, St. Georgi, SS. Boris and Gleb, St. Ioan[2] Ishkov, St. Catherine, St. Prokopi, and of Christ; and six stone churches were damaged by fire, and the seventh was the Varangian Church. And accursed men likewise having no fear of God, nor remembering the judgment of God, and having no pity for their fellows, plundered other peoples' property. Repay them, Lord, according to their deeds!

The same year they took the *Posadnik*-ship from Mikhail and gave it to Semen Klimovich. The same year *Vladyka* David erected a stone church at the gate of the Nerev quarter, to St. Volodimir.

A.D. 1312. A.M. 6820. *Knyaz* Mikhail armed himself against Novgorod, and withdrew his lieutenants and cut off the corn from Novgorod, and he occupied Torzhok and Bezhitsy and the entire district. And in the spring, when the roads were bad, the *Vladyka* David went to Tver and concluded a peace; the *Knyaz* opened the gates and sent his lieutenants into Novgorod.

The same year the *Vladyka* David founded a stone church in the Nerev quarter in his own court, in the name of the holy Father Nikola.

A.D. 1313. A.M. 6821. The *Posadnik* of Ladoga with the men of Ladoga went out to war, and for our sins the *Nemtsy* went all over lake Ladoga and burned it.

In the same year the stone Church of St. Nikola in the Nerev quarter was consecrated, which *Vladyka* David built; and he made daily service in it, and attached monks to it.

[1] *Greblya*.
[2] John.

A.D. 1314. A.M. 6822. The Korel people killed the townsmen in the Korel town[1] who were Russian and brought in *Nemtsy* to themselves. And the men of Novgorod with the lieutenant Fedor went against them, and the Korel people surrendered, and the men of Novgorod killed the *Nemtsy* and the Korel traitors.

The same year Fedor of Rzhev came to Novgorod from *Knyaz* Yuri from Moscow; and seized the lieutenants of Mikhail and held them in the *Vladyka's* Court. And the men of Novgorod with *Knyaz* Fedor went to the Volga, and *Knyaz* Dmitri Mikhailovich came out from Tver, and halted on the opposite side of the Volga, and thus they remained until the frost; *Knyaz* Mikhail being at that time in the Horde. After this they concluded a peace with Dmitri, and thence they sent to Moscow for *Knyaz* Yuri, with reservation of all the rights of Novgorod; and they themselves returned to Novgorod.

The same winter before the great Fast *Knyaz* Yuri came to Novgorod to the throne with his brother Afanasi,[2] and the men of Novgorod were glad at their desire.

Bread was dear in Novgorod in the same winter; in Pleskov bad men took to looting in the villages and the houses in the town and storehouses in the town; and the men of Pleskov killed about fifty of them; and then it became quiet.

A.D. 1315. A.M. 6823. The *Veliki Knyaz* Yuri summoned to the Horde by the *Tsar*, went from Novgorod on Lazar Saturday, March 15, leaving his brother Afanasi[2] in Novgorod.

The same year *Knyaz* Mikhail came from the Horde into Russia, bringing with him Tartars of the accursed Taitemer. And the men of Novgorod with *Knyaz* Afanasi having heard, went out to Torzhok, and stayed about six weeks there gathering information. And then *Knyaz* Mikhail with all the people of the Low Country and with the Tartars went to Torzhok. And the men of Novgorod with *Knyaz* Afanasi[2] and with the men of Novi-torg went out against them into the field. It was by the infliction of God: for both forces having met there was a terrible slaughter, and no little evil was done; and there they killed many good men and *Boyars* of Novgorod: Andrei Klimovich, Yuri Mishinich, Mikhail Pavshinich, Silvan, Timofei Andreyanov, son of the *Tysyatski*, Anani Meluyev, Afonasi[2] Romanovich

[1] sc. Keksholm.
[2] i.e. Athanasius.

besides many worthy merchants, and God knows how many other men of Novgorod and Novi-torg; the rest of them fled into the town and shut themselves in the town with *Knyaz* Afanasi. And *Knyaz* Mikhail sent word to the men of Novgorod in Torzhok: " Give up to me *Knyaz* Afanasi and Fedor of Rzhev and I will conclude peace with you." And the men of Novgorod said: " We will not deliver over Afanasi, but will all die honourably for St. Sophia." Then *Knyaz* Mikhail again sent: " Give up Fedor of Rzhev to me," and not wishing to give him up, they gave him up, and against their will paid for themselves 50,000 silver *grivnas*, and they concluded a peace and kissed the Cross. And after the peace, *Knyaz* Mikhail summoned to him *Knyaz* Afanasi and the *Boyars* of Novgorod, and seized them, and sent them as hostages to Tver; and the rest of the men in the town he began to sell for as much as each would fetch, and he took away all their arms and belongings. The battle was on February 10, the day of the Holy Martyr Kharlampi. And *Knyaz* Mikhail sent his lieutenants into Novgorod and they gave the *Posadnik*-ship to Semen Klimovich.

A.D. 1316. A.M. 6824.   The lieutenants of *Knyaz* Mikhail left Novgorod, and *Knyaz* Mikhail went against Novgorod with the whole of the Low Country. And the men of Novgorod raised defences round the town on both sides, and the whole of the Novgorod district, the men of Pleskov, of Ladoga, of Russa, the Kórel, and Izhera, and Vod people came together. And the *Knyaz* halted short of the town at the village of Usti[1], and so not accepting peace, he withdrew, having accomplished nothing, but receiving great hurt, for in the retreat they lost the way among the lakes and swamps, and began to die of hunger. They even ate horse flesh, and others tearing off the leather of their shields ate it. They burned and threw away their belongings and arms and came back on foot to their homes, having suffered no little harm.

The same year before *Knyaz* Mikhail had reached the town they seized Ignat Besk and beat him at a *Veche*, and then threw him from the bridge into the Volkhov, for they thought he had held traitorous communication with Mikhail; but God knows.

At that same time Danilo Pistsev was murdered on the meadow land[2] by his own slave; for he had calumniated him before the citizens, saying thus: " He tried to send me with letters to *Knyaz* Mikhail."

[1] sc. The Mouths; cf. p 12.
[2] *Rel*, water-meadow, near Novgorod.

A.D. 1317. A.M. 6825. The men of Novgorod sent *Vladyka* David to *Knyaz* Mikhail seeking to ransom their brothers, who were with the *Knyaz* as hostages, but the *Knyaz* did not listen to him. The same year the *Nemtsy* came into lake Ladoga, and killed many merchants of Obonezh.[1]

A.D. 1318. A.M. 6826. When the river was high the men of Novgorod went to war over sea, and ravaged much and took Lyuderev the town of the Sum *Knyaz* and Bishop and returned to Novgorod all well.

The same year the *Veliki Knyaz* Yuri left the Horde with Tartars, and with all the men of the Low Country and went to Tver against *Knyaz* Mikhail, and sending Telebeg, summoned the men of Novgorod, and having come to Torzhok they concluded [an agreement] with *Knyaz* Mikhail not to side with either: because they did not know where *Knyaz* Yuri was; and they returned to Novgorod. And *Knyaz* Yuri having come with a force to within forty *versts* of Tver, *Knyaz* Mikhail went out against him there from Tver; and they joined battle, and there was great slaughter, many heads fell on *Knyaz* Yuri's side; and they took his brother Boris and his wife, and brought them into Tver and there they put her to death. And he himself fled to Novgorod, and summoned the men of Novgorod after him, all Novgorod and Pleskov went with him, taking *Vladyka* David with him; and having come to the Volga they concluded peace with *Knyaz* Mikhail, both to go to the Horde, and to release Yuri's wife and brother. And all the men of Novgorod returned to Novgorod in the spring, and *Knyaz* Yuri went to Moscow and thence to the Horde.

A.D. 1319. A.M. 6827. The *Tsar* killed *Knyaz* Mikhail of Tver in the Horde and gave the title of *Veliki Knyaz* to Yuri, and gave over to him Mikhail's son Kostyantin and his *Boyars*. And *Knyaz* Yuri sent his brother Afanasi to Novgorod.

A.D. 1320. A.M. 6828. *Knyaz* Yuri went to war against *Knyaz* Ivan of Ryazan; and they concluded a peace.

A.D. 1321. A.M. 6829. *Knyaz* Yuri went to war against Dmitri Mikhailovich of Tver and came to Pereyaslavl with his forces. And *Knyaz* Dmitri sent thither the *Vladyka*

[1] i.e. from the shores of Lake Onega.

of Tver, and they concluded a peace for 2,000 in silver and Dmitri not to take to himself the title of *Veliki Knyaz.*

The same year, on June 26, there was a sign in the sun before morning service; the sky being clear, the sun suddenly grew dark for about an hour, and was like a moon of five nights; and there was darkness as on a winter night; and it filled out gradually and we were glad.

A.D. 1322. A.M. 6830. *Knyaz* Yuri came to Novgorod, called by the men of Novgorod, and gave orders to repair the battering rams.

At the same time the *Nemtsy* came to make war on the Korel town,[1] and did not take it.

The same year the *Veliki Knyaz* Yuri went with the men of Novgorod to Viborg, a town of the *Nemtsy*[2]; and they beat at it with six rams, for it was strong; and they killed many *Nemtsy* in the town and hanged others, and others they led away to the Low Country.   And having laid siege to it for a month they attacked it, and did not take it, but for our sins several good men fell.

The same year *Knyaz* Afanasi, brother of Yuri, died; he had been shorn into the monastic order, and they laid him in the Holy Saviour's in the *Gorodishche.*

The same year *Knyaz* Dmitri Mikhailovich went to the Horde, and obtained the title of *Veliki Knyaz.*

The same year a powerful envoy came into Russia from the Horde, named Akhmyl, and he did much harm in the Low Country; he slew many Christians, and others he took away to the Horde.

And *Knyaz* Yuri having come from Viborg went to the Low Country, the men of Novgorod having much beseeched him to lead them there.   And while he was at the [river] Urdoma, *Knyaz* Alexander Mikhailovich came from Tver, and there fell on him, so that *Knyaz* Yuri with a small party ran away and fled to Pleskov; and they plundered all his baggage.

And the Lithuanian *Knyaz* Davidko was then in Pleskov, and the men of Novgorod called him from there according to their kissing of the Cross, and put him in the deacon Afanasi's Court.

A.D. 1323. A.M. 6831. The men of Novgorod went with *Knyaz* Yuri and established a town at the mouth of the Neva on Orekhov[3] island; and great ambassadors from the

---

[1] sc. Keksholm, on lake Ladoga.
[2] *Nemetski gorod*, on the north shore of the Gulf of Finland.
[3] Walnut island.

king of the *Svei* having come there, they concluded an everlasting peace with the *Knyaz* and with Novgorod, on the old terms.[1]

The same year the Lithuanians ravaged the [valley of the] Lovot, but the men of Novgorod drove them out, and killed them, and some escaped.

The same year the people of Ustyug[4] quarrelled with the men of Novgorod; they captured the men of Novgorod who had gone to the Yugra country,[2] and robbed them.

A.D. 1324. A.M. 6832. The men of Novgorod with *Knyaz* Yuri went beyond the *Volok*[3] and took Ustyug[4] by assault, and came to the Dvina and there the *Knyazes* of Ustyug sent envoys to the *Knyaz* and people of Novgorod, and concluded a treaty of peace on the old terms.[5] And the men of Novgorod returned all well, and *Knyaz* Yuri went from *Zavoloche* to the Horde by the [river] Kama.

The same year they completed Christ Church in stone, and *Vladyka* David consecrated it.

The same winter David, *Vladyka* of Novgorod, died on February 5, the Commemoration Day of the Holy Martyr Agafa, and they laid him in the porch of St. Sophia by the side of Kliment. Then the men of Novgorod with the *Igumens*, the priests and the monks and all Novgorod having consulted, chose Moisei, the appointed of God, former Archimandrite of St. Georgi. He had of his own free will gone out to his own monastery of the Holy Mother of God at Kolomtsy[6]; and they led him up to the threshold[7] and set him in the *Vladyka's* Court till the Metropolitan should summon him.

A.D. 1325. A.M. 6833. *Knyaz* Olexander Mikhailovich came back from the Horde, and with him came Tartar collectors, and there was much hardship in the Low Country.

The same year *Vladyka* Moisei went to Moscow to be confirmed by the Metropolitan, and when he was there they brought [the body of] the *Veliki Knyaz* Yuri, son of Danilo, grandson of Alexander,

---

[1] *Poshlina*, lit. duty, tariff.

[2] See Introduction, p. x, etc.

[3] *Volok*=portage; sometimes called *Volok Dvinsk* in contrast to *Volok Lamsk;* " *Zavoloche* "=" beyond the *Volok*,"sc. the basin of the N. Dvina, and N.E. Russia generally; cf. Introduction pp. ix–xi, etc., and Index.

[4] i.e. " Yugmouth," a town on the N. Dvina, at its junction with the Yug.

[5] *Poshlina*.

[6] Near Novgorod.

[7] A platform thus called (*seni*=threshold, or porch), specially placed in the interior of churches for ceremonies of consecration.

from the Horde, and the Metropolitan Peter, Moisei, Varsonofi, Bishop of Tver, Prokhor, Bishop of Rostov, and Grigori, Bishop of Ryazan, buried him on Saturday of the first week in Lent; and *Knyaz* Ivan deeply lamented him and all the people with great lamentation, both great and small; for *Knyaz* Dmitri Mikhailovich had killed him in the Horde without the *Tsar's* word, and it was not well for himself; for as a man sows so shall he reap.

A.D. 1326. A.M. 6834. *Vladyka* Moisei came to Novgorod on Tuesday in Palm week, confirmed. On August 23 of the same year a fire broke out in Boyanya Street and all was burnt up to half the Rogatitsa Street; and the Slavkov Street was burnt from St. Dmitri up to the field, and the Church of St. Kliment was burnt.

The same year the *Tsar* killed *Knyaz* Dmitri Mikhailovich in the Horde.

The same winter the Metropolitan Peter of all Russia died in Moscow, and they laid him in the Church of the Holy Mother of God which he himself had begun to build in stone. Through his prayers God performed miracles at his tomb.

The same year envoys arrived from Lithuania, the brother of Gedimin, *Knyaz* of Lithuania, Voini, *Knyaz* of Polotsk, Vasili, *Knyaz* of Minsk, and Fedor Svyatoslavich, and they concluded a peace with Novgorod and with the *Nemtsy.*

A.D. 1327. A.M. 6835. There was a tumult in Novgorod, and they plundered the house of Ostafi[1] Dvoryaninets and entirely burned it.

The same year *Vladyka* Moisei erected the Church of the Nativity of the Holy Mother of God in the Desyatina.[2]

The same year on the day of the Assumption of the Holy Mother of God *Knyaz* Alexander Mikhailovich killed a great many Tartars in Tver and in other towns, and he killed some merchants of Khopyl. For an important envoy named Shefkal had come from the Horde with a large number of Tartars, and *Knyaz* Olexander sent envoys to the men of Novgorod, wishing to flee into Novgorod; but they did not receive him.

The same year *Knyaz* Ivan Danilovich sent his lieutenants to Novgorod, and himself went to the Horde.

[1] Eustaphi, Eustathius.
[2] In Novgorod.

The same winter a very great force of Tartars came, and they took Tver and Kashin and the Novi-torg district, and to put it simply, laid waste all the Russian Land, God and St. Sophia preserved Novgorod alone, and *Knyaz* Olexander fled to Pleskov, and his brother Kostyantin and Vasili to Ladoga.   And the Tartars sent envoys to Novgorod, and the men of Novgorod gave them 2,000 in silver, and they sent their own envoys with them, with numerous presents to the *Voyevodas.*

And then, too, the Tartars killed *Knyaz* Ivan of Ryazan.

A.D. 1328. A.M. 6836.   The *Veliki Knyaz* Ivan Danilovich with Kostyantin Mikhailovich, and with Fedor Kolesnitsa sent by the men of Novgorod, went to the *Tsar* to the Horde.   And the *Tsar* let them go, commanding them to seek out *Knyaz* Alexander.   And *Knyaz* Ivan sent his own envoys to *Knyaz* Alexander in Pleskov, and the men of Novgorod on their own part sent *Vladyka* Moisei and the *Tysyatski* Avram,[1] bidding him go to the Horde; and he did not obey.

The same year Yurev of the *Nemtsy*[2] was burnt down, with all its churches, and the houses of stone crumbled and fell; and 2,000 and 500 and thirty *Nemtsy* perished in the fire, and four Russians.

A.D. 1329. A.M. 6837.   The *Veliki Knyaz* Ivan Danilovich, grandson of Olexander,[3] came to the throne in Novgorod on March 26, the festival of the Archangel Gabriel.   And the *Knyazes* Kostyantin and Vasili of Tver and Olexander of Suzdal, besides many other Russian *Knyazes*, were with him.

The same year they killed in Yurev an honourable man, Ivan Sypa, the Novgorod envoy.

The same year the Metropolitan named Feognast, a Greek by birth, came to Novgorod.

The same year *Knyaz* Ivan, with all the *Knyazes* and with Novgorod, went to war on Pleskov; and hearing this the men of Pleskov turned out Olexander from amongst them, and sent envoys to *Knyaz* Ivan and to the men of Novgorod to Opoka with greeting, and concluded a peace.

The same winter the *Knyazes* of Ustyug killed the men of Novgorod who had gone against the Yugra country.

The same year in the absence of the *Knyaz* and of the men of Nov-

[1] Abraham.

[2] *Yurev Nemetski,* German Dorpat, on the river Embach, a tributary of Lake Chud, near Pskov, as opposed to Yurev Polski, near Moscow.

[3] sc. Alexander Nevski.

gorod a fire broke out at Ondreshek's house in the Carpenters' quarter[1]; the fire extended to St. Fedor's; and on the same Sunday nearly the whole of Ilya Street was burnt, also the Lyubyanitsa Street, and the Churches of St. Saviour and St. Luke were burnt.

A.D. 1330. A.M. 6838.   *Vladyka* Moisei was shorn into the *schema*[2] of his own will; and the men of Novgorod with all Novgorod respectfully entreated him to retain his seat on the throne, but he did not listen, but blessed them and said: " Select from among yourselves a man worthy of such a thing, but I bless you." And the men of Novgorod having deliberated much were without a *Vladyka* for about eight months; and all Novgorod and the *Igumens* and priests chose Grigori *Kaleka*[3] nominated of God, a good and humble man, a priest of the Church of Holy Kosma and Demyan in Kholop Street, he was shorn in the holy angelic fashion in January, and was named Vasili and they put him in the *Vladyka's* Court until they should send him to the Metropolitan. The same winter Fedorko and Semenko arrived from Volynia as envoys from the Metropolitan in Passion Week, summoning Vasili for confirmation.

A.D. 1331. A.M. 6839.[4]   The same year Vasili was confirmed in Volynia for Novgorod. The same year on November 30, the day of the Apostle St. Andrew, there was a darkening of the sun lasting from one to three.

[The same year *Vladyka* Vasili laid the foundation of a stone wall extending from St. Volodimir to the Church of the Holy Mother of God, and thence to that of Boris and Gleb.

The same year on the day of the Birth of St. Ioan, in the month of June, Vasili departed to Volynia for confirmation, and with him went the *Boyars* Kusma Tverdislavl and Valfromei[5] Ostafiev, the son of the *Tysyatski*, and they arrived in Volodimir of Volynia, by the providence of God and the help of the Holy Spirit, and they celebrated the great festival of the Holy Mother of God, and they confirmed him on the Day of the Apostle St. Titus. A sign then appeared in the heavens: a bright star over the church. He was confirmed by the Metropolitan Feognast, by birth a Greek, and the

---

[1] *Plotniki.*
[2] cf. p. 34.
[3] i.e. the cripple.
[4] For this year the record in different handwritings stands as follows; that in brackets is supplied from another text.
[5] Varfolomei, Bartholomew.

Vladykas: Grigori of Polotsk, Afanasi of Volodimir, Fedor of Galich, Marko of Peremyshl, and Ioan of *Kholm.*

At that same time envoys came to the Metropolitan from *Knyaz* Alexander, from Pleskov, and from Gedimin, and from all the Lithuanian *Knyazes*, bringing with them Arseni desiring to appoint him to the *Vladyka*-ship in Pleskov, thinking Novgorod of no account they had puffed themselves with their pride. But God and St. Sophia always lay low presumptuous thoughts, for the men of Pleskov violated their kissing of the Cross to Novgorod, they had set up *Knyaz* Alexander on their throne by Lithuanian hands; so Arseni with the men of Pleskov went disgraced from the Metropolitan from Volynia to Kiev. *Vladyka* Vasili left the Metropolitan on the Day of Simon Stylites[1]; as he approached Chernigov, there *Knyaz* Fedor of Kiev at the prompting of the devil set upon him murderously with a *Baskak* and fifty men. And the men of Novgorod were aware in time and halted to defend themselves; only by a little was it not a disaster for them, and the *Knyaz* was disgraced and rode away, though he did not escape punishment from God: his horses all died.

And thence the *Vladyka* went to Bryansk and reached Torzhok on the day of the holy Martyr Akepsim.[2] And the people of Novitorg were glad of their *Vladyka;* but they were sad in Novgorod, because there was no news, for the report had spread, that the Lithuanians had taken the *Vladyka* and had killed his children.

The same year the *Veliki Knyaz* Ivan went to the Horde with *Knyaz* Kostyantin.

The same year *Vladyka* Vasili, *Vladyka* of Novgorod arrived in Novgorod from Volynia in the month of December on a Sunday, the day of the holy Father Patapi, having received the sacred dignity from the Metropolitan Feognast; and the men of Novgorod were glad of their *Vladyka;* and this was under *Knyaz* Ivan, *Posadnik* Valfromei and the *Tysyatski* Ostafi.]

A.D. 1332. A.M. 6840. Turbulent men rose in Novgorod, and took the *Posadnik*-ship from Fedor Ahmyl and gave it to Zakhari Mikhailovich, and they plundered the house of Semen Sudokov, and they plundered the villages of his brother Senefont.[3]

The same year the *Veliki Knyaz* Ivan returned from the Horde and threw upon Novgorod his wrath, asking from them silver for the

[1] September 13.
[2] November 16.
[3] Xenophon.

country beyond the Kama, and in addition seized Torzhok and Bezhitsy against his kissing of the Cross.

The same year they took the *Posadnik*-ship from Zakhari and gave it to Matvei Koska.

A.D. 1333. A.M. 6841.   *Knyaz* Ivan came to Torzhok with all the *Knyazes* of the Low Country and of Ryazan, and sent into Novgorod and removed the lieutenants; and himself sat in Torzhok from Epiphany till the second week of Lent, despoiling the district of Novgorod.   And the men of Novgorod sent envoys to him calling him to Novgorod: the Archimandrite Lavrenti, Fedor Tverdislavich and Luka Valfromeyev; but he did not accept their prayer, and did not listen to them, and he did not grant peace, and went away.

The same year Vasili, *Vladyka* of Novgorod, raised the stone wall[1] in two years, and the Archimandrite Lavrenti of St. Yuri[2] raised the walls of St. Yuri forty *sazhens*,[3] with embrasures.

[1333][4]   The same year *Vladyka* Vasili covered the side of Saint Sophia with lead and renewed the great cross on St. Sophia and took off the coverings at the side and put up a stone wall by the help of God, in two years.   And give him, Lord God and Saint Sophia in this world and in the next remission of his sins, him and his children, the people of Novgorod! The same year the men of Novgorod sent *Vladyka* Vasili to the *Veliki Knyaz* Ivan with a request, and he came to him to Pereyaslavl with Terenti Danilovits and Danil Mashkovits and they offered him five hundred *roubles*[5] if he would renounce his privileges, according to the kissing of the Cross; and the *Vladyka* requested him much, that he would take peace, and he did not listen.

The same year *Vladyka* Vasili having come from the *Veliki Knyaz* Ivan, went to Pleskov, and the people of Pleskov received him with great honour, because a *Vladyka* had not been in Pleskov for seven years, and he christened *Knyaz* Olexander's son Mikhail.

---

[1] sc. and finished it in two years.
[2] George.
[3] One *sazhen*=1⅛ fathom.
[4] At this point the Synodal text as a continuous whole comes to an end; what follows is borrowed from a text called " Continuation of the Annals of Novgorod " which belongs to the Archæographical Commission; the Synodal text has small records for 1337, 1345 and 1352, but as these are the same in the " Continuation " they have not been printed separately.
[5] cf. Appendix.

The same year God put into the heart of the Lithuanian *Knyaz* Narimont, called in baptism Gleb, the son of Gedimin, *Veliki Knyaz* of Lithuania, and he sent to Novgorod, wishing to bow down to Saint Sophia; and the people of Novgorod sent Grigori to Olexander for him, and called him to them; and he arrived at Novgorod, wishing to worship, in the month of October; and they received him with honour, and he kissed the Cross to Great Novgorod[1] as for one man. And they gave him Ladoga, and Orekhov, the Korel town[2] and the Korel land and half Koporya for patrimony and heritage and to his children. The same year the Metropolitan Feognast came back to Russia having been at *Tsargrad*[3] and in the Horde.

A.D. 1334. A.M. 6842. Second of the Indiction. *Vladyka* Vasili went to the Metropolitan in Volodimir. The same year the *Vladyka* put the top on the stone wall.

The same year the *Veliki Knyaz* Ivan Danilovich came back from the Horde, and the men of Novgorod sent Valfromei Yurevich to him, and he received them with love.

The same winter the *Veliki Knyaz* Ivan Danilovich came to Novgorod in Sexagesima Week, on Thursday, February 16, the day of the holy Martyr Pamphil.

A.D. 1335. A.M. 6843. *Vladyka* Vasili founded a Church to the Holy Mother of God in Zverinets,[4] and *Vladyka* Moisei founded a stone monastery Church of the Holy Resurrection by the river Derevyanitsa. The same year *Vladyka* Vasili with his children, with *Posadnik* Fedor Danilovich and the *Tysyatski* Ostafi and with all Novgorod, laid the foundations of a stone fortification on the opposite side, from St. Ilya to St. Paul, under the *Veliki Knyaz* Ivan Danilovich.

The same year, for our sins, there were great fires in Russia; Moscow, Vologda, Vitebsk were burnt, and Yurev of the *Nemtsy* was entirely burnt down.

The same year the *Veliki Knyaz* Ivan wished to go with the men of Novgorod and with the whole of the Low Country against Pleskov, and he had a friendly conference with the men of Novgorod, and they deferred the march; but they did not grant peace to the men of Pleskov.

[1] *Veliki Novgorod.*
[2] sc. Keksholm, on lake Ladoga.
[3] Constantinople.
[4] Near Novgorod.

K

The same year *Vladyka* Vasili completed the Church of the Holy Mother of God in Zverinets, and Moisei the other of the Holy Resurrection, of stone.

The same year the *Veliki Knyaz* Ivan having come to Torzhok from Novgorod, the Lithuanians ravaged the district of Novi-torg, while there was peace, and the *Veliki Knyaz* having sent [a force] burned the Lithuanian town of Osechen and Ryasna, and many others.

The same year the *Veliki Knyaz* called to him the *Vladyka*, the *Posadnik* and the *Tysyatski* to Moscow, as well as the leading *Boyars*, to be honoured; and *Vladyka* Vasili went, and saw much great honour.

The same autumn ice and snow drifted into the Volkhov, carrying away fifteen stays of the great bridge; God knows whether this was in punishment or in mercy. God did not allow any bloodshed among the brethren: the people stood on either side of the Volkhov having taken up arms against each other at the prompting of the devil, but God guarded [against it] and they united in love.

A.D. 1336. A.M. 6844. *Vladyka* Vasili, *Vladyka* of Novgorod, founded a stone church, [in honour of] the entrance of our Lord Jesus Christ into Jerusalem, on June 25, St. Fevronia's Day, where a small palace[1] had stood. The same year they completed the new bridge over the Volkhov.

The same year the *Veliki Knyaz* Ivan went to the Horde.

The same year the God-loving *Vladyka* Vasili fenced St. Sophia with a new fence[2] and put up gilded brass doors in St. Sophia.

The same year Pleskov was entirely burnt down; all the houses within the wall, and the churches.

A.D. 1337. A.M. 6845. At the instigation of the devil the common people rose against the Archimandrite Esif, and they held a *Veche*, shut Esif in the Church of St. Nikola, and the rioters sat round the church night and day keeping watch on him.

The same winter the *Veliki Knyaz* Ivan quarrelled with the men of Novgorod, and he sent a force to the Dvina[3] beyond the *Volok*,[4] not remembering the kissing of the Cross, and there by the power of

1 *Terem.*
2 *Tyn.*
3 sc. the N. Dvina.
4 cf. p. 123.

the Cross they were disgraced and beaten. Whoso diggeth a pit for another shall fall into it himself.

The same year *Vladyka* Vasili went on his visitation to Pleskov, but the men of Pleskov would not grant him jurisdiction, so the *Vladyka* left having cursed them.

The same year the whole of Moscow was burnt down; and then there came heavy rain and flooded everything; both in the cellars and in the squares wherever anything had been carried out.

The same year Toropets was burnt down and flooded.

The same year *Knyaz* Olexander went from Pleskov to the Horde, having been in Pleskov ten years.

The same year the Church of the Entrance of our Lord Jesus Christ into Jerusalem was completed, and it was consecrated by the most reverend *Vladyka* Vasili, on September 21, the day of the Holy Martyr St. Kondrat; and it was a refuge to Christians. It was nine weeks in building.

The same winter the Korel people having fetched the *Nemtsy*, killed many Russians of Novgorod and of Ladoga, who were trading amongst them, and all the Christians who lived amongst them, and they themselves fled into the town of the *Nemtsy*[1] and then slew many Christians from the town of the *Nemtsy*.

A.D. 1338. A.M. 6846. The water was big in the Volkhov as it never had been before, three weeks after Easter Day on Wednesday, and it carried away ten stays of the great bridge; at the same time it carried away the bridge over the stream Zhilotug, and much harm was done.

The same year *Vladyka* Vasili ordered the Church of the Entrance of Our Lord Jesus Christ into Jerusalem to be painted by Isaia a Greek, with others, on May 4, the Day of the Holy Martyr Selivan; they began to paint it the same day.

The same spring the men of Novgorod went with *Posadnik* Fedor to the Neva, and stood before Orekhov, conversing through envoys with the *Nemetski Voyevoda* Sten; and there was no peace; and so the men of Novgorod returned to Novgorod. The *Nemtsy* warred much with the Korel people around lake Onega, and afterwards, having come up, they set fire to the town[2] at Ladoga but did not take the fort.[3]

After that the brave men of Novgorod went with their *Voyevodas*

---

[1] *Nemetski Gorod*, sc. Viborg, on the N. shore of the Gulf of Finland.
[2] *Posad.*   [3] *Gorod.*

and ravaged the districts round the *Nemetski* and Korel towns[1] and devastated their country considerably, burning their crops and killing their cattle; and they returned all well with captives.

The same year the *Nemtsy* came from their town[2] to ravage the [town of] Toldoga, and from there they wished to go to the country of the Vod people, but they took nothing; for they[3] had taken precautions.   But the men of Koporya issued out with Fedor Vasilevich and beat them; and here they killed Mikhei of Koporya, a good man, and wounded Fedor's horse under him, but he himself suffered no harm; for they had gone out in a small body.

And *Knyaz* Narimont remained in Lithuania; and they sent urgently for him, but he would not come; he even withdrew his son Alexander from Orekhov, leaving only his lieutenant.

The same year the damaged bridge was repaired by order of *Vladyka* Vasili; for he urged on the work himself; he began and finished it with his own men; and he did much good for the Christians.

And *Knyaz* Alexander was made a grant by the *Tsar*, and he came away from the Horde to his own patrimony[4] in Tver, and having sent to Pleskov, he had his wife and children brought to him.

The Archimandrite Lavrenti of St. Georgi died this same year, and they installed Esif.

The same winter they sent envoys to Novgorod from the *Nemetski* town Viborg from *Voyevoda* Petrik concerning peace, saying: "The *Knyaz* of the *Svei* knows not that a rupture had occurred with Novgorod; but the *Voyevoda* Smen[5] had done it of his own mind." And the men of Novgorod sent Kusma Tverdislavich and Olexander Borisovich on a mission, and they returned with a peace, having concluded a peace on the terms agreed upon with the *Veliki Knyaz* Yuri on the Neva; but concerning the *Kobylich* Korel[6] they agreed to ask the *Knyaz* of the *Svei*.

A.D. 1339. A.M. 6847.   The *Veliki Knyaz* Ivan went to the Horde. On his advice the Tartars summoned to the Horde Alexander and Vasili Davidovich of Yaroslav, and all the

---

[1] In Finland.
[2] sc. Viborg.
[3] sc. the Vod people.
[4] *Otchina.*
[5] Sten ?
[6] A part of the Korel country or people.

Knyazes. And *Knyaz* Alexander had first sent his son Fedor to the Horde, expecting news from there. And the *Tsar* sent for him, and he went to the Horde, and Vasili of Yaroslav against whom *Knyaz* Ivan, his father-in-law, put out 500 men to intercept him, but he beat them off. For *Knyaz* Ivan had already left the Horde and the men of Novgorod sent envoys to him.

The same year, on August 13, there was a sign from the ikon of the Holy Mother of God in St. Lazar at evening service; tears as it were flowed from both its eyes, and two wax cups were placed under it; the next morning the whole town learning about this, they and the *Igumens* and priests and readers in their gowns went with crosses to see it.

The same year the men of Novgorod sent Kusma Tverdislavl and Olexander Borisovich with others, and the *Vladyka* on his part sent his nephew Matvei, beyond sea on a mission to the *Knyaz* of the *Svei;* they found him in Lyudovl town in the Murman country and concluded a peace with him on the terms of previous documents; and regarding the Korel people they spoke thus: " If ours escape to you, slay or hang them, if yours to us, we will do the same by them; that they make no treachery between us; but these we will not deliver, who have been baptised into our faith; also there are but few of them left, the rest have all died by the wrath of God."

And to *Knyaz* Ivan they sent Selivester Volosevich and Fedor Ovramov with the tribute.[1]   And the *Knyaz* sent his envoys re quiring another tribute: " and in addition give me the *Tsar's* demand, what the *Tsar* has demanded from me."   And they said: " That has never been amongst us since the beginning of the world, and thou hast kissed the Cross to Novgorod on the terms of the old Novgorod dues and according to Yaroslav's *Gramota.*"[2]

The same year they finished the painting of the *Vladyka's* Church.

The same autumn, on October 5, the surrounding quarter from St. Volodimir was burnt.

On the 29th of the same month the pagan Tartars killed *Knyaz* Olexander and his son Fedor in the Horde.   For *Tsar* Ozbyak[3] had summoned him with deceit, intending to kill him, saying thus: " The *Tsar* desires to make thee a grant."   And they listening to the deceitful words of that pagan, and having gone, were both killed; and received a bitter and violent death.

The same year the *Veliki Knyaz* Ivan Danilovich withdrew his

[1] *Vykhod.*
[2] Charter.   [3] Uzbeg.

lieutenants from Novgorod, and he was not at peace with Novgorod.

A.D. 1340. A.M. 6848.   The *Veliki Knyaz* Ivan Danilovich died in Moscow, as a monk, and in the *schema*[1]; and all the *Knyazes* went to the Horde; his son Simeon, Vasili of Yaroslav, Kostyantin of Tver, Kostyantin of Suzdal, with other *Knyazes*.

And some adventurers having gone from Novgorod made an attack on Ustyuzhna and burned it; but going in pursuit of them they[2] took back the captives and plunder from the boatmen; and after that they ravaged the district of Belo-Ozero.[3]

The same year on Tuesday in Trinity week, on June 7, the day of the Holy Martyr Fedor, a fire broke out in Rozvazha Street, in the field beyond St. Fedor's; the Nerev quarter was burnt, even so far as St. Yakov, and hitherwards to Chudinets Street, and all the churches and houses; from there it flung itself into the town, and the *Vladyka's* Court was burnt and the Church of St. Sophia; and all the houses and churches in the town, and the Lyudin quarter, up to St. Alexis' Church, also churches and houses and hitherwards up to the Prussian Street: for so great and fierce was the fire, with storm and gale, that they thought it was the end [of all things]; the fire went burning over the water, and many people were drowned in the Volkhov; and the fire threw itself across the Volkhov to the other side[4] and there by evening service time the whole of that side rapidly burned, from the Fedor stream into Slavno and up to the fields, and stone and wooden churches, and houses; from many churches they had no time to carry out either images or books, nor from out of the houses; and whatever anyone brought out and laid either in the fields or in the gardens, or in the fosse or in boats or canoes, all was taken by the flames; and whatever else was brought out wicked men carried it off, who fear not God, nor expect the resurrection of the dead, nor God's judgment, nor the repayment according to deeds; and it was not only that they robbed people, their own brothers and Christians, killing some who were guarding their goods, and taking it to themselves, but even in the sacred churches which every Christian ought to protect, even abandoning his own house.   But instead of repenting, we rather commit greater

[1] cf. p. 34.
[2] sc. the people of Ustyuzhna, on the river Mologa, a tributary of the Volga.
[3] The White Lake, in N. Russia.
[4] sc. the E. or mercantile half of the town.

sin, even seeing the punishment of God on them: in the Church of
the Forty Holy Martyrs which had been fitted out and adorned with
ikons, paintings, and metallic work and ikon-frames; shutting
themselves in the church they plundered all the goods, whosesoever
they were; and they did not allow anyone to carry out the images or
books,'but when they themselves ran out from the church all was
enveloped in fire; and they murdered two watchmen. In the
Church of the Holy Mother of God in the market place a priest was
burnt; though others say that they murdered him while guarding
property; because this church was entirely burnt and the ikons
and the books, but of this man the fire did not touch even a hair;
but they plundered all the property; in the Church of the Holy
Friday the watchman was burnt with his son; in consequence of
that fire that church collapsed, also that of the Holy Martyrs Boris
and Gleb in Podol[1]; and many people were burnt in their houses;
for the fire took on rapidly; and the great bridge was burnt to the
water's edge. And they had not time to carry the image out of St.
Sophia, and there was much harm. The whole of Smolensk was
burnt down in the same year, in the night of the Transfiguration.
They made a new bridge again across the Volkhov the same year.

The same year *Knyaz* Simeon came from the Horde, and sent to
collect tribute in Torzhok, and began to act violently. And the
Novi-torg people sent with greeting to Novgorod; and they sent
Matvei Valfromeyevich, Terenti Danilovitch with his brother, and
Valfromei, *Posadnik* Ostafi's son, and Fedor Avramov, with armed
men; and having gone they came upon Torzdok unexpectedly and
seized the lieutenants of *Knyaz* Mikhail Davidovich, Ivan Rybkin's
son, and the son of the collector Boris Smenov; also their wives and
children, and put them in fetters, and they stayed in Torzhok for a
month and strengthened it. And they had previously sent Kusma
Tverdislav to the *Knyaz* from Novgorod with complaints: "Thou
hast not yet taken thy seat among us, yet thy *Boyars* are already
doing violence." And they sent messengers from Torzhok to
Novgorod that the men of Novgorod should take to horse and come
to Torzhok, but the common people did not desire this. On this
the people of Novi-torg, seeing that a force would not come from
Novgorod, the common people rose against the *Boyars* crying out:
" Why did you call in the men of Novgorod, and they have seized
the *Knyaz*'s men, and we shall perish for that." And putting on
their armour they broke by force into the houses and took away from

[1] The " Lower " town, a part of Novgorod.

the captains the *Knyaz's* lieutenants and the collectors with their wives, and turned the men of Novgorod out of the town. And the Novi-torg nobles fled to Novgorod with only their souls, those who could, and they plundered their houses and razed their dwellings, and killed Smen's grandson at the *Veche,* and then devastated their villages.

In the winter of the same year, on December 6, Nikola Day, the people of Bryansk killed *Knyaz* Gleb Svyatoslavich; at the same time the Metropolitan was there and he could not calm them, till he came out from the Church of St. Nikola.

The same winter *Knyaz* Simeon came to Torzhok with a force, with the whole of the Low Country, and the men of Novgorod began to assemble the whole of the district in the town, and they sent the *Vladyka* and the *Tysyatski* Avraam with other *Boyars* to the *Knyaz,* and they concluded a peace according to the old charters on all the terms of Novgorod; and they kissed the Cross. And they gave the *Knyaz* a tax on the district, and on the Novi-torg people 1,000 *roubles;* and the Metropolitan was also there; and the *Knyaz* sent a lieutenant into Novgorod.

A.D. 1341. A.M. 6849. *Vladyka* Vasili covered St. Sophia with lead, which had been burnt, and painted the images and fitted up an image-case.

The same winter the Metropolitan Feognast, a Greek by birth, came to Novgorod with many people; the feeding and the gifts weighed heavily on the *Vladyka* and the monasteries.

The same year the pagan *Tsar* Ozbyak died.

The same winter the pagan *Veliki Knyaz* Gedimin of Lithuania died.

The same autumn the *Vladyka* built a large palace.[1]

The same winter the young *Knyaz* Mikhail Olexandrovich came from Tver to Novgorod to the *Vladyka,* his god-father, to be taught reading and writing.

Bread was cheap this year, but horned cattle died.

A.D. 1342. A.M. 6850. The men of Pleskov sent envoys with greeting to Novgorod: "A *Nemetski*[2] force fully armed is advancing against Pleskov; we bow to you, our masters, defend us." And making no delay, the men of Novgorod went quickly on Good Friday, others following on Easter Eve,

[1] *Terem.*
[2] "German," here.

having sealed up all their communal property; and when they reached Meletovo the men of Pleskov sent greeting: "We bow to you; there is no army coming against us; there is an army of *Nemtsy*, but they are building a fort[1] on the border on their own land." And they wanted to go to Pleskov, and then they listened to their request, and came back to Novgorod all well.

The same year *Vladyka* Vasili founded the Church of the Holy Annunciation in the *Gorodishche* [in place of the one] destroyed, by order of the *Veliki Knyaz* Semen Ivanovich, on Monday, May 27, in St. Peter's Fast, the day of St. Kliment, establisher of the Canons.

The same year *Vladyka* Vasili ordered a big bell to be cast for St. Sophia, and brought masters[2] from Moscow, a good man named Boris.

The same year the men of Pleskov gave themselves over to Lithuania, renouncing Novgorod, and the *Veliki Knyaz*. They fetched into their midst *Knyaz* Olgerd from Lithuania, son of Gedimin, with the Lithuanians; they had first turned out Olexander Vsevolodits. And Olgerd had his son baptised in the name of Andrei, and he set him in Pleskov, and himself departed to Lithuania.

The same year the men of Pleskov beat the *Nemtsy*, pursuing them up to their town Novogrodek on the border, killing about 300 of them. And the *Nemtsy* came in great strength to Izborsk with battering rams, and stood before the town eleven days and nearly took it; but they killed many *Nemtsy*, and there also they killed Voinev, son of the Lithuanian *Knyaz*, and several Lithuanians and men of Izborsk fell; and the *Nemtsy* withdrew.

The same year a fire broke out in Novgorod in Danislav Street, extending along the bank to the fosse, and up the hill to the Churches of the Forty Saints and SS. Kuzma and Damian, and three churches were burnt, St. Nikola and the stone Church of St. Yakov; and a watchman also was burnt there, and the good man Esif Davidovich; the third was the Church of St. Georgi; and much evil was done. And the people took fright, and dared not dwell in the town, but over the fields, others settled on the water-meadows, others along the banks, in boats. And the whole town was to be seen in motion; the people wandered about for a week and longer; people endured much harm and loss at the hands of miscreants who fear not God. And the *Vladyka* with the *Igumens* and priests ordained a fast, and visited the monasteries and churches throughout the town with

[1] Or town, *Gorod*.
[2] sc. experts.

crosses, praying to God and to His Immaculate Mother, that He might avert from us His just wrath.

The same year *Knyaz* Simeon went to the Horde to the pagan Zyanibek who had taken his seat on the *Tsar's* throne after killing his two brothers, and the *Knyaz* came back into Russia.

On October 25, the day of the Holy Martyrs Markyan and Marturi, the servant of God, the *Posadnik* of Novgorod Volfromei, son of Yuri Mishinich, died, and the *Vladyka* Vasili with the *Igumens* and priests, laid his body in his father's tomb in the Church of the Forty Saints. Grant, Lord, that his soul may rest in peace with all the Saints!

The same year Luka Valfromeyev not listening to Novgorod and the blessing of the Metropolitan and the *Vladyka* collected a party of peasant adventurers and went to the Dvina beyond the *Volok*, and put up the fort[1] of Orlitsk; and gathering a number of the Yem people, he took by assault all the country beyond the *Volok* and the villages along the Dvina. And at the same time his son Ontsifor[2] went off to the Volga, and Luka going out to fight with a party of 200, was killed by the people beyond the *Volok*; and the news came to Novgorod: " Luka has been killed! " and the common people rose against Ondreshko and *Posadnik* Fedor Danilov, saying that they had sent men to kill Luka, and they plundered their houses and villages, and Fedor and Ondreshko fled to the town of Koporya where they stayed all the winter until the Great Fast. And at that time Ontsifor came and beat with his forehead against Novgorod against Fedor and Ondreshko: " They sent men to kill my father," and the *Vladyka* and the men of Novgorod sent the Archimandrite Esif with nobles to Koporya for Fedor and Ondreshko; and they came and said: " We had not plotted the killing of our brother Luka, nor the sending of anyone against him." And Ontsifor with Matvei summoned a *Vladyka Veche* at St. Sophia, while Fedor and Ondreshko summoned another in Yaroslav's Court. And Ontsifor and Matvei sent the *Vladyka* to the *Veche*, but not waiting the *Vladyka's* return from that *Veche*, they attacked the Yaroslav Court and there seized Matvei Koska and his son Ignat, and put them in the church. And Ontsifor fled with his confederates. That was in the morning; and by mid-day the whole town was up in arms; this side for itself, and that side for itself, until *Vladyka* Vasili with his lieutenant Boris made peace between them. So the Cross was exalted and the devil disgraced.

[1] *Gorod.*
[2] Onesiphorus.

A.D. 1343. A.M. 6851. The men of Pleskov with *Knyaz* Ostafi, 5,000 strong, went to war into the country of the *Nemtsy* to the town of Medvezhya Golova; and the men of Pleskov ravaged eight days and eight nights, and it happened on lake Ostrechno on the day of the Descent of the Holy Spirit, the *Nemtsy* came upon them and arrayed a force against the men of Pleskov. And the men of Pleskov stood their ground and there was a great battle. God aided *Knyaz* Ostafi and the men of Pleskov; they killed their *Knyaz* and many men of Velnevik[1] and *Nemtsy*. And of the men of Pleskov, they killed *Posadnik* Korman, Olufer and other *Boyars*. God give rest to their souls among the Saints! And *Posadnik* Danila of Pleskov cut off his armour and ran.

The same year the Metropolitan Feognast, the Greek, went to the Horde, to the pagan *Tsar* Zhenbek. And Kalantai maligned him to the *Tsar* and they robbed him, and took him and tortured him, saying: " Give the annual tribute." He would not agree to this, but put down six hundred *roubles* ransom, and he then returned safely to Russia. The same year on August 8, the day of the holy Father Emelyan, Vasili, *Vladyka* of Novgorod, completed the stone Church of the Holy Annunciation in the *Gorodishche*, and it was consecrated on the 24th of the same month, the day of the Holy Martyr Evtikhi. Grant him, Lord, many years of life in this world, and, in the next, place him at Thy right hand, who laboured much for Thy church!

A.D. 1344. A.M. 6852. There was a great tumult beyond the Narva. The Chud people attacked the *Boyars* of their country in the Kolyvan district and in the Rugodiv[2] district, killing 300 of them; then the men of Velnevik,[1] with the men of Yurev rose against them and killed fourteen thousand of the Chud people, and the rest fled to the Island country[3]; and the men of Velnevik[1] followed them up into the Island country,[3] and did not take them, but themselves drew back defeated.

A.D. 1345. A.M. 6853. The third of the Indiction. *Vladyka* Vasili founded the Church of the Holy Friday which had been destroyed in the great fire, by order of God's servant Andrei, son of the *Tysyatski*, and of Paul Petrilovits. The same day

[1] sc. Velyad, the town of Fellin, in Livonia.
[2] sc. Narva.
[3] *Ostrovskaya zemlya.*

Vladyka Vasili founded the Church of SS. Kuzma and Damian in Kuzma-Demyan Street, by order of God's servant Anani Kuritski, the second week after Easter. The same year at the instance of the Archimandrite Esif the Church of St. Georgi was renovated and roofed with new lead, under the *Veliki Knyaz* Simeon Ivanovich, by God's providence and with the help of Georgi the holy Martyr for Christ. The same year, on the day of the Holy Father Simon Stylites,[1] the Church of the Holy Friday was completed. The same year, in the Autumn, on the day of SS. Kuzma and Demyan, the Church of SS. Kuzma and Demyan was completed.

The same year a southerly wind arose, with snow, and drove the ice into the Volkhov, and carried away seven stays, the *Posadnik* had only just had time to cross to the Commercial Side at mid-day, with the whole of the *Veche*, on the day of the *Archistrategos* Michael.[2]

Then they took the *Posadnik*-ship from Ostafi Dvoryaninits and gave it to Matvei Valfromeyevich. By God's grace there was no ill-will between them.

The same year there was great confusion in Lithuania; the town of Vilna expelled Olgerd with his brother Kestuti, and the *Veliki Knyaz* Evnuti flung himself over the wall and escaped to Smolensk, while Narimont went off to the Horde to the *Tsar*. Knyaz Evnuti took refuge in Smolensk and after being there a little, went to Moscow to the *Veliki Knyaz* Simeon, and here he was baptised in the name of the Father, the Son, and the Holy Ghost, by *Knyaz* Simeon, and his name was called Ioan.

A.D. 1346. A.M. 6854. *Vladyka* Vasili went to Moscow to the *Knyaz* and to the Metropolitan to call the *Veliki Knyaz* to Novgorod, and there the Metropolitan Feognast blessed Vasili, *Vladyka* of Novgorod, and gave him a cross-covered vestment.

The same winter *Knyaz* Simeon, great-grandson of brave *Knyaz* Alexander, came to Novgorod to the throne on the Festival of St. Fedor Sunday[3] and took his seat on his throne; and having remained in Novgorod three weeks he went to the Low Country on the *Tsar's* business.

The same year the Lithuanian *Knyaz* Olgerd came with his brother *Knyazes* and with all the Lithuanian land, and halted in the Shelon

[1] September 14.
[2] November 21.
[3] 1st Sunday in Lent.

country[1] at the mouth of the Pshaga river, calling to the men of Novgorod: " I wish to meet you; your *Posadnik* Ostafi Dvoryaninits had abused me, he called me a hound." And he took Shelon and Luga[2] by assault, and he imposed a contribution on the towns of Porkhov and Opoka. And the men of Novgorod rode out against him to Luga, and having returned to the town, they summoned a *Veche*, and killed *Posadnik* Dvoryaninits at the *Veche* saying: " It is owing to thee that they have taken our district."

A.D. 1347. A.M. 6855. Slavno was burnt from Smenov Beskov's house as far as Nutna Street.

A.D. 1348. A.M. 6856. Magnush, King of the *Svei*, sent to the men of Novgorod saying: " Send your philosophers to a conference, and I will send my own philosophers, that they may discuss about faith; they will ascertain whose faith is the better; if your faith is the better, then I will go into your faith, but if our faith is the better, you will go into our faith, and we shall all be as one man. But if you do not agree to uniformity, then I will come against you with all my forces." And *Vladyka* Vasili and *Posadnik* Fedor Danilovich and the *Tysyatski* Avraam and all the men of Novgorod having taken counsel together, replied to Magnush: " If thou wishest to know whose is the better faith, ours or yours, send to *Tsargrad*[3] to the Patriarch, for we received the Orthodox faith from the Greeks; but with thee we will not dispute about the faith. As to what grievances there may be between us, we will send about that to thee to the conference." And the men of Novgorod sent to Magnush the *Tysyatski* Avraam, Kuzma Tverdislav, and other *Boyars*. And Avraam and the others arriving at Orekhovets wished to go to Magnush, but Magnush was then on Berezov[4] island with all his forces. And the men of Orekhov beat with their foreheads to Avraam not to leave their town, but Kuzma Tverdislav with others went to Magnush; and Magnush replied to Kuzma: " I have no grievance whatever against you "; but he said thus: " Adopt my faith, or I will march against you with my whole force "; and he dismissed Kuzma and the others. On their return to Orekhovets they all shut themselves in the town, and Magnush came up against the town with his whole force, and began baptizing

[1] West of lake Ilmen.
[2] The places in these districts.
[3] Constantinople.
[4] " Birch-tree."

the Izhera people into his own faith, and let loose his troops among
those who refused baptism. And hearing that the king had turned
his force on the Izhera people, the men of Novgorod sent Ontsifor
Lukinits, Yakov Khotov and Mikhail Fefilatov[1] against them with a
small company[2] and through the prayers of the Holy Mother of God,
and with the help of St. Sophia and of the holy Martyrs Boris and
Gleb, God aided Ontsifor; they killed 500, and others they took
alive, and executed the traitors, and the men of Novgorod returned
all well, having lost only three men.

And *Posadnik* Fedor Danilovich with the lieutenants of the
Veliki Knyaz and all the men of Novgorod and of Pleskov, with the
whole of the Novgorod district and a few men of Novi-torg went to
Ladoga, and to *Knyaz* Simeon Ivanovich they sent envoys, saying:
" Come to us, Sire,[3] to defend thy patrimony according to thy
kissing of the Cross; the king of the *Svei* is coming against us." And the
Veliki Knyaz Simeon replied to the men of Novgorod: " I come
gladly to you."   And after long delay the *Knyaz* went to Novgorod;
but on reaching [the village of] Sitno from Torzhok, he turned back
to Moscow, and sent his brother Ivan to Novgorod.   And *Knyaz*
Ivan came to Novgorod but did not go to the men of Novgorod at
Ladoga.   In the meanwhile King Magnush captured the town of
Orekhovets on Transfiguration Day, and he seized Avraam and
Kuzma with eight other *Boyars*, and let all the others go out of the
town, and himself went away from it, leaving a force behind in
Orekhovets.   And *Knyaz* Ivan hearing of the capture of Orekhovets,
by the *Nemtsy*, went back from Novgorod without the benediction
of the *Vladyka*, and not listening to the petition of the men of
Novgorod.   And the men of Novgorod went from Ladoga, and
halted by Orekhovets.

At the same time, on the night of the death of Ioan the Theologian, a fire broke out in Volosov Street which was partially burnt
down, also a part of Dobrynya Street and a goodly part of Prussian
Street; the Church of the Holy Mother of God was partially burnt,
also Chudinets Street, as far as the field, and the Lyudgoshcha
Street and four wooden churches; but before that, in the same
autumn, the Church of St. Flor in Lyudgoshcha Street was burnt,
and one church during dinner-time.

The same year the God-loving Vasili, *Vladyka* of Novgorod,
ordered the painting of the Church of the Holy Resurrection in the

[1] Theophylaktov.
[2] Druzhina.   [3] *Gospodin.*

Derevyanitsa Street, and it was completed on the day of the Conception of Ioan the Baptist.

The same autumn the men of Novgorod halted by Orekhov, investing it from our Lady's Fast[1] till the Great Fast [Lent]; then on Monday before Easter they approached the town with siege-engines, and on the dawn of Tuesday in Passion Week they took the town by the grace of God and the mediation of St. Sophia, through the prayers of the Most Holy Mother of God our Sovereign Lady, and by the power of the Honourable Cross, in which we repose our trust, also with the aid of the sacred Martyrs Boris and Gleb, on Tuesday, the day of Commemoration of the discovery of the sacred and honourable Head of Ioan the Forerunner,[2] and they slew the *Nemtsy* and took others alive, and set their brothers of Novgorod, Yakov Khotov and Olexander Borisovich in Orekhov.

A.D. 1349. A.M. 6857. The King of Cracow[3] with a large force seized the country of Volynia by deceit, and did much injury to the Christians, and he converted the sacred churches to the Latin service hated of God.

A.D. 1350. A.M. 6858. The men of Novgorod went to war against the *Nemtsy*, with Boris the son of the lieutenant, Ivan Fedorovich the *Tysyatski*, the *Voyevodas* Mikhali Danilovich, Yuri Ivanovich, and Yakov Khotov; and came to the town of Viborg on Monday the 21st day of March, and burned the whole of the town.[4] On the next day the *Nemtsy* came out of the town[5] and the men of Novgorod fell on them, and the *Nemtsy* fled into the town,[5] and there they killed several *Nemtsy*, and ravaged and burned the district near the town[5] and killed many *Nemtsy*, both women and children, and took others alive; and they returned to Novgorod all well.

The same year the men of Novgorod went to Yurev,[6] and made an exchange with the *Nemtsy* of the Swedish captives taken at Orekhov for Avraam and Kuzma, Alexander and Andrei and the company who had been over sea in the Swedish King Magnush's country. And they returned all well to Novgorod by the mercy of God, and by the power of the honourable Cross in which they trusted they

[1] In August.
[2] March 9.
[3] *Krakovsky*, sc. Poland.
[4] *Posad.*
[5] *Gorod.*
[6] sc. Dorpat.

reached Novgorod on the 9th day of June, the day of the Holy Martyr Alexander.

On the 16th day of the same month they took the *Posadnik*-ship from Fedor Danilovich and gave it to Ontsifor Lukin.

The same year *Vladyka* Vasili erected a new stone palace in his own Court, next to [the church of] the Nativity [of Christ].

The same year the men of Novgorod drove *Posadnik* Fedor out of Novgorod, together with his brother Mikhail, and Yuri and Ondreyan; their houses they pillaged, and they plundered the whole of Prussian Street. And Fedor, Mikhail, Yuri and Ondreyan fled to Pskov, and after being there a short while they went to Koporya.[1]

A.D. 1352. A.M. 6860.[2] The nobles and the common people of Novgorod beat with their foreheads to *Vladyka* Vasili, *Vladyka* of Novgorod, to go to Orekhov to establish the fort there; he went and established the fort and returned to Novgorod. Envoys arrived from Pskov praying *Vladyka* Vasili thus: " It has pleased God, the Holy Trinity, God hath spoken to thy children bidding the men of Pskov to live until thou, Sire,[3] shouldest come to the [church of the] Holy Trinity and bless thy children the men of Pskov." And making no delay he went, taking with him the Archimandrite Mikifor, the *Igumens* and priests, and arrived at Pskov and performed a service in Holy Trinity, in [the churches of] the Holy Mother of God, on Sneta Hill, of St. Mikhail, of Ioan the Theologian, and again in that of the Holy Trinity; he went in procession round the town with crosses, and blessed all the men of Pskov his children. And leaving the town and reaching Proshchenek[4] on Sunday, he stopped in the evening one *verst* beyond Proschenek, by the Cherekha river, and here he was taken ill; he was taken into the monastery of St. Mikhail at the mouth of the Uza river, on the Shelon; here he died on Tuesday, the day of the Holy Martyr Uakimf.[5] And they brought him to Novgorod on Thursday, July 5, the day of the Holy Father Lampad, *Vladyka* Moisei, *Vladyka* of Novgorod, the *Igumens* and the priests and all Novgorod attending; and they laid him in the porch of St. Sophia.[6]

1 No record for 1351.
2 This is the last entry in the Synodal text.
3 *Gospodin.*
4 A place near Pskov.
5 Hyacinth.
6 Here ends this last entry of the Synodal text; all that follows is from the " Continuation of the Annals of Novgorod " text, cf. p. 128.

There was a very great plague in Pleskov. The same year envoys arrived in Novgorod from Pleskov calling the *Vladyka* to Pleskov to bless the people. And the *Vladyka* heard their prayer and went and blessed the people of Pleskov, and on his way back to Novgorod going from Pleskov he was seized with a severe illness, and died at the Uza river on the 3rd day of July, Tuesday, at nine of the day, the day of the Holy Martyr Akinf.[1]

The same year *Vladyka* Moisei erected a stone church in the name of the Assumption of the Holy Mother of God in the Volotov [field].[2] The same year they led *Vladyka* Moisei with prayers on to his own throne in St. Sophia.

The same year there was a great plague in Novgorod; it came on us by God's loving kindness, and in His righteous judgment, death came upon people, painful and sudden, it began from Lady Day till Easter; a countless number of good people died then. These were the symptoms of that death: a man would spit blood and after three days he was dead. But this death did not visit Novgorod alone; I believe it passed over the face of all the land; and whom ever God commanded, that man died, and whomever he saved, him he admonished and punished, that the rest of our days we may live in the Lord virtuously and sinlessly.

The same spring Feognast, Metropolitan of all Russia, died after a long illness.

A.D. 1353. A.M. 6861. The *Veliki Knyaz* Simeon Ivanovich of all Russia, and his two sons died.

The same year *Vladyka* Moisei of Novgorod sent his envoys to *Tsargorod*[3] to the *Tsar*[4] and to the Patriarch, asking for their benediction, and for redress in improper matters brought upon him compulsorily by the Metropolitan.

The same year the men of Novgorod sent Smen Sudokov as their own envoy to the *Tsar*[5] to the Horde, asking for the bestowal of the title of *Veliki Knyaz* on Konstyantin *Knyaz* of Suzdal. And the *Tsar* refused, and bestowed it on *Knyaz* Ivan Ivanovich, and the men of Novgorod remained on hostile terms with the *Veliki Knyaz* for one year and a half; but there was no harm done.

A.D. 1354. A.M. 6862. Ontsifor Lukin voluntarily relinquished the *Posadnik*-ship which they then gave to

[1] Hyacinth.
[2] Near Novgorod.
[3] Constantinople.
[4] sc. the Emperor.
[5] sc. the Tartar *Tsar* (Khan of the Golden Horde).

L

Bakun Tverdislavich, and Olexander the brother of Dvoryanintsov was appointed *Tysyatski*.

The same year the envoys of *Vladyka* Moisei of Novgorod returned from *Tsargrad* and brought with them vestments ornamented with crosses and documents, with bestowal of great favour from the *Tsar* and from the Patriarch, and a gold seal. Ivan Kantakuzin was then the Greek *Tsar*, and the Patriarch was Filofei,[1] previously Metropolitan of Iraclia.[2]

A.D. 1355. A.M. 6863. The Metropolitan Alexi arrived in Russia, having been appointed in *Tsargrad*.

A.D. 1356. A.M. 6864. A stone church to the Annunciation of the Holy Mother of God was erected in Ilya Street.

A.D. 1355. A.M. 6863. *Vladyka* Moisei erected a stone church to St. Mikhail in the Skovorodka.[3]

A.D. 1356. A.M. 6864. They erected a stone church to St. Georgi in the Lubyanitsa [Street] where formerly a wooden church had stood. The same year they erected a church to the Forty Saints, of stone; the previous one had also been of stone, but had collapsed from old age and from the great conflagrations. The same year three wooden churches were built: St. Nikola in Yakov Street, St. Sava in Kuzma-Demyan Street, and St. Nikola in Lyatka.[3]

The same autumn the water was high.

A.D. 1357. A.M. 6865. *Vladyka* Moisei erected the stone Church of the Holy Spirit and monastery. The same year *Vladyka* Moisei erected the Church of the Holy Mother of God in Radokovichi.[4]

The same year there was a great thunder storm; the *Igumen* of St. Nikola in Lyatka was struck, and others; and in the Rogatitsa [Street] one was struck dead, while others by the mercy of God remained alive.

A.D. 1358. A.M. 6866. They erected the wooden Church of the Twelve Apostles.

[1] Philotheos.
[2] Heraclea.
[3] Near Novgorod.
[4] A part of Novgorod.

A.D. 1359. A.M. 6867. *Vladyka* Moisei erected the stone Church of St. Prokopi in the *Knyaz's* Court.

The same year Lazuta erected the Church of St. Ioan of stone in the German Court.

The same year *Vladyka* Moisei left his office of his own free will on the day of the Holy Father Moses, on account of his ill health; and all Novgorod implored him to remain, but he would not; but blessed them saying: " Choose a man for yourselves, whomever God gives you."

And having deliberated much, the *Posadnik* and the *Tysyatski*, and all Novgorod and the *Igumens* and priests decided not to make choice of any man for themselves but decided to take advice from God and to trust to his mercy, whomever God and St. Sophia should choose, him let him[1] point out. And they selected three men: Olexei, monk and almoner of the House of St. Sophia, Sava, *Igumen* of the Ontonov monastery, and Ivan, a priest of St. Barbara; and they placed three lots on the altar in St. Sophia, declaring: " Whomsoever God and St. Sophia, the Wisdom of God may desire, to have as servant at his altar, his lot will he leave on His altar." And God and St. Sophia chose for high priest of St. Sophia and as shepherd of his speaking sheep the good, intelligent and all-discriminating monk Olexei, and left his lot on His altar; and all Novgorod led him honourably up to the threshold[2] on the 15th day of September, the day of the martyr for Christ St. Nikita; and then seated him till the Metropolitan should summon him for confirmation. For the Metropolitan was at that time in Kiev, and they sent envoys to him. The same year Alexei, the itinerant monk, was appointed deacon and a priest in Tver by Fedor, Bishop of Tver.

The same spring God inflicting it on account of our sins, and the devil acting with his help, and by the advice of wicked men, there was a great tumult in Novgorod; they took the *Posadnik*-ship from Ondreyan Zakharich, but not all Novgorod, only the Slavno quarter, and they gave the *Posadnik*-ship to Selivester Lentiev. And no small confusion arose in the Yaroslav Court and there was a fight: because the Slavno men had come up unexpectedly in arms, and dispersed the men from across the river[3] who were without arms, and they attacked and robbed many nobles, and killed Ivan Borisov Likhinin.

[1] *Sic.*
[2] cf. p. 123.
[3] Zarechane.

And then the two sides armed themselves against each other; the Sophia side sought to avenge the dishonour to its brothers, and the Slavno side fought for their lives and property. And they stood opposite to each other for three days, for the Slavno men had dismantled the bridge. And *Vladyka* Moisei came out from the monastery taking with him Olexei, and the Archimandrite and the *Igumens*, and blessed them, saying: " My children, do not cause strife among yourselves, exultation to the pagans, and devastation to the sacred churches and this place; engage not in battle." And they accepted his word, and dispersed; and they sacked Selivester's villages, and many villages of the Slavno quarter were seized; and also many innocent people perished then. And they gave the *Posadnik*-ship to Mikita Matveyevich, and so they were reconciled. God did not suffer the devil utterly to exult, but Christianity was exalted to generation and generation.

A.D. 1360. A.M. 6868. Olexei went to Volodimir to be confirmed as *Vladyka*, summoned by envoys from the Metropolitan, and there went with him the Novgorod *Boyars*, *Posadnik* Olexander and Yuri Evanov.

And in the *Vladyka's* absence there was a fire in Novgorod; the Podol,[1] and the Gornichar[2] quarter, and seven wooden churches were burnt.

The same year there was a great tumult in the Horde; many *Tsars* with their wives and children were killed, and the men of the ranks fought against each other.

The same year *Knyaz* Dmitri Kostyantinovich of Suzdal returned to Volodimir from the Horde to asume the office of *Veliki Knyaz*.

And Olexei was confirmed Archbishop of Novgorod in Volodimir in the most renowned Church of the Holy Mother of God of Vladimir by the most venerable Metropolitan of all Russia, Olexei, in the presence of the *Veliki Knyaz* Dmitri Kostyantinovich, on July 12, the day of the Holy Martyrs Golendukha and Prokl; he returned to Novgorod, and was met by the *Igumens* and priests with the crosses at St. Ilya's, by the *Posadnik* and the *Tysyatski* and all Novgorod; and all rejoiced with a great gladness on that day.

The same year the *Veliki Knyaz* Dmitri sent his lieutenants to Novgorod, and the men of Novgorod placed the *Knyaz's* lieutenants amongst them, and gave them jurisdiction, having arrived at an agreement with the *Knyaz*.

[1] Lower town.
[2] " Potters."

The same year Semeon Ondreyevich with his pious mother founded a stone Church to St. Fedor in Fedor Street.

The same year there was a great plague in Pleskov, and the men of Pleskov sent envoys to the *Vladyka* with prayer and beating of the forehead, that, having come, thou mightest bless us, thy children. And the *Vladyka* went and blessed them; and went round the town of Pskov with crosses and performed three liturgies and returned to Novgorod; and thenceforward the men of Pleskov were better deserving of God's mercy, and the plague ceased.

The same year, in Philip's Fast,[1] there was a sign in the moon; it appeared in the clear sky as if covered with a dark covering.

The same year the Korel town[2] was burnt unexpectedly, and much harm was done to life and property; and the people of the town had only their souls left.

That spring, during Lent [it was] as though a fiery dawn appeared from the east ascending over the sky.

A.D. 1361. A.M. 6869.   They completed the stone Church of St. Fedor in Fedor Street.

A.D. 1362. A.M. 6870.   *Vladyka* Moisei erected a stone Church of the Holy Annunciation in Mikhail Street.

The same year Alexei, *Vladyka* of Novgorod, erected the stone Church of the Holy Nativity at the threshold, and he himself consecrated it, together with the *Igumens* and priests and with the choir of St. Sophia, on September 1, the day of the Holy Father Simon Stylites.

The same year the men of Pleskov detained the *Nemetski* merchants and those from the sea coast[3] and from over sea[4], saying: " The people of Yurev and of Velnev[5] have taken from us our land and water."

Moisei, *Vladyka* of Novgorod, died in the winter of the same year; and *Vladyka* Alexei assembled the *Igumens* and priests and all the church hierarchy and a multitude of Orthodox Christians, both men and women, and immediately took him honourably and laid him with his own hands into the tomb, in St. Mikhail's in the monas-

---

[1] In November.
[2] sc. Keksholm, on lake Ladoga.
[3] *Pomorski.*
[4] *Zamorski.*
[5] sc. Velyad, or Fellin.

tery at Skovorodka,[1] on January 25, the day of the Holy Father Grigori the Theologian.

A.D. 1363. A.M. 6871. *Nemetski* envoys and others from Yurev and from Velnev[2] came to Novgorod for settlement with the men of Pleskov; and the men of Pleskov also came to Novgorod, and having deliberated much, they departed without having concluded peace; and Novgorod merchants were detained in Yurev.

The same year the Church of the Holy Mother of God in the Volotov [field] in the Moisei monastery was painted by order of the God-loving Alexei, *Vladyka* of Novgorod.

The same year Novgorod envoys, one *Boyar* from each quarter of the town, went to Yurev of the *Nemtsy*.[3] And the *Nemtsy* agreed in love with the men of Pleskov, and there was peace between them; and the men of Pleskov released the *Nemetski* merchants, and the *Nemtsy* released the Novgorod merchants.

A.D. 1364. A.M. 6872. They erected a stone Church in Torzhok in the name of the God-befitting Transfiguration of our Lord God the Saviour Jesus Christ, at the instance of God-fearing merchants of Novgorod, and with the aid of all Orthodox Christians; and in the winter Alexei, *Vladyka* of Novgorod, consecrated it with the priests and deacons and all the choir of St. Sophia.

A.D. 1365. A.M. 6873. *Vladyka* Alexei erected the stone Church of [Our Lady's] Meeting[4] at the gates of the Ontonov monastery; and in Lyatka[5] Lazuta erected a stone Church to St. Nikola. The same year with the benediction of *Vladyka* Alexei they began to build in Pleskov a stone Church of the Holy Trinity, on the old foundations.

A.D. 1366. A.M. 6874. Young men with the captains Esif Valfromiyevich, Vasili Fedorovich and Olexander Obakunovich, went off to the Volga without the word of Novgorod. They all returned safely to Novgorod the same year; and for that the *Veliki Knyaz* Dmitri Ivanovich was angry and

[1] Near Novgorod.
[2] Velyad, or Fellin.
[3] *Yurev Nemetski*, Dorpat.
[4] i.e. St Mary's Meeting with Elizabeth (Luke I, 40, etc.)
[5] Near Novgorod.

broke off peace with the men of Novgorod saying thus: " Why did you go to the Volga and rob many of my merchants? " In the winter of the same year men from the *Knyaz* seized Vasili Danilovich and his son in Vologda; he was coming from the Dvina[1]; he knew not of this and was not on his guard.

A.D. 1367. A.M. 6875. The men of Novgorod sent envoys to the *Veliki Knyaz* Dmitri Ivanovich and concluded a peace with him. And the *Veliki Knyaz* released Vasili and his son Ivan, and sent his own lieutenant into Novgorod.

The same year, for our sins, there was no understanding between Pleskov and Novgorod; and a force of *Nemtsy* and men of Velnev[2] came and ravaged about Izborsk, all the Pleskov district as far as the Great river,[3] and having forded the Great river they came to the town of Pleskov and burned the town[4] around the fort[5] and did much damage, and then retired, suffering no harm, because neither *Knyaz* Alexander nor the *Posadnik* Lenti,[6] nor any other good men were in the town at that time; many were away in travel. And then the men of Pskov sent envoys to Novgorod with greeting and complaint: " Brothers, what care are you taking for us, your brothers? " And at that time Novgorod merchants had been detained in Yurev and in other towns of the *Nemtsy*, and *Nemetski* merchants were detained in Novgorod; only the kissing of the Cross of Novgorod with the *Nemtsy* had not been broken, and, therefore, the men of Novgorod did not hasten to occupy the land of the *Nemtsy* for the men of Pleskov. The same winter the men of Pleskov sent their *Posadnik* Anani, and Paul to Novgorod and beat with their foreheads to Alexei, *Vladyka* of Novgorod, to consecrate their Church of the Holy Trinity; and the *Vladyka* sent to them his spiritual father Ioan and his archpriest and archdeacon; and the Church of the Holy Trinity was consecrated with the benediction of Alexei, *Vladyka* of Novgorod, on January 30, the day of the Holy Martyr Popolit.[7] They then sent Sava Kuprov as envoy to the Country of the *Nemtsy*.

A.D. 1368. A.M. 6876. On May 12, the day of the Holy Martyr Epifani, there was a bad fire in Novgorod;

---

[1] sc. the N. Dvina.
[2] Velyad, Fellin.
[3] *Velikaya reka*, on which Pskov is situated.
[4] *Posad*.
[5] *Gorod*.
[6] Leontius.
[7] Hippolytus.

the whole *Detinets-gorod*[1] was burnt, also the *Vladyka's* Court, and the Church of St. Sophia was partially burnt, and of the Nerev quarter half the streets up to Danislav Street, and all the Carpenters' quarter[2] from St. Nikita to Radokovitsi,[3] and churches were burnt and several people.

And the same year the *Nemtsy* came with a large force; the Bishop himself came, and the *Meister* and Commanders, to Izborsk. And the men of Novgorod went out against them and went as far as Pleskov; and the *Nemtsy* fled from Izborsk, having cut their battering rams.

The same winter Volodimir, brother of the *Veliki Knyaz*, came to Novgorod.

A.D. 1369. A.M. 6877.   The Slavno quarter was completely burnt from Nutna Street to St. Ilya.

The same year they founded a stone church in Yarishev Street, and another of stone in Rogatitsa [Street], to St. Eupati.

A.D. 1370. A.M. 6878.   The men of Novgorod went with the men of Pleskov to Novogrodek of the *Nemtsy*, and they withdrew without taking it, because it was strong, and several people were shot from the town.

The same year they completed the Churches of St. Vasili and St. Eupati, and Alexei, *Vladyka* of Novgorod, with the priests, consecrated them.

The same year Olgerd with the Lithuanians was near Moscow and burned the outer town.[4]

A.D. 1371. A.M. 6879.   They erected a stone Church of St. Nikola in Russa.[5]

The same year there was a fire which spread from Ilya Street to the Carpenters' quarter[2]; all the *Podol*[6] was burnt and the quarter as far as Kilova Street. These many fires are because of our sins, that we might repent of our wickednesses; but we return to even greater. What is worse than this evil, namely, to take an oath falsely before God, to kiss the Cross and then violate it ? and that evil

[1] Citadel.
[2] *Plotniki.*
[3] A part of Novgorod.
[4] *Posad.*
[5] At the S. end of lake Ilmen.
[6] Lower town.

is often done among us; and, therefore, God inflicts the most severe punishments on us according to our deeds.

The same year Yuri Ivanovich, *Posadnik* of Novgorod, Selvester Lenteyevich,[1] the *Tysyatski* Olisei[2] and Olexander Kolyvanov went to a conference and concluded a peace with the *Nemtsy* near Novo-grodek.

The same year the town of Torzhok was completely burnt, for our sins; and here was not the end of the evil.

A.D. 1372. A.M. 6880. The men of Novgorod went to Torzhok to build up the town; and they sent Mikhail's lieutenants away from Torzhok. And *Knyaz* Mikhail came with a force to Torzhok, and burned the whole town, and the Christians suffered great distress: some were burnt with fire in their houses with their property, others took refuge in St. Saviour's, and were there suffocated; very many were burnt, others escaping from the fire were drowned in the Tvertsa river. And good women and girls foreseeing their violation at the hands of the men of Tver, for they were stripping them to utter nakedness, as even the pagans did not do, from shame and grief drowned themselves in the river; monks and nuns were all stripped. First of all Olexander Obakunovich met them in the open, and there laid his bones for St. Saviour and for the wrongs of Novgorod; and with him they killed Ivan Shakho-vich and another Ivan Timofeich, and Grigori Shchebelkov; and several others fell there, but some escaped. Others again were taken, and were led away captives to Tver, men and women, a countless number. They also took a great deal of property, what was left from the fire, and many of the silver frames from off the pictures. And who, my brethren, can help grieving over this? Those who remained alive, seeing how those others suffered violent and bitter death, the churches burnt and the town utterly laid waste: for such wrong-doing had never been suffered even from the pagans. And they filled five pits with dead bodies of the killed, drowned and burnt; and others were burnt so that nothing was left, and others drowned without being heard of, and floated down the river Tvertsa.

The same year they dug a trench around the Lyudin and the Nerev quarters and the outer parts of the town.[3]

[1] Leontievich.
[2] Elisha.
[3] *Zagorodie.*

A.D. 1373. A.M. 6881. *Knyaz* Volodimir came to Novgorod a week before the festival and stayed in Novgorod until Peter's Day,[1] and went away.

The same year the Volkhov flowed back for seven days.[2]

A.D. 1374. A.M. 6882. They erected the Church of Saint Saviour in stone in Ilya Street, and Alexei, *Vladyka* of Novgorod, consecrated it with the *Igumens* and priests and the choir of St. Sophia.

A.D. 1375. A.M. 6883. There was a sign in the sun on the 29th day of July, a Sunday, the day of the holy Martyr Kalinnik.

The same year the *Veliki Knyaz* Dmitri Ivanovich with all the *Knyazes* and with all the forces of Russia went against *Knyaz* Mikhail of Tver; and they stood near Tver four weeks and occupied the whole district, burned the town[3] and took away to different parts a very great many captives; and they had raised stockades[4] around the town of Tver, and thrown two bridges across the Volga. And the *Veliki Knyaz* sent for the men of Novgorod, and the men of Novgorod upholding the honour of their *Knyaz* came quickly in three days to Tver.   And *Knyaz* Mikhail seeing the force of Novgorod coming against him, sent *Vladyka* Eufemi to the *Veliki Knyaz* and surrendered to the *Veliki Knyaz* on all his terms.   And the men of Novgorod stood four days before Tver, and concluded peace on all the terms of the *Veliki Knyaz* and of Novgorod.

The same winter *Vladyka* Alexei resigned the Archbishopric voluntarily, retiring to Derevyanitsa,[5] and Novgorod fell into great grief.   After much deliberation they sent the Archimandrite Sava, Maxim Ontsiforovits with *Boyars* to the Metropolitan, that he should bless his son *Vladyka* Alexei into the House of St. Sophia, with the rank of sanctity proper to him.   And the Metropolitan blessed his son, *Vladyka* Alexei, and he dismissed the Archimandrite Sava and the *Boyars* with great honour; and they brought the blessing of the Metropolitan on *Vladyka* Alexei and on all Novgorod.

And the men of Novgorod held a *Veche* in Yaroslav's Court, and from the *Veche* they sent Ivan Prokshinich, the lieutenant of

[1] July 11.
[2] sc. owing to floods lower down.
[3] *Posad.*
[4] *Ostrog.*
[5] sc. the monastery on the river of this name.

the *Veliki Knyaz, Posadnik* Yuri, and the *Tysyatski* Olisei, together with many *Boyars* and good men to the *Vladyka* in Derevyanitsa,[1] and the *Vladyka* accepted their petition; and they elevated *Vladyka* Alexei in his own Archiepiscopal dignity into the House of St. Sophia on March 9, the day of the Forty Holy Martyrs, and the men of Novgorod were glad of the *Vladyka*.

A.D. 1376. A.M. 6884. For the second time in three years the Volkhov flowed backwards,[2] seven days. The same spring the Metropolitan Mark from the Holy Mother of God, from Mount Sinai, arrived in Novgorod, seeking charity. After a while the Archimandrite Vnifanti[3] from St. Michael came from Jerusalem also asking for charity.

The same year *Vladyka* Alexei went to the Metropolitan, and with him the Archimandrite Sava, Yuri Ontsiforovich, Vasili Kuzminich, Vasili Ivanovich and many other *Boyars*, on the 13th day of August, the day of the Holy Confessor Maxim. And the Metropolitan received his son *Vladyka* Alexei with love, as did the *Veliki Knyaz*. And he stayed two weeks in Moscow; and the Metropolitan dismissed him with a blessing, and the *Veliki Knyaz* and his brother Volodimir with great honour. And the *Vladyka* returned to the House of St. Sophia on the 17th of October, Friday, the day of the holy Prophet Osea.

The same winter the Metropolitan Kiprian[4] sent from Lithuania his envoys bringing documents[5] from the patriarch to the *Vladyka* in Novgorod, and it said thus: " The Patriarch Filofei has blessed me for[6] all the Russian Land." And Novgorod having heard the document[5] gave them answer: " Send to the *Veliki Knyaz;* if the *Veliki Knyaz* accepts thee as Metropolitan for all the Russian Land, then also shalt thou be our Metropolitan." And having heard this reply from Novgorod the Metropolitan Kiprian[4] did not send to the *Veliki Knyaz* in Moscow.

A.D. 1377. A.M. 6885. Young men from Novgorod went off to Novogrodek of the *Nemtsy* on the Ovla river, and they stood many days before the town, and took the whole outer town and ravaged the entire district and brought away many

[1] sc. the monastery on the river Derevyanitsa.
[2] sc. into lake Ilmen, owing to floods lower down.
[3] Boniface.
[4] Cyprian.
[5] *Gramotas, Gramoty.*
[6] sc. to be over.

captives to Novgorod, and themselves returning all well to Novgorod, with *Voyevoda* Ivan Fedorovich, Vasili Borisovich and Maxim Ananinich.

The same spring there was a fire in Novgorod, it broke out in Lyudgoshcha Street and extended to Yakov Street, and seven wooden and three stone churches were burnt. The same year the Church of the Holy Mother of God in the Mikhalitsa [Street] was struck by lightning and burnt.

The same year the Lithuanian *Knyaz* Olgerd died in Lithuania.

The same year, on May 29, the day of the Holy Martyr Kalinnik, the Archimandrite Sava of Novgorod died, and he was followed [to the grave] by *Vladyka* Alexei of Novgorod, and by the *Igumens* and priests with lamps and candles, and they laid him in the Church of the Holy Mother of God in the Ontonov monastery.

The same year they completed the stone Church of the Holy Martyrs Boris and Gleb in the Carpenters' quarter,[1] and *Vladyka* Alexei, with the priests and the choir of St. Sophia, consecrated it.

The same year the Tartars took Nizhni Novgorod.[2]

The same winter the Russian Metropolitan Alexei died in Moscow.

A.D. 1378. A.M. 6886. They completed the stone Church of the Holy Effigy in Dobrynya Street; and *Vladyka* Alexei with priests and the choir of St. Sophia, on its festival day, consecrated it.

The same year the Tartars went to the Suzdal Country against *Knyaz* Dmitri; and the *Knyaz* sent out his son *Knyaz* Ivan with a force against them, and they fought on the Pyana river; and *Knyaz* Ivan was drowned here, and others were killed.

The same winter *Knyaz* Ondrei Olgerdovich of Lithuania fled to Pskov, and kissing the Cross to the men of Pskov, he went through Novgorod to Moscow to the *Veliki Knyaz* Dmitri and the *Knyaz* received him.

A.D. 1379. A.M. 6887. Eight streets were burnt down in Novgorod, the fire breaking out in Lukin Street, and twelve churches, the fire extending to Chudinets Street.

The same year the Tartars came into the Russian Land, against the *Veliki Knyaz* Dmitri. And the *Knyaz* went out against them, and it was on the Ovozha river, and there both forces met and God aided the *Veliki Knyaz*, and the Tartars turned shoulder and fled.

[1] *Plotniki.*
[2] " Lower Newtown," on the Volga.

The same year they founded two stone churches: one to the Holy Mother of God in the Mikhalitsa [Street] and the other to the Holy Frola and Lavra[1] in Lyudogoshcha Street.

The same year the Lithuanian *Knyaz* Yuri Narimantovich came to Novgorod.

A.D. 1380. A.M. 6888. All Novgorod beat with the forehead to their lord[2] *Vladyka* Alexei, that thou shouldst undertake to go to the *Veliki Knyaz* Dmitri Ivanovich; and the *Vladyka* received the petition[3] of his children of all Novgorod, and went to the Low Country a week before Flower[4] Sunday, and with him went Yuri Ivanovich, Mikhail Danilovich, Yuri Ontsiforovich, Iev Obakunovich, Ivan Fedorovich and many other *Boyars* and men of substance. And the *Knyaz* received them with love, and kissed the Cross to Novgorod on all the old rights of Novgorod and on the old charters.

The same year, in the month of August, news came to the *Veliki Knyaz* Dmitri and to his brother *Knyaz* Volodimir from the Horde that the pagan race of Ishmaelites was rising against the Christians; for there was some weak man *Tsar* among them, and *Knyaz* Mamai was controlling all their affairs and he was savagely enraged against the *Veliki Knyaz* and all the Russian Land.

And having heard this, that a great Tartar force was coming against him, the *Veliki Knyaz* Dmitri Ivanovich gathered many soldiers and went against the godless Tartars, trusting in the mercy of God and in His Immaculate Mother, the Mother of God, the eternal Virgin Mary, calling to his aid the honourable Cross. For he entered their country beyond the Don, and there was there a clean field[5] at the mouth of the river Nepryadva, and there the pagan Ishmaelites had ranged themselves against the Christians. And the Moscovites, of whom many were inexperienced, were frightened and in despair of their lives at sight of the great numbers of Tartars, others turned to flight, forgetful of the Prophet's saying that one shall reap one thousand and two shall move ten thousand, if God does not abandon them.

And the *Veliki Knyaz* Dmitri with his brother Volodimir ranged their troops against the pagan Polovets people, and raising their

[1] Florus and Laurus.
[2] *Gospodin.*
[3] Lit. forehead-beating.
[4] sc. Palm.
[5] sc. treeless country.

eyes humbly to heaven, and sighing from the depth of their hearts, said, in the words of the psalm: " Brothers, God is our refuge and our strength." And both forces immediately met, and there was a fierce battle for a long time, and God terrified the sons of Hagar with an invisible might, and they turned their shoulders to wounds,[1] and they were routed by the Christians, and some were struck down with weapons, and others were drowned in the river, a countless number of them.

And in the encounter *Knyaz* Fedor Belozerski was killed, also his son *Knyaz* Ivan; and other *Knyazes* and captains went in pursuit of the aliens. The godless Tartars fell from dread of God and by the arms of the Christians; and God raised the right hand of the *Veliki Knyaz* Dmitri Ivanovich and of his brother *Knyaz* Volodimir Andreyevich for the defeat of the aliens.

And this was because of our sins: the aliens take up arms against us, that we might renounce our wrong doings and hatred of our brethren, from our love of silver, and from wrong judging and violence; but God is merciful and man-loving; He is not angry with us utterly, and is not at enmity for ever.

The *Knyaz* gained this victory on September 8, on a Saturday, the day of the Birth of the Mother of God. And the *Veliki Knyaz* Dmitri with his brother *Knyaz* Volodimir halting over the bones of the Tartars and many Russian *Knyazes* and captains, glorified with supreme great praise the Immaculate Mother of God, having stoutly fought with the aliens for God's holy churches, for the Orthodox faith and for all the Russian Land; and he himself, preserved by God, came back to his own great capital city of Moscow, his patrimony, with his brother Volodimir.

A.D. 1381. A.M. 6889. They founded a stone church in Slavkov Street to St. Dmitri.

The same autumn the Lithuanian *Knyaz* Skrigailo with an army of *Nemtsy* invested Polotsk, and they suffered much hardship and sent to Novgorod praying for Christian aid: " You should help us "; but they received no help from Novgorod, they only sent an envoy, Yuri Ontsiforovich, to the Lithuanian *Knyaz* Yagailo. And God and St. Sophia protected their house; and they went away and did not take the town.

The same year there was a tumult in Lithuania, God inflicting on them His anger: they rose against each other, and killed the

[1] sc. fled.

Veliki Knyaz Kestuti Gediminovich and his *Boyars,* but his son Vitovt escaped to the *Nemtsy.*[1] Much mischief was done to the Lithuanian country; for Kestuti had deprived Yagailo of the sovereignty.

A.D. 1382. A.M. 6890. The Tartar *Tsar* Tektomysh came against the Russian Land with a large force, and ravaged much of the Russian Land; he took Moscow town and burned it; also Pereyaslavl, Kolomno, Serpukhov, Dmitrov, Volodimir and Yurev.[2]

And the *Veliki Knyaz* seeing the enormous number of godless Tartars did not take stand against them; but retired to Kostroma with his wife and children, *Knyaz* Volodimir to the *Volok,*[3] and his mother and his wife to Torzhok; the Metropolitan to Tver, and Gerasim *Vladyka* of Kolomna removed to Novgorod. And who of us, my brethren, would not be terrified by this, seeing such confusion in the Russian Land? for as the Lord said through the Prophet: " If ye hearken unto me I shall put your fear into your enemies and ye shall enjoy the fruit of the earth; but if ye hearken not unto me, ye shall flee when none pursueth you; I shall send fear and dread on to you, and one hundred of you shall run from five, and from one hundred ten thousand."

The same year they completed the stone Church of St. Dmitri in Slavkov Street, and *Vladyka* Alexei consecrated it with the *Igumens* and priests and the choir of St. Sophia; and in a few days it crumbled to pieces.

The same year *Vladyka* Dionisi of Suzdal came to Novgorod from *Tsargrad*[4] from the Patriarch Nil with a blessing and with charters, and by command of *Vladyka* Alexei he went to Pskov teaching the law of God, and strengthening the faith in the true Christian Orthodox religion, in order that God might establish the Orthodox faith in the last years untroubled by wicked men prompted of the devil.

A.D. 1383. A.M. 6891. They dug a trench round the Sophia side, up to the old earthen wall.

The same year they founded two stone churches: one to St. Philip in Nutna Street and the other to St. Ioan in Radokovitsi,[5] and they completed that of St. Dmitri in Slavkov Street.

[1] sc. the German parts of the Baltic provinces.
[2] sc. Yurev Polski, N.E. of Moscow.
[3] sc. Lamsk, N.W. of Moscow.
[4] Constantinople.
[5] A part of Novgorod.

The same year *Knyaz* Vasili, the son of the *Veliki Knyaz*, went to the Horde summoned by the *Tsar*.

The same autumn *Knyaz* Mikhail of Tver went to the Horde, seeking the title of *Veliki Knyaz*.

Knyaz Patriki Narimantovich came to Novgorod and was received by the men of Novgorod; and they gave him for his maintenance the town of Orekhov, the Korel town,[1] and half of the town of Koporya, and Lusko village.

A.D. 1384. A.M. 6892. The townsmen of Orekhov and of the Korel town came to Novgorod complaining of *Knyaz* Patriki: and *Knyaz* Patriki incited the Slavno quarter to rise; and caused confusion in Novgorod. And the Slavno people sided with the *Knyaz* and they held a *Veche* in Yaroslav's Court, while another *Veche* met at St. Sophia; and both were in arms as for battle, and they dismantled the great bridge; but God and St. Sophia preserved us from civil war. But they took away those towns from the *Knyaz*, and they gave him [the two towns of] Russa and Ladoga.

The same year the men of Novgorod raised a stone wall on the road in Luga, by the grace of St. Sophia and the encouragement of the great *Archistrategos* Mikhail, and with the blessing of their father *Vladyka* Alexei, in only thirty and three days.

The same year a fire broke out at St. Lazar's in the Nerev quarter, and the Church of St. Lazar and another, that of St. Peter, were burnt.

The same year there was a darkness for many days and nights, and birds could not see whither to fly, and kept falling to the ground and into the water, and people dared not go on the lakes or on the rivers; and there was grief and trouble amongst Christians. This is God punishing us, brethren, for our sins, showing us the way to repentance, in order that we should repent of our wicked ways. Having punished us, have mercy on us, O Lord! And there was light, and we were glad.

The same autumn they completed the stone Church of St. Philip in Nutna Street, and *Vladyka* Alexei consecrated it, and they completed another to St. Ioan in Radokovitsi.[2]

A.D. 1385. A.M. 6893. The town of Pskov was entirely burnt down; the church of the Holy Trinity was alone

[1] sc. Keksholm, on lake Ladoga.
[2] A part of Novgorod.

preserved by God. The same year, in the month of June, on the 14th day, in Peter's Fast, the day of the Holy Prophet Elisei, the whole of the Commercial Side of Novgorod was burnt down and all the churches, God preserved only that of the Holy Mother of God in the Mikhalitsa [Street], through the prayers of the Holy Mother of God. And seventy persons were burnt; for the fire was very fierce.

In the winter of the same year, on January 1, there was a sign in the sun, on the day of the Holy Father Vasili.

A.D. 1386. A.M. 6894. The town of Orekhov was burnt down, and the end of Mikitin Street in Novgorod was burnt. The same year they completed the stone Church of St. Kliment in Ivorov Street.

The same year the Lithuanians killed *Knyaz* Svyatoslav of Smolensk. The same winter the *Veliki Knyaz* Dmitri came to Novgorod with an army and with his brother *Knyaz* Volodimir, being angered against Novgorod on account of the Volga men. And he halted at [the village of] Yamny, and *Vladyka* Alexei went and concluded a peace on all the old terms; and for the guilty, for the Volga men the *Veliki Knyaz* took 8,000 *roubles* from Novgorod.

The same winter *Posadnik* Fedor Timofeyevich, Timofei Yurievich and some *Boyars'* sons went beyond the *Volok* to get the 5,000 *roubles* which Novgorod had imposed on the country beyond the *Volok*[1] for it was the men from beyond the *Volok* who had been to the Volga.

A.D. 1387. A.M. 6895. They raised an earth rampart round the commercial side. The same year *Vladyka* Alexei blessed all Novgorod to build up a town[2] of stone at Porkhov; and the men of Novgorod sent Ivan Fedorovich and Fatian Esifovich, and they built the town of Porkhov in stone.

In the winter of the same year *Knyaz* Vasili Dmitrievich, son of the *Veliki Knyaz*, came away from the Horde.

A.D. 1388. A.M. 6896. *Vladyka* Alexei resigned voluntarily the Archbishopric, retiring to the monastery of the Holy Resurrection on the Derevyanitsa on the *Vladyka's* mid-way festival[3]; having blessed his children, the *Posadnik* and *Tysyatskis* and all Novgorod, having sat in the House of St.

---

[1] *Zavolochkaya zemlya, Dvinskaya zemlya,* sc. the basin of the N. Dvina, N.E. Russia generally.
[2] sc. town-wall.
[3] i.e., half-way between Easter and Pentecost.

M

Sophia thirty years short of one year and five months, and all Novgorod entreated him much to remain in the House of St. Sophia until they should know who would be Metropolitan of the Russian Land, but he did not listen to them, but blessed them, saying: " Select for yourselves three men [one of] whom God will give you." And the men of Novgorod did so. And after much deliberation the *Posadnik* and the *Tysyatski* and all Novgorod, and the *Igumens* and the priests would not make a choice for themselves from men, but decided to receive advice from God, and to trust in His mercy, and selected three men: Ioan, *Igumen* of St. Saviour from Khutin, Parfeni, *Igumen* of the Holy Annunciation, and Afanasi, *Igumen* of the Holy Nativity, and they placed three lots on the altar in St. Sophia, resolving thus: " Whomever God and St. Sophia shall desire to serve at Their altar, his lot will they leave on Their altar." And the priests began to sing the midday service, and the men of Novgorod held a *Veche* at St. Sophia, and at the end of the service the arch-priest Ismaelo brought out the lot of Afanasi, then that of Parfeni; and God and St. Sophia and God's altar chose the good, humble and meek Ioan, *Igumen* of St. Saviour, leaving his lot on their altar; and all Novgorod raised him to the threshold[1] with honour on May 7, the day of the Ascension of our Lord, the commemoration day of the Holy Father Pakhomi. There was at that time no Metropolitan in the Russian Land.

The same autumn at midnight of October 26, a southerly wind arose and drove the ice from the lake into the Volkov, which broke away nine stays of the great bridge.

Also God did not wish to see bloodshed between brothers at the prompting of the devil; for three of the quarters of the St. Sophia side rose against *Posadnik* Esif Zakharinich, and summoning a *Veche* at St. Sophia, they went like a large army, every one armed, to his dwelling, and took his house and demolished his rooms. And *Posadnik* Esif fled across the river to the Carpenters' quarter[2]; and the entire commercial side rose in his favour, and began to strip[3] people, and to beat off the ferry-men from the shore, and to cut up the vessels, and so they were without peace for two weeks, and then they came together in love. And they gave the *Posadnik*-ship to Vasili Ivanovich.

The same autumn, on December 8, *Vladyka* Ivan[4] went to Moscow,

---

[1] cf. p. 123.
[2] *Plotniki.*
[3] sc. rob.
[4] *Ioan,* John.

summoned by envoys of the Metropolitan, for confirmation in the Archbishopric, and with him went the *Boyars* of Novgorod: *Posadnik* Vasili Fedorovich, and the *Tysyatski* Efim Faleleyevich, Yev Obakunovich, Timofei Evanovich, and many other *Boyars;* and he arrived in Moscow on January 10; and Ivan was established *Vladyka* of Novgorod on January 17, on the day of the Naming of the Church of the Holy and Great *Archistrategos* Michael, on Sunday, the day of the Holy Father Antony, by the most reverend the Metropolitan Pimen of all Russia. And *Vladyka* Danilo of Smolensk and the *Vladyka* of Ryazan were at the confirmation. And they made high festival on that day with laudations and chants in the presence of the *Veliki Knyaz* Dmitri Ivanovich, and he returned to Novgorod on February 8, on Pharisees' Sunday, the day of the Holy Father Parfeni, and the *Igumens* and priests of the Slavno quarter, the *Posadnik*, the *Tysyatski*, and all Novgorod met him with crosses; and they rejoiced with great gladness on that day for their *Vladyka*.

A.D. 1389. A.M. 6897. The *Veliki Knyaz* Dmitri Ivanovich died in Moscow on May 9, the day of the Holy Prophet Isaiah.

And in that spring there was a great plague in Pskov, the symptoms being in the glands. *Vladyka* Ivan went in the same spring to Pskov, and through his prayers the plague ceased in Pskov, and *Vladyka* Ivan returned to Novgorod, and all those with him, in good health.

The same year *Posadnik* Grigori Yakunovich erected the stone Church of the Intercession of the Holy Mother of God at the gate.

The same year *Knyaz* Simeon Olgerdovich came to Novgorod on the day of the Assumption of the Holy Mother of God, and the men of Novgorod received him with honour.

The same winter Alexei, *Vladyka* of Novgorod, died, on February 3, on the day of St. Simeon, the Accepted of God.

A.D. 1390. A.M. 6898. *Knyaz* Vasili Dmitrievich took his seat on the throne of the *Veliki Knyaz*, and the men of Novgorod took peace with him on the old terms. The same year the men of Novgorod went to a conference with the *Nemtsy*, but did not take peace. And the men of Novgorod went to war with Pskov, and the men of Pskov beat with their foreheads to Novgorod and took peace; and they returned from [the village of] Soltsa.

The same year they erected a stone church to Holy *Tsar* Kostyantin and his mother Olena,[1] and *Vladyka* Ivan consecrated it; and they established a new monastery of St. Nikola at the end of Lyudgoshcha and Chudinets Streets by the cemetery.

The same autumn there was à great plague in Novgorod; all this came upon us because of our sins; a great number of Christians died in all the streets. And this was the symptom in people: a swelling would appear, and having lived three days [the man] would die. Then they erected a church to St. Afanasi in a single day, and *Vladyka* Ioan, *Vladyka* of Novgorod, consecrated it, with all the *Igumens* and priests and with the choir of St. Sophia; so by God's mercy and the intercession of St. Sophia, and by the blessing of the *Vladyka*, the plague ceased.

The same winter the Church of St. Dmitri in Danislav Street was burnt down with all the images, and books and all the church stores, and very much property was burnt, for the fire took on rapidly.

A.D. 1391. A.M. 6899. There was a fire, and it went from Borkova Street up to the [stream] Gzen,[2] and on the other side of the river from Mikitin Street to Rodokovitsi [street]; eight wooden churches were completely and three stone churches partially burnt, and fourteen men, women and children perished on June 5, the day of the holy Martyr Dorofei. On the 21st of the same month, the day of the holy Martyr Ulyan, a fire broke out in Prussian Street at the Church of the Presentation of the Holy Mother of God, and the whole of the Lyudin quarter was burnt up to St. Alexei, when seven wooden churches were completely and four stone churches partially burnt.

The same autumn the men of Novgorod sent envoys to a conference with the *Nemtsy* at Izborsk: *Posadnik* Vasili Fedorovich, *Posadnik* Bogdan Obakunovich, *Posadnik* Fedor Timofeyevich, the *Tysyatski* Esif Faleleyevich, Vasili Borisovich, and merchants; and the envoys of the *Nemtsy* came from over sea from the town of Lubek, from the Goth coast,[3] from Riga, Yurev,[4] Kolyvan,[5] and from many other towns; then they took peace with the *Nemtsy*.

The same winter the same envoys of the *Nemtsy* came to Novgorod, and took their merchandise; and kissed the Cross, and began to

[1] Constantine and Helena.
[2] In Novgorod.
[3] sc. Gothland.
[4] Dorpat.
[5] *Yurev Nemetski* or Revel.

build their court anew, because for seven years there had been no stable peace.

The same winter the Metropolitan Kiprian came to Novgorod; and *Vladyka* Ioan met him at St. Saviour's in Ilya Street with crosses with the *Igumens* and priests, and with many Christians; and he stayed two weeks in Novgorod: he spoke much to Novgorod that they should tear up the charter[1] which the men of Novgorod had concluded, not to be summoned by the Metropolitan to Moscow. And Novgorod did not accept his word, and they did not tear up the charter, and the Metropolitan departed from Novgorod, nursing great displeasure against Novgorod.

A.D. 1392. A.M. 6900. Yuri Ontsiforovich erected a church to the Assumption of the Holy Mother of God and established a monastery.

The same year the *Veliki Knyaz* Vasili Dmitrievich came away from the Horde, and took Nizhni Novgorod and took away the *Knyazes* and their wives as hostages. And *Knyaz* Simeon fled to the Horde.

The same year some *Nemtsy*[2] pirates came from over sea into the Neva, taking the villages on both sides of the river to within five *versts* of the town of Oreshek.[3] And *Knyaz* Simeon with the townsmen coming upon them, killed some and scattered others and brought captive interpreters to Novgorod; and then he went to his kinsmen in Lithuania, abandoning the town.

The same year they raised an earth rampart round the commercial side.

The same year the *Veliki Knyaz* Vasili Dmitrievich went to the Horde summoned by the *Tsar*.

The same year *Posadnik* Bogdan Obakunovich with his brothers and men of his street erected a stone Church to St. Simeon in Chudinets Street and it was consecrated on his festival day.

The same year, in the month of June, *Posadnik* Vasili Fedorovich died after entering the monastic order, and they laid him in St. Nikola's. The same autumn *Posadnik* Mikhail Danilovich died, having entered the monastic order.

A.D. 1393. A.M. 6901. The *Veliki Knyaz* Vasili Dmitrievich broke the peace with Great Novgorod[4] about the

---

[1] sc. treaty, *gramota*.
[2] Here probably Swedish.
[3] Orekhov.
[4] *Veliki Novgorod.*

charter which Great Novgorod had written,[1] not to be summoned by the Metropolitan to Moscow, saying thus: " that you send the charter back to the Metropolitan, and as regards your having kissed [the Cross] the Metropolitan will absolve you from the sin." And Great Novgorod would not have that, and the *Veliki Knyaz* took from Novgorod the neighbouring town of Torzhok and its districts, Volok-Lamsk, and Vologda, and ravaged many districts. And the men of Novgorod took the town of Ustyug, Ustyuzhna, and many other districts from the *Veliki Knyaz*, and there was much bloodshed at that time on both sides. And the men of Novgorod not wishing to see more bloodshed between Christians, sent envoys to the *Veliki Knyaz* with a petition for the old terms, and they sent the sworn charter to the Metropolitan, and the Metropolitan sent word: " I accept your sworn charter, and absolve you from your sin, and bless you." And the *Veliki Knyaz* received the petition of Novgorod and took peace on the old terms.

They erected a stone church on the Lisitsa Hill[2] to the Holy Mother of God.

Knyaz Vitovt Kestutievich took his seat as *Knyaz* in Lithuania, and the men of Novgorod took peace with him on the old terms.

Knyaz Kostyantin Belozerski came to Novgorod, and they received him.

A.D. 1394. A.M. 6902. The people of Danislav [Street] erected a stone church to St. Dmitri and *Vladyka* Ivan consecrated it on his festival day.

The same year the men of Novgorod went to war against Pskov and stood before the town for a week; and during that time a fight occurred in a raid of the men of Novgorod on the men of Pleskov, and there they killed *Knyaz* Ivan of Koporya and Vasili Fedorovich, and God knows who else fell on both sides, and the men of Novgorod withdrew from the town, at enmity with the men of Pleskov.

At that time the men of Novgorod took away the *Posadnik*-ship from Esif Zakharinich and gave it to Bogdan Obakunovich.

The same autumn the *Vladyka's* Court and adjacent premises were burnt down; and many streets outside the town were also burnt down; the top of St. Sophia was partly burnt; eight stone churches were partly, and two wooden churches completely burnt. They erected a wooden Church of St. Saviour at the end of Kuzma-Demyan Street, and established a monastery.

[1] sc. had concluded, and possessed.
[2] "Fox's hill."

Knyaz Andrei arrived with envoys from Pskov, and left Novgorod without taking peace. *Vladyka* Mikhail of Bethlehem arrived from *Tsargrad*[1] sent by the Patriarch Antoni, bringing to Novgorod two charters[2] of instructions for Christians.

A.D. 1395. A.M. 6903. The Metropolitan Kiprian came to Novgorod with the Patriarch's envoy during the Great Fast, and demanded the right of jurisdiction, but the men of Novgorod refused him. He stayed throughout the whole spring in Novgorod up to Peter's Fast,[3] and *Vladyka* Ivan gave great honour to the Metropolitan and to the Patriarch's envoy. And the Metropolitan Kiprian on departing from Novgorod blessed his son the *Vladyka* Ioan and all Great Novgorod.[4]

The same year Isak Onkifov[5] erected a stone church to the Feast of St. Mikhail in the Arkadi monastery.

Nemtsy Sveo[6] came to the new town of Yam[7] and retired; and *Knyaz* Kostyantin with the townsmen killed some of them; the rest took to flight.

The same autumn *Knyaz* Vitovt of Lithuania took the town of Smolensk and placed his lieutenant there, and *Knyaz* Yuri Svyatoslavich fled to Ryazan.

A.D. 1396. A.M. 6904. *Vladyka* Ivan went to Moscow to the Metropolitan Kiprian, summoned by the Metropolitan, and remained in Moscow two days, and the Metropolitan immediately let him go with his blessing and with honour, and he returned to Novgorod on Tuesday in Holy Week.

The same year the *Nemtsy* came to the Korel country, and ravaged the Kyur and the Kyulola villages, and burned the church; and *Knyaz* Kostyantin pursued them with the Korel people and captured the native interpreters and sent them to Novgorod.

The whole Ontonov monastery was burnt, and the Church of the Holy Mother of God, which had been leaded, was destroyed by fire, also the Church of the Purification.

There was a sign from the image of the Holy Sovereign Lady in St. Eupati's in Shcherkova Street: wine appeared to flow from the ikon.

---

[1] Constantinople.
[2] *Gramoty*, sc. books.
[3] In June.
[4] *Veliki Novgorod*.
[5] sc. Akinf, Hyacinth.
[6] Swedes.
[7] Yamburg.

By order of *Vladyka* Ivan they covered with lead the top of St. Sophia, which had been damaged by fire.   The Church of St. Ioan in the Rostkin monastery was burnt, together with the images and books.

The same year *Knyaz* Vitovt of Lithuania went against Ryazan and ravaged its districts.

A.D. 1397. A.M. 6905.   Isak Onkifov erected a stone Church of the Birth of the Holy Mother of God in the Desyatina.   The same year envoys came from Pskov to Great Novgorod: *Knyaz* Grigori Ostafievich, *Posadnik* Sysoi, *Posadnik* Roman, Philip Kozachkovich, with their friends, and they beat with their foreheads to the Lord[1] *Vladyka* of the Great Novgorod, *Vladyka* Ioan: " That thou, Lord, shouldst bless thy children of Great Novgorod, that our Lord the Great Novgorod might forgive his displeasure, and receive us on the old terms." And *Vladyka* Ioan blessed Great Novgorod, his children: " That you, my children, accept my blessing and forgive the men of Pskov your displeasure, and receive back your younger brothers on the old terms; for you see, my children, the last days, you should all be as one brother in Christianity." And *Posadnik* Timofei Yurievich, the *Tysyatski* Mikita Fedorovich and all the *Posadniks* and *Tysyatskis*, the *Boyars* and the whole Great Novgorod received the blessing of their. Lord Father *Vladyka* Ivan, and they withdrew their displeasure from the men of Pskov, and took peace on the old terms, on the 18th day of June,. the day of the holy Martyr Lentei.[2]   Because there had not been peace for four years, and there was gladness and rejoicing among the Christians, and the devil seeing the good of the Christians, lamented, seeing himself discomfited, and the foes of the Christians were obscured.

After this *Knyaz* Vasili Ivanovich of Smolensk arrived in Novgorod and they received him.

After this a fire broke out in Shcherkova Street opposite the [Church of the] Forty Saints; and the whole of Shcherkova Street along the quay was burnt, also the Yanev quay, except three houses, and the whole of Rozvazha quay, the whole of the Kuzma-Demyan quay, and as far as Kholop Street, on the day of the Holy Martyr Andrew Stratilat.[3]

The same autumn the *Nemtsy* came and took seven villages of the

[1] *Gospodin.*
[2] Leonti.
[3] *Stratelates*, August 31.

Yam town[1] and burned them. The Church of the Exaltation[2] was burnt with all the pictures and books. And then *Posadnik* Esif Faleleyevich died, having entered the monastic order. *Knyaz* Patriki Narimantovich arrived in Novgorod and they received him.

The same year the *Veliki Knyaz* Vasili Dmitrievich sent his *Boyars*, Andrei Alberdov with others, to the whole Dvina colony[3] beyond the *Volok*,[4] saying thus: " That you should give allegiance to the *Veliki Knyaz* and leave Novgorod; and the *Veliki Knyaz* will defend you against Novgorod and will stand up for you." And the men of the Dvina, Ivan Mikitin, the *Boyars* of the Dvina, and all the people of the Dvina gave their allegiance to the *Veliki Knyaz* and kissed the Cross to the *Veliki Knyaz;* and the *Veliki Knyaz* against his kissing of the Cross to Novgorod seized Volok-Lamsk with its districts, Torzhok and its districts, Vologda and Bezhitsy; and then put off from himself his kissing of the Cross to Novgorod and threw up the sworn charter. And the men of Novgorod put off from themselves their kissing of the Cross, and threw up the charter they had sworn to the *Veliki Knyaz*.

And after this the Metropolitan Kiprian sent his bailiff Kliment to Great Novgorod to his son *Vladyka* Ivan, saying thus: " Come to Moscow, thy Father the Metropolitan summons thee on sacred business." And the *Vladyka* let the Metropolitan's *Boyar* go back to Moscow, and himself resolved to go to his Father the Metropolitan; and the *Posadnik*, the *Tysyatski*, and the whole of Great Novgorod, beat with their foreheads to their Father the Lord *Vladyka* Ioan: " That thou give a good word and thy blessing to the *Veliki Knyaz*, for thy children, for Great Novgorod."

And the men of Novgorod sent as envoys to the *Veliki Knyaz Posadnik* Bogdan Obakunovich, Kyuril Dmitrievich, and other men of substance, with their Father the *Vladyka*.

And *Vladyka* Ioan gave to the *Veliki Knyaz* his good word and blessing, and the envoys from Novgorod a petition, saying thus: " That thou, my Lord and son, *Veliki Knyaz*, receive my benediction and good word, and the petition of Novgorod; that thou withdraw thy displeasure from thy free men of Novgorod, and receive them on the old terms; that there be no more shedding of blood among Christians, my son, during thy reign. And what thou hast taken from Novgorod against thy kissing of the Cross, the country beyond

---

[1] Yamburg.
[2] Of the Cross.
[3] *Sloboda*.
[4] Volok Dvinsk, in N. Russia. See Introduction, pp. ix, x, etc.

the *Volok*[1], Torzhok, Vologda and Bezhitsy, that thou give up all that, and that it come to Novgorod as of old. And as regards the common jurisdiction on the borderland, forego, my son, that, for that, Lord *Veliki Knyaz*, is not the old custom."

And the *Veliki Knyaz* would not except the blessing and the good word of the *Vladyka*, nor the petition from the Novgorod envoys; and he did not withdraw from Novgorod his displeasure, and he granted no peace, but the Metropolitan Kiprian dismissed his son *Vladyka* Ioan with honour and with his blessing.

A.D. 1398. A.M. 6906. In the spring, after Easter, the men of Novgorod said to their Lord Father *Vladyka* Ivan: " We cannot, Lord Father, endure this violence of our *Veliki Knyaz* Vasili Dmitrievich; that he has taken the surrounding villages and districts away from Novgorod, and from St. Sophia, which belonged to our fathers and grandfathers; but intend to recover the outlying parts and districts of St. Sophia which belonged to our fathers and grandfathers." And they kissed the Cross to stand as one man how to recover the outlying parts and districts of St. Sophia and Great Novgorod. And *Posadnik* Timofei Yurievich, *Posadnik* Yuri Dmitrievich, Vasili Borisovich, the *Boyars*, the sons of *Boyars*, the men of substance, the sons of merchants, and all their soldiers beat with their foreheads: " Bless, O Lord Father *Vladyka*, our attempt to recover the outlying parts and districts of St. Sophia; we shall either recover our patrimony for St. Sophia and for Great Novgorod, or we shall lay down our heads for St. Sophia and for our Lord Great Novgorod.[2]" And *Vladyka* Ivan blessed his children and the *Voyevodas* of Novgorod and all the soldiers, and Novgorod sent forth its brothers, saying to them thus: " Go, seek the outlying parts and the districts of St. Sophia and our patrimony." And the *Voyevodas* of Novgorod, *Posadnik* Timofei, *Posadnik* Yuri, and Vasili and all the soldiers went off to the Dvina beyond the *Volok*, to Orlets town, and there met them coming from the Vel district the *Vladyka's* superintendent Isai, saying to them thus: " Sirs, *Voyevodas* of Novgorod, the *Veliki Knyaz's Boyar* Andrei, with Ivan Mikitin and with the Dvina men, having invaded the Vel district of St. Sophia on Easter Day, they ravaged the St. Sophia district and levied a poll tax; and *Knyaz* Fedor of Rostov has come from the *Veliki Knyaz* with a column of troops to keep garrison on the Dvina to guard the town,

[1] sc. the country of the N. Dvina. See Introduction, p. ix, etc.
[2] *Gospodin Veliki Novgorod.*

to hold judgment and to levy taxes on the Novgorod districts; and the captains of the Dvina, Ivan and Konon, with their friends, have divided the Novgorod districts and *Boyars* amongst themselves." And the *Voyevodas* of Novgorod having heard this, said to their brother *Voyevodas*: " Since our Lord the *Veliki Knyaz* has done this in concert with the covenant-breaking Dvina *Voyevodas*, better were it for us, brothers, to die for St. Sophia than to suffer wrong at the hands of our *Veliki Knyaz*." And they went against the Belo-Ozero[1] districts of the *Veliki Knyaz* and took the Belo-Ozero districts by assault, after ravaging and firing them; and burnt the old town of Belozersk, and the *Knyazes* of Belozersk and the *Voyevodas* of the *Veliki Knyaz* came out from the new town, and beat with their foreheads to the Novgorod *Voyevodas* and all the soldiers, and they took from them a ransom of sixty *roubles*, and they took countless plunder and took a countless quantity of cattle; and ravaged the Kubensk districts and ravaged around Vologda, and ravaged and burnt the town of Ustyug, and they remained at Ustyug four weeks.

And then the *Voyevodas* sent Dmitri Ivanovich, Ivan Bogdanovich, and with them sons of *Boyars*, and they ravaged the districts of the *Veliki Knyaz* to within one day of Galich,[2] and they ravaged and burnt the districts, and took a countless number of captives and they took ransom for the captives because their boats would not hold them, and other plunder they threw away. And thence they went along the Dvina to the town of Orlets, ravaging the districts of the *Veliki Knyaz*, and coming to Orlets town they stood before it four weeks, and set up battering rams, and invested the town, and began to batter with them. And the Dvina men came from out of the town and began to beat with their foreheads with lamentation to the *Voyevodas* and to all the Novgorod soldiers.

And the Novgorod *Voyevodas* and all the soldiers, at the word of their Lord Novgorod, accepted the petition of the Dvina men and forgave them their displeasure, and seized the *Voyevodas* of the country beyond the *Volok*, Ivan and Konon with their friends, and others they punished with death; and they put Ivan and his brother Afanasi, Gerasim and Radivon in fetters who had led the Dvina country into evil. And from *Knyaz* Fedor of Rostov they took away the fines or taxes which he had used to raise, but gave him and his friends their lives. And from the merchants of the *Veliki*

1 " White-Lake."
2 *Galich Meriazhski*, town in N. Russia.

Knyaz they took a ransom of 300 *roubles* per head, and from the people of the Dvina, for their defection and their fault, the *Voyevodas* and all the soldiers of Novgorod took 2,000 *roubles*, and 3,000 horses, for there were 3,000 of the men of Novgorod, or less.   O merciful God! to have traversed so much Russian Land, and at such a strong town as this, there was no harm done to the people[1]; one man alone was killed from the town: the young *Boyar* Levushka, son of *Posadnik* Fedor; but the town they plundered.

Vladyka Ioan, *Vladyka* of Novgorod, erected a church of stone by the gates, to the Holy Resurrection, and consecrated it himself with the priests and the choir of St. Sophia.   Mikhail Krupa erected a church of stone to St. Nikola in Chudinets Street in the Lyudgoshcha quarter.

The same autumn with the blessing of *Vladyka* Ivan envoys went from Novgorod to the *Veliki Knyaz* Vasili Dmitrievich: the Archimandrite Parfeni, *Posadnik* Esif Zakharinich, the *Tysyatski* Anani Kostyantinovich, and the men of substance, Grigori and David, and they took peace with the *Veliki Knyaz* on the old terms.

The same winter the *Voyevodas* of Novgorod, *Posadnik* Timofei, *Posadnik* Yuri, and *Boyars* and sons of *Boyars* and all the soldiers returned to Novgorod sound and well, and the men of Novgorod were glad of their brothers; and they threw the traitor Ivan Mikitin from the bridge; and Gerasim and Radivon beat with their foreheads to their Lord Great Novgorod with lamentation, and Novgorod granted them their lives, and they had themselves shorn into the monastic order; but Alfan[2] escaped on the way.

A.D. 1399. A.M. 6907.   *Knyaz* Vitovt Kestutievich of Lithuania sent to Novgorod a declaration of war saying thus: " You have dishonoured me; you were to have stood by me, and I was to have been your *Veliki Knyaz*, and I was to have protected you; whereas you have not stood by me."   And the men of Novgorod sent back the declaration of war from them to *Knyaz* Vitovt.

The same year for our sins a fire broke out in the Lyubyanitsa [Street], and the Carpenters' quarter[3] was burnt up to the Fedor stream; and the whole Slavno quarter was burnt, and twenty-two stone churches were partially burnt, and five side-chapels, and one

[1] i.e. " and to have suffered no harm in the siege of so strong a town."
[2] Or Anfailo.
[3] *Plotniki.*

wooden church, and how many persons were burnt God knows, and some were drowned in the Volkhov, on the day of the holy Martyr Memnon.[1] So fierce was the fire, with a hurricane, that it swept burning over the water.

Knyaz Andrei Dmitrievich, brother of the *Veliki Knyaz* Vasili, came to Novgorod on the day of the holy Father Osif, *Vladyka* of Selun,[2] and he stayed in Novgorod from Volodimir Day to St. Simon the Summer-speeder's Day,[3] and he departed from Novgorod and the *Vladyka* Ioan, the *Posadnik* and the *Boyars* gave the *Knyaz* great honour.

The *Veliki Knyaz* Mikhail Olexandrovich of Tver died, in the month of August, having taken the monastic order, and they laid him in the Church of St. Saviour.

The same year the *Vladyka* of Novgorod, *Vladyka* Ioan, with his sons the men of Novgorod erected a church of stone of the Intercession of the Holy Mother of God, in Zverinets,[4] and *Vladyka* Ioan himself with the priests and the choir of St. Sophia consecrated it on October 1, the day of the Intercession of the Holy Mother of God. O most Immaculate Sovereign Mother of God, Mother of Christ our God, keep Thy church steadfast in Thy name, O Lady, holy and indestructible to the end of the whole world! Accept, Sovereign Lady, the prayer of Thy slave *Vladyka* Ioan, granting him Thy grace and Thy spiritual blessing as shepherd of Christ's talking flock; and grant him, Sovereign Lady, long life with all his children, the men of Novgorod, together with those who have served Thy holy house, Sovereign Lady; and in the world to come help, Sovereign Lady, to place him by Thy great mercy at the right hand of Thy son our God!

The same year the Tartar *Tsar* Temir Kutlui sent his envoys to *Knyaz* Vitovt Kestutievich of Lithuania saying thus: " Deliver to me our fugitive *Tsar* Takhtomysh; and whatsoever he may have about him, that is thine." And *Knyaz* Vitovt having heard this replied to the *Tsar's* envoy: " I will not deliver up *Tsar* Takhtomysh; but I wish to meet the *Tsar*." And *Knyaz* Vitovt went with all his *Knyazes* and with all the forces of Lithuania against the *Tsar* Temir Kutlui; and reaching the Vorskla he halted there in the Tartar country.

[1] September 1.
[2] Joseph, Bishop of Salonika, February 7.
[3] July 27–September 13.
[4] Near Novgorod.

And the *Tsar*, having heard of the arrival of *Knyaz* Vitovt, sent envoys to him with a last word: " Inasmuch as thou hast come to fight us, and hast refused to deliver up the fugitive *Tsar*, and we have not encroached on thy lands, nor taken from thee any of thy towns or villages; therefore, let God and the truth be for all of us."[1]

And so both armies came into conflict, and there was such a fierce battle as had never been between Lithuania and the Tartars. And no small disaster befell the children of Lithuania for their sins; and here they killed the *Veliki Knyaz* Andrei Olgerdovich and his brother *Knyaz* Mikhail Evnutievich in the encounter, and in all seventy-four noble *Knyazes*; and of *Voyevodas* and other Lithuanians who laid their bones there, only God knows the number; and *Knyaz* Vitovt seeing this turned and fled, and the Tartars followed in pursuit of them for 500 *versts*,[2] as far as the town of Kiev, and from the town of Kiev they took a ransom of 500 *roubles*, and set their own lieutenants there; and they took from the Pechersk monastery a ransom of thirty *roubles*. For thus did God bring the pagan Tartars upon the land of Lithuania because of the pride of their *Knyaz*; for God had given Vitovt to the land of Lithuania as its *Veliki Knyaz*, for the sins of the Christians. For *Knyaz* Vitovt had previously been a Christian, and his name was Alexander, but he renounced the Orthodox faith and Christianity, and adopted the Polish[3] faith, and perverted the holy churches into service that is hateful to God, and he thought thus: he would conquer the Russian Land and Novgorod and Pskov, but he thought not of the Lord saying through the Prophet, how: " One shall reap a thousand; and two shall move ten thousand." If God be for the Christians, who shall come against us? And this battle was on the 5th day of August, on the eve of St. Saviour's, the day of the holy Martyr Eusegni.

The same autumn there was a darkening of the sun; and there was darkness, and the sun disappeared, and the form of a scythe appeared in the sky, and then the sun appeared emitting blood-red rays with smoke, in the month of October, on the day of the holy Martyr Anastasia.[4]

The same winter *Vladyka* Ioan went to Pskov on visitation, and the men of Pskov gave great honour to their Lord father *Vladyka*

[1] sc. judge between us.
[2] About 330 miles.
[3] *Lyadskaya vera;* Lyakh, a Pole.
[4] November 11.

Ioan; and they gave him jurisdiction to judge for a month, as of old.   And *Vladyka* Ioan left for Novgorod, and blessed his children, the men of Pskov.

A.D. 1400. A.M. 6908.   *Vladyka* Ioan laid the foundation of the *Detinets*[1] wall from [the Church of] SS. Boris and Gleb in the month of July, on the Commemoration Day of the holy Martyr Golendukha [and the Church of] the Holy Resurrection at the gate was freshly painted by order of *Vladyka* Ioan.   They erected a stone church in Yanev Street to *Tsar* Kostyantin and his mother Olena,[2] and it was consecrated by *Vladyka* Ioan.

The same autumn Klimenti Vasilievich, *Posadnik's* son, went as envoy from Novgorod to Lithuania to *Knyaz* Vitovt, and took peace on the old terms.

A.D. 1401. A.M. 6909.   *Vladyka* Ioan went to Moscow from Novgorod to the Metropolitan Kiprian, summoned by him on ecclesiastical business, on Wednesday of the fourth week in Lent, March 6, and the Metropolitan received him.

The same autumn the *Vladyka's* town at Molvotitsy was burnt.

The same year against the peace and against their kissing of the Cross, by order of the *Veliki Knyaz*, Anfal Mikitin and Gerasim Rostriga with a force of the *Veliki Knyaz* came against the Dvina beyond the *Volok*; and took all the Dvina country by assault by surprise, on St. Peter's Day,[3] hanged some of the Christians and slew others, and took their cattle and their belongings.   They seized Ondrei Ivanovich and the *Posadniks* of the Dvina, Esip Filipovich and Naum Ivanovich.   And Stepan Ivanovich, his brother Mikhail, and Mikita Golovna collecting around them the Vod people, and overtaking Anfailo and Gerasim fought them at Kolmogory and recovered from them the Novgorod *Boyars* Andrei, Esif and Naum.   At the same time the *Veliki Knyaz* Vasili Dmitrievich sent his *Boyars* Alexander Pol and Ivan Narin, with a body of 300 men, against Torzhok; they seized Simeon Vasilievich and Mikhail Fefilatov, against their kissing of the Cross, and took their property out of St. Saviour's.

The same autumn the people of Smolensk accepted Yuri Svyatoslavich as their *Knyaz*, and killed *Knyaz* Roman of Bryansk, lieutenant of *Knyaz* Vitovt.   And *Knyaz* Vitovt came to Smolensk with

---
[1] Citadel.
[2] Constantine and Helena.
[3] July 11.

all the forces of Lithuania, and remained by the town for four weeks, and they beat on the town with guns [*sic*] and he withdrew from the town and took peace with *Knyaz* Yuri on the old terms. And the people of Smolensk with their *Knyaz* Yuri put to death those of their *Boyars* who had been in secret communication with *Knyaz* Vitovt.

A.D. 1402. A.M. 6910. There was a sign in the sky, a tailed star, having a bright ray in the west, which lasted all the month of March.

Knyaz Roslav[1] Olgovich of Ryazan ravaged the country of Lithuania, and *Knyaz* Simeon Olgerdovich attacked him, captured *Knyaz* Roslav and led him to *Knyaz* Vitovt, and destroyed his force and captured some of them.

The men of Novgorod took peace with *Knyaz* Yuri of Smolensk. *Knyaz* Oleg of Ryazan died.

The same year the *Veliki Knyaz* Vasili let Simeon and Mikhail, the two men of Novgorod whom he had seized, go from Moscow back to Novgorod.

The Chudinets quarter erected a stone Church of the Decapitation of St. Ioan the Forerunner, and the Chernichinets quarter erected a stone church to St. Barbara, and the three sons of *Posadnik* Kyuril Ondreyanovich built a side chapel to St. Mikhail in Prussian Street.

And this winter from St. Georgi's Day up to March, horses could go over the Volkhov.

A.D. 1403. A.M. 6911. The Novgorod merchant-butchers erected in [the town of] Russa a stone church to SS. Boris and Gleb. The Carpenters' quarter[2] as far as Slavkova Street was burnt, and Rogatitsa [Street] as far as St. Eupati, the Lyubyanitsa [Street] as far as St. Luke, and the entire Slavno quarter, and fifteen stone churches were partially burnt; the fire occurred on August 16, the Day of the Holy Effigy; but the *Knyaz* quay and the Gothic[3] Court did not catch fire.

Knyaz Simeon Olgerdovich took the towns of Smolensk and Vyazma, and he captured the *Knyazes* Ivan Svyatoslavich and Alexander Mikhailovich.

The same year there was a plague with swellings in Pskov, and

[1] Rodislav.
[2] *Plotniki.*
[3] i.e. Hanseatic.

the stone Church of St. Dmitri was burnt throughout; the *ikons* and books and much property were burnt.

A.D. 1404. A.M. 6912. *Knyaz* Vitovt of Lithuania came with all his forces up to the town of Smolensk and remained near the town three months, and withdrew.

Vladyka Ioan arrived in Novgorod on the 15th day of July, having been with the Metropolitan Kiprian in Moscow three years and four months; and *Igumens* and priests and the choir of St. Sophia and all Novgorod met him in Novgorod at St. Nikola in Yaroslav Court with crosses; and there was great rejoicing over their *Vladyka*.

The same year *Knyaz* Yuri Svyatoslavich went from Smolensk to Moscow to bow to the *Veliki Knyaz* Vasili that he might defend him from the *Veliki Knyaz* Vitovt; and at that time traitors delivered over the town of Smolensk to the Lithuanian *Knyaz* Vitovt; on hearing that his town was taken, *Knyaz* Yuri of Smolensk came to Novgorod and the men of Novgorod received him.

A.D. 1405. A.M. 6913. In Yanev Street fifteen houses were burnt and six persons; and then the Lyudin quarter and Prussian Street as far as St. Mikhail's were burnt, and in the *Detinets*[1] the fire extended to the *Vladyka's* Court; five wooden churches were burnt and two of stone were partially burnt, and the Church of Boris and Gleb was entirely burnt, also thirty people.

Posadnik Vasili Ivanovich died, having entered the monastic order.

The Lithuanian *Knyaz* Vitovt took the Pleskov settlement at Kolozhe against the peace, and halted at Voronats two days, ravaging many of the Pleskov districts, making surprise attacks, and killed many Christians, and took others into captivity.

A.D. 1406. A.M. 6914. *Knyaz* Peter, brother of the *Veliki Knyaz* Vasili Dmitrievich, came to Novgorod and stayed in Novgorod a week and a half. The same year heavy ice came from the lake[2] and broke away a stay of the great bridge, on Easter Day, April 11.

There was a fire in Novgorod in the *Knyaz's* Court, on the commercial side, and six persons perished; the fire extended from the Gothic[3] Court to Pleskov Court.

[1] Citadel.
[2] sc. Lake Ilmen.
[3] Hanseatic.

N

The town of Pskov[1] was burnt down on the Day of the [Descent of the] Holy Ghost; only Dovmont's wall and the Krom[2] did not burn.

The Metropolitan Kiprian died in Moscow.

The men of Pskov went to war on Polotsk, and they nearly took the town, and after ravaging the districts of Polotsk, they withdrew. A Master of Riga,[3] named Korto, came up to Pskov with all the forces of the *Nemtsy*, and retired after ravaging the districts.

Three churches were erected: the Nativity of St. Ioan the Forerunner, in the Rostkin monastery, SS. Peter and Paul in the Nerev quarter, and St. Nikita in the Carpenters' quarter.

The same autumn *Knyaz* Yuri left Novgorod for Moscow.

The same winter the men of Pskov went to ravage the country of the *Nemtsy* under the leadership of *Knyaz* Danilo Alexandrovich, lieutenant of the *Veliki Knyaz*, and the *Nen* *y* met them beyond Novogrodek. And they fought there, an·   od helped *Knyaz* Danilo and the men of Pskov against the pagan *·mtsy*, and they pursued them fighting fifteen *versts* as far as Kiry..,iva; they took some alive and brought them to Pskov.

There was then a plague with glands in Pskov.

A.D. 1407. A.M. 6915. *Vladyka* Feodul[4] of Trebizond came to Novgorod from *Tsargrad*[5] for alms.

On the 6th day of June a great calamity ι fell: the Nerev quarter was burnt as far as the town wall, and St. Sophia was entirely burnt, and the *Vladyka's* Court and Lyudgoshcha Street, and twelve churches of stone were partially burnt and six of wood were burnt down.

The men of Pskov invaded the country of the *Nemtsy*, led by Kostyantin, brother of the *Veliki Knyaz;* and they took their town of Porkh, and after ravaging many villages, they went back to Pskov and *Knyaz* Kostyantin went away to Moscow.

The same year *Knyaz* Simeon Olgerdovich came to Novgorod, and the men of Novgorod gave him the appanages which had been his previously.

The *Nemtsy* entered the Pskov country and camped at Komen,[6]

---

[1] Pskov = Pleskov.
[2] A part of Pskov.
[3] sc. of the German Order of Knights.
[4] Theodoulos.
[5] Constantinople.
[6] The town of *Kamen-Bely*—White Stone.

short of Pskov. And the men of Pskov coming out of the town attacked them, but the *Nemtsy* defeated the men of Pskov and killed three *Posadniks* of Pskov: Ephrem Kortats, Elentei[1] Lubka, Penkrat, and many others fell on both sides. And the *Nemtsy* went away, having caused much evil to the Christians; and there was lamentation and not gladness in Pskov.

Vladyka Ioan erected a stone church on the [river] Verenda to the Transfiguration of St. Saviour and consecrated it himself, and he established a monastery. They erected a stone church to St. Vlas in the Lyudin quarter. The two cousins, Yuri Dmitrievich, the *Posadnik*, and Yakov, erected a wonderful stone church to Mikhail the *Archistrategos* of Khony[2] in the Arkadi monastery.

A.D. 1408. A.M. 6916. *Knyaz* Kostyantin Dmitrievich came to Novgorod as lieutenant from his brother the *Veliki Knyaz* sili.

Vladyka Ioa covered St. Sophia with lead and built a large gold-topped cupola.

The same winter Edegei, father-in-law of Shadebeg the Tartar *Tsar*, went with a great force to war against Moscow on November 23; and the *Tsar* himself camped before Moscow, and spread his troops over the Russian Land, and they took the towns of Pereyaslavl, Rostov, Nizhni-Novgorod, and Serpukhov, and they slew many Christians, and took others into captivity. And they ravaged as far as Klin, to the boundaries of Tver, cutting down Christians all the time like grass; and took from the town of Moscow a ransom of three thousand *roubles;* and on leaving the Russian Land they took the town of Ryazan.

A.D. 1409. A.M. 6917. *Knyaz* Danilo died in Pskov, and *Posadnik* Timofei Yurievich in Novgorod.

Vladyka Ioan built a house of stone where they bless the water every month, also a bakery of stone.

The same year the men of Pskov took peace with Lithuania and with the *Nemtsy*, having been at war with the *Nemtsy* three years.

Posadnik Esif Zakharinich died.

The same winter, on the 30th day of November, the Day of the Holy Apostle Andrew, there was a terrifying wonder in the Church of St. Mikhail at Skovorodka[3]: there was a noise in the dome; and

[1] i.e. Leonti.
[2] Khony, near Hierapolis, in Phrygia.
[3] Near Novgorod.

the priests and monks of St. Mikhail heard this noise for two days and two nights.

A.D. 1410. A.M. 6918.   The Metropolitan Foti[1] arrived in Novgorod from *Tsargrad*, appointed by the Patriarch Matvei under *Tsar* Manuel.

Knyaz Volodimir Andreyevich died in Moscow, and *Posadnik* Yuri Dmitrievich in Novgorod.

There was a sign from the image of the Holy Mother of God to which prayers were offered in the Church of St. Georgi at the end of Lubyanka[2] Street.

The same year on the 15th day of July there was a battle[3] between King Yagailo Olgerdovich, named Volodislav, with the *Veliki Knyaz* Vitovt Kestutievich of Lithuania and the Prussian *Nemtsy* in their country of Prussia between the towns of Dubravna and Ostrod, and they killed the Master[4] and the *Morshold*[5] and the *Kuntury*,[6] and defeated the entire army of the *Nemtsy;* and took the towns of the *Nemtsy*, only three towns did not surrender to the King and Vitovt. The same autumn the Poles[7] and the Lithuanians had three battles with the *Nemtsy*, and thrice they defeated the *Nemtsy;* and in all these battles many Christians, both Lithuanians and Poles,[7] were slain by the *Nemtsy*.   And they stood before the fortified town of Marien[8] eight weeks, and took two outlying forts of Marien, but the upper third fort they did not take; and they campaigned in the land of the *Nemtsy* eleven and a half weeks.

The same year *Knyaz* Danilei Borisovich, whose old patrimony was Nizhni Novgorod, seized the capital city of Volodimir, taking its people captive, and burning it; and the Tartars stripped the gold-topped Church of the Holy Mother of God.

The same year the Archimandrite Varlam erected a stone church in the gateway of Lisitsa monastery, in the name of the most righteous Varlam, *Igumen* of St. Saviour of Khutin; and in Russa they erected two stone churches: to St. Georgi, and to the Annunciation of the Mother of God.

The same year the men of Novgorod began to trade among

[1] Photius.
[2] Lyubyanitsa.
[3] The battle of Tannenberg.
[4] sc. of the Order of Teutonic Knights.
[5] Marshal.
[6] Commanders.
[7] *Lyakhi.*
[8] Marienburg near Danzig, the capital (since 1307) of the Teutonic order.

themselves in *lopatses*[1] and Lithuanian *groshes* and *Nemetski artugs*,[2] doing away with *kunas*,[3] in the *Posadnik*-ship of Grigori Bogdanovich and the *Tysyatski* Vasili Esifovich.

On December 21 there was a sign from the image of the holy Martyrs Guri, Samon and Aviv, in the Church of St. Sophia.

The same winter *Posadnik* Kiril Ondreyanovich died, having entered the monastic order.

Yagailo and Vitovt again went to Marien town, and after defeating the forces of the *Nemtsy*, took peace.

A.D. 1411. A.M. 6919. The *Svei* having come to make war took the Novgorod town of Tiversk; the men of Novgorod went quickly against the *Svei* only three days after this news, with *Knyaz* Simeon Olgerdovich; and having come to the *Sveiski* country they ravaged and burned their villages, and killed many *Svei* and captured others, and took and burned an outwork of Viborg on March 26, the day of the Festival of the Archangel Gabriel, and returned to Novgorod with a large number of captives. And the *Voyevodas* of the Novgorod troops were: *Posadnik* Yuri Ontsiforovits, *Posadnik* Foma Esifovits, *Posadnik* Alexander Fominits, Ivan Danilovits, Gregori Bogdanovits, Ofonos Esifov, *Posadnik's* son, Mikhailo Ivanovits, *Posadnik's* son, Andrei Ivanovits, Ivan Fedorovits, *Posadnik's* son, Foma Troshcheikin, Dmitri Ivanovits, Esip Philipovits, Avram Stefanovits.

And the *Nemtsy* at Viborg killed only one man: Paul of Nutna Street.

Vladyka Ioan erected a miracle-working church of stone to the Holy Confessors.

By order from Novgorod the *Posadnik* of the Dvina, *Voyevoda* Yakov Stepanovits went from the country beyond the *Volok* to make war against the Murman people, and ravaged their country.

The same winter *Vladyka* Ioan went to Moscow to the Metropolitan Foti.

A.D. 1412. A.M. 6920. They erected a stone church to St. Nikola at Porkhov, another of wood to St. Nikola by the bridge on the [river] Veryazh, in the monastery, and a third of wood to the Holy Trinity at Klopsko.[4]

[1] Properly *lobtsi* or *lobki*, skins of the little foreheads of squirrels.
[2] A Swedish copper coin.
[3] Squirrel skins.
[4] Near Novgorod.

Lugven[1] went away to Lithuania and withdrew the lieutenants from the Novgorod townships.

And *Knyaz* Vasili of Moscow and Ivan of Tver went to the Horde to *Tsar* Zeleni-Sultan, the son of Takhtamysh.   And King Yagailo and Vitovt and Lugven[1] sent a challenge to Novgorod on January 2. And the King and Vitovt spoke thus: " You undertook to be on our side; if the *Nemtsy* combine against us, you would combine against the *Nemtsy;* and that we should stand as one man together and strengthen ourselves on both sides against all chances if this should happen; but if this should not be necessary, then nothing would come of it; and we moreover sent our *Boyars* Nemir and Zinovi Bratoshich [to find out] whether you stand by the aforesaid word. And you replied to Nemir: 'Novgorod cannot do this; we are at peace both with Lithuania and with the *Nemtsy*. We took over *Knyaz* Lugven[1] from amongst you; and with the *Nemtsy* we have taken perpetual peace, and we are at peace with the *Ugry* people,[2] and with all on our borders.'   And you having forgotten your word have not kept it, to be on our side; and besides, your people have upbraided us, dishonoured us, and put us to shame, calling us pagans; and above all, you have received our enemy Fedor, the son of Yuri Svyatoslavich."

And Lugven[1] spoke thus: " You kept me with you and fed me; but now it pleases not my elder brethren, the King and Vitovt, and it pleases me not because I am with them as one man; and I renounce the kissing of the Cross."

And *Knyaz* Fedor said to the men of Novgorod: " Do not be at enmity with Vitovt on my account "; and he went off to the *Nemtsy*.

A.D. 1413. A.M. 6921. *Vladyka* Ioan with the *Voyevodas* of Novgorod and their soldiers who had been in Viborg, and by Christian help, erected the stone Church of the Festival of the Archangel Gavril[3] in Khrevkov Street, and he consecrated it himself on his festival day.   And Ivan Morozov erected a stone church to the Conception of St. Ioan the Forerunner in the Desyatina.

Tver was burnt down.

The same year in the patrimony of *Knyaz* Andrei Dmitrievich, ten *versts* beyond the town of Mozhaisk, abundant grace and pardon

[1] sc. *Knyaz* Simeon Olgerdovich.
[2] sc. Hungarians.
[3] sc. Gabriel.

to people appeared from the image of the Holy Mother of God; to the blind, the lame, the feeble, the deaf and the dumb; it is not possible to name or count them; the mind of man cannot express how great is God's love of man and how great is his mercy towards men.

And *Vladyka* Ioan went to Pskov.

A.D. 1414. A.M. 6922. The Metropolitan Foti went to Lithuania and Vitovt robbed him.

The *Vladyka's* house in the monastery in the Derevyanitsa was burnt, and the stone Church of the Holy Mother of God was partially burnt, and a man was burnt.

The same spring envoys from Novgorod went to Lithuania: *Posadnik* Yuri Ontsiforovich, Ofonos[1] Fedorovich, *Posadnik's* son, and Fedor Tryablo; and they took peace with Vitovt on the old terms.

There was a heavy sickness among the Christians.

A fire broke out in the Nerev quarter on August 3, which extended from St. Volodimir to the [stream] Gzen; eight stone and five wooden churches were burnt.   They completed the stone Church of St. Euphemia in the Carpenters' quarter[2] the same autumn.

Vladyka Ioan was shorn into the *schema*.[3]   *Posadnik* Kiril Dmitrievich died.   The same winter on January 20, *Vladyka* Ioan retired from the Archbishopric, having occupied the Archbishopric thirty years less three.

A.D. 1415. A.M. 6923. The water flowed backwards.[4]

The Tartars ravaged the country round Elets, and Moscow and Smolensk were burnt; and there was a sign in the sun on June 7.

Posadnik Fedosi Obakunovich died, in the monastic order.   They erected a Church of the Holy Trinity in the monastery on the [river] Vidogoshch.

The same year the men of Novgorod deliberating in Yaroslav's Court, and holding a *Veche* at St. Sophia, placed three lots with their names written on the altar: Samson, monk of St. Saviour at Khutin, Mikhail, *Igumen* of St. Mikhail at Skovorodka,[5] and Lev, *Igumen* of the Holy Mother of God at Kolmovo[5]; and at the end of

[1] Athanasius.
[2] *Plotniki.*
[3] cf. p. 34.
[4] sc. into the lake, owing to floods lower down.
[5] Near Novgorod.

the holy service the old Archpriest Vasili brought out to the *Veche*, first Lev's lot, then Mikhail's, and Samson's remained on the altar; then *Posadnik* Ondrei Ivanovich and the *Tysyatski* Olexander Ignatievich with the men of Novgorod, raised Samson honourably to the threshold[1] of the house of St. Sophia on Sunday, August 11, the day of the holy Martyr the Deacon Eupl. The same day the wooden Church of the Holy Resurrection of the Lord on Krasnaya Gorka[2] in the Carpenters' quarter was consecrated, and a monastery was established. The same autumn they completed two stone churches in the Lyudin quarter: that of the Holy Exaltation [of the Cross] of the Lord, and that of St. Luke.

The same autumn, by the sufferance of God, and the will of *Knyaz* Vitovt of Lithuania, [Vitovt] by his own wish having collected the Christian Bishops residing within his province—Feodosi of Polotsk, Isaak of Chernigov, Dionisi of Lutsk, Gerasim of Volodimir, Khariton of Holm, Eufimi of Turov—over those Bishops, put as Metropolitan, Gregory the Bulgarian, at Kiev on November 15.

The same winter, on February 23, in Sexagesima Week, Samson went to the Metropolitan for confirmation as *Vladyka;* and with him envoys from Novgorod: Vasili Obakunovich, the *Tysyatski* Vasili Esifovich, and the *Tysyatski* Olexander Ignatievich; and they reached Moscow.

A.D. 1416. A.M. 6924. On March 9, the day of the Forty Martyrs, after the full service on Monday, and on Thursday of that week, the 12th, God granted grace in the Church of the Holy Mother of God by the tomb of the Metropolitan Peter: the shortened leg of a man was made whole; on the 15th in the second week of Lent, a nun's hand was cured. On that day the Metropolitan Foti confirmed Samson as Deacon, and on Saturday 21st, the third of Lent, he made him full priest, and on the 22nd, on Sunday in Mid-Lent on the day of the holy Father Vasili, he was confirmed *Vladyka* of Great Novgorod in the Church of the *Archistrategos* Mikhail, and was named Simeon by the Metropolitan, and there were present with the Metropolitan at the confirmation five *Vladykas*: Grigori of Rostov, Mitrofan of Suzdal, Antoni of Tver, Timofei of Sarsk, and Isaki of Perm; and the *Veliki Knyaz* Vasili Dmitrievich was present together with his brothers Yuri and Kostyantin; and he came to Novgorod on April 16, on Great Thursday

[1] cf. p. 123.
[2] The Red Hill.

[in Holy Week]. And *Posadnik* Ivan Bogdanovich, the *Tysyatski* Boris Vasilievich, with the *Igumens* and the priests and the choir of St. Sophia met him with the crosses at the end of the Slavno quarter, and the men of Novgorod were glad of their *Vladyka*.

And on that day *Vladyka* Simeon performed a holy liturgy in St. Sophia, at his own altar granted to him by God.

They erected a church to St. Ilya in Prussian Street.

The same autumn two stone churches were completed: that of St. Peter, Metropolitan of Russia, and of St. Afanasi, by the efforts of *Vladyka* Simeon.

A.D. 1417. A.M. 6925. *Posadnik* Yuri Ontsiforovich died, having been dumb one year and three months. On June 10 there was a thunderstorm and in the Church of St. Eupati in Rogatitsa [Street] the images were burnt.

Vladyka Ioan died on the 24th of the same month the day of the Birth of St. Ioan the Forerunner, in the monastery on the [river] Derevyanitsa, and he was laid in the porch of the Holy Resurrection. And *Knyaz* Ivan, son of the *Veliki Knyaz* Vasili, died in Moscow.

The same year six stone churches were completed: the Holy Trinity at Kolmovo,[1] St. Nikola, St. Mina in Danislav Street, St. Andrew in Shchitna[2] Street, St. Andrei by St. Saviour's at Khutin,[1] and St. Nikola in Kholop town.[3]

The same year Gleb Semenovich, a *Boyar* of *Knyaz* Yuri, with some fugitives from Novgorod, together with Simeon Zhadovski and Mikhail Rossokhin, and with men of Ustyug and of Vyatka, the patrimony of the *Veliki Knyaz*, went from Vyatka secretly in boats to the country beyond the *Volok;* they ravaged Borok, a district of the sons of Ivan Vasilievich, and also took and burnt the districts of Yemtsa and Kolmogory, and captured the Novgorod *Boyars* Yuri, Ivanovich and his brother Samson. Ivan Fedorovich and his brother Afonosi with Gavrilo Kirilovich and Isak Ondreyevich, having come up with them on an island by Morzh, rescued their brethren Samson and Yuri, and all the captives and the cattle, and let them[4] go free. And Vasili Yurievich, *Posadnik's* son, Simeon Ivanovich, Gavrilo Kirilovich and his brother Grigori with men from the country beyond the *Volok* pursued the robbers and pillaged Ustyug.

1 Near Novgorod.
2 " Shieldmakers."
3 In Novgorod.
4 sc. the fugitives.

At that time the men of Novgorod took peace with the *Nemtsy*.

The same summer and winter there was a fearful plague among the people in Novgorod, and in Ladoga, in Russa, Porkhov, Pskov, Tver, Dmitrov, and in Torzhok, and throughout their districts and villages. And how can I relate the fearful and terrible misery that there was during the whole plague? What grief the living had for the dead, for the deaths increased so in towns and villages that the living had barely time to make the dead tidy for burial; so many died every day, that they had not time to bury them; and many houses were closed unoccupied. First of all it would hit one as if with a lance, choking, and then a swelling would appear, or spitting of blood with shivering, and fire would burn one in all the joints of the body; and then the illness would overwhelm one; and many after lying in that illness died. But to many Christians God was merciful: they left this life entering the angelic order after receiving holy unction from the *Vladyka*. And two *Posadniks* died in the same order: Ivan Olexandrovich and Boris Vasilievich.

And *Vladyka* Simeon with all the seven congregations, with the Christians and with crosses went round the whole of Great Novgorod, praying God and His Immaculate Mother to withhold the wrath of God; and the Christians on horseback and afoot drew logs from the forest and built a church to St. Anastasia which was consecrated the same day by the *Vladyka* Simeon who performed a holy liturgy; with the remainder of the logs, they erected a church to St. Ilya in Prussian Street. And the people of Novi-torg put up a church to St. Afanasi likewise in a single day, and performed a liturgy.

A.D. 1418. A.M. 6926. There was a sign in the Church of the Holy Martyr Anastasia: blood seemed to come from both sides of the robe of the image of the Holy Mother of God, on April 19.

The same month this happened in Novgorod at the instigation of the devil: a certain man Stepanko seized hold of the *Boyar* Danilo Ivanovich, Bozha's grandson, and, holding him, cried out to the people: "Here, sirs! help me against this miscreant." And seeing his cry[1] folk dragged him like a miscreant to the people, beating him with wounds nearly to death, and they led him from the *Veche* and hurled him from the bridge. And a certain man of the people, Lichko's son, wishing him well, caught him up into his boat; but the people, enraged against that fisherman, plundered his house. And

[1] *Sic.*

the aforesaid *Boyar*, wishing to avenge his dishonour, caught the
impostor and put him to torture, and wishing to cure the evil,
raised up still greater trouble; I will not recall the spoken words:
" Vengeance is mine."   And the people learning that Stepanko had
been seized, began to summon a *Veche* in Yaroslav's Court, and a
multitude of people assembled, and they kept shouting and crying
for many days: " Let us go against that *Boyar* and plunder his
house."   And they came armed and with a banner to Kuzma-
Demyan Street, sacked his house and many other houses, and
ravaged the quay in Yanev Street.   And the people of Kuzma-
Demyan Street became afraid at these robberies that worse would
befall them, surrendered Stepanko, and coming to the *Vladyka*
prayed him to send him to the meeting of the people.   And the
prelate heard their prayer and sent him with a priest and one of his
own *Boyars*, and they received him.   And again they became
enraged like drunkards, against another *Boyar*, Ivan Ievlich,[1]
of Chudinets Street, and on his account pillaged a great many
Boyars' houses, as well as the monastery of St. Nikola in the Field,
crying out: " Here is the treasure house of the *Boyars*."   And
again the same morning they plundered many houses in the Lyudgoshcha Street, calling out: " They are our enemies."   And they
came to Prussian Street, but there they beat them off successfully.
And from that hour the mischief began to increase.   Returning
to their own, the commercial side, they said: " The Sophia side is
going to arm against us, and to plunder our houses."   And they
began to ring throughout the whole town, and armed men began to
pour out from both sides as for war, fully armed, to the great bridge.
And there was loss of life too.   Some fell by arrows, others by arms,
they died as in war, the whole town trembled at this terrible storm
and great rebellion and a ·dread fell on the people on both sides.
And *Vladyka* Simeon shed tears from his eyes on hearing of the
internecine war between his children, and he ordered those under
him to gather his congregation; and the *Vladyka*, having entered
the Church of St. Sophia, began to pray with tears, and arraying
himself in his vestments with his clergy he ordered them to take the
Lord's Cross and the image of the Holy Mother of God, and went to
the bridge, and there followed him the priests and servants of the
church and all who called themselves Christians, and a great multitude, shedding tears and saying: " O Lord, make it to cease by the

[1] Son of Job (Yev.).

prayers of our lord.[1] " And God-fearing people fell in tears at the
feet of the prelate saying: " Go, Lord, and may the lord cause this
internecine war to cease, through thy blessing." And others said:
" May this evil be on the heads of those who began the fighting."
And on reaching the middle of the bridge the prelate raised the life-
giving Cross and began to bless both sides. And those who looked
at the honourable Cross wept. The opposite side, hearing of the prelate's arrival, *Posadnik* Fedor Timofeich came with other *Posadniks*
and *Tysyatskis* and bowed to the *Vladyka;* and the *Vladyka* heard
their prayer and sent the Archimandrite Varlam and his spiritual
father, and an archdeacon to Yaroslav's Court to bestow the
blessing on the acting *Posadnik* Vasili Esifovich and on the *Tysyatski*
Kuzma Terenteyevich, to go to their homes; and they dispersed
through the prayers of the Holy Mother of God and with the blessing
of *Vladyka* Simeon, and there was peace in the town.

That same year four stone churches were erected: All Saints in
Chernitsyn Street, St. Sava in Kuzma-Demyan Street, St. Ilya by
St. Saviour's in the general monastery of Christ's Resurrection at
Khutin, and St. Nikola on the [stream] Pidba.

The same autumn *Vladyka* Simeon went on his periodic visitation
to Pskov and sat there for a month in judgment.

A.D. 1419. A.M. 6927. On May 1 the Slavno and Carpenters'
quarters[2] as far as the Fedor stream were
burnt down; twenty-four churches were burnt, and that of the
Holy Fathers was entirely destroyed by fire; a large quantity of the
property of the Christians was burnt, and many people were drowned
in the Volkhov and many were burnt.

The same year *Posadnik* Ivan Bogdanovich died.

During evening service on April 9, Sunday, there was a violent
storm of wind, and clouds and very thick rain; the water from the
springs ran like a strong river; lightning flashed, and there was
terrible thunder, and it killed the watchman Andrei in the Church
of the Holy Mother of God by the town gates; the chain of the
candelabra from the ceiling of the cupola was all torn; and the Holy
Gates were burnt; it caused damage in [the churches of] St. Ioan the
Forerunner, of St. Nikola and of St. Vasili, but by God's mercy the
churches were spared, but below the churches in the gateway two
men were killed, others fell down as dead, and others were struck

---

[1] *Gospodin*, sc. the *Vladyka*.
[2] *Plotniki.*

deaf; some lost their legs, and others were struck dumb, but by the mercy of God they were assuaged with water and carried to their homes, where, after having lain down a little on their beds, by the grace of God they got up again; and at that same time the *ikons* in the Church of St. Kostyantin were scorched.

The same year the Murman people[1] to the number of 500 men coming in vessels and boats made war on the Korel[2] villages in [the district of] Arzuga and on the villages[3] of the country beyond the *Volok*, namely: Nenoksa, the monastery of St. Nikola in the Korel[2] country, Konechny village, the Yakov gulf, the Ondreyan shore, Kig and Kyar islands, Mikhail monastery, Chiglonim and Khechinima; they burned three churches and slew Christians and monks. But the men from beyond the *Volok* destroyed two boats of the Murman people; the others escaped out to sea.

The Archimandrite Varlam erected a church in the Yurev monastery to the Nativity of the Mother of God, and Mikhail Yurievich put up a wooden church to St. Mikhail at Kolmovo, and *Igumen* Fedosi put up a stone church to the Holy Trinity in Klopsko in sixty days.

The same year the Lithuanian Metropolitan Grigori of Kiev died, who had been appointed by order of Vitovt's Bishops, and not by the Patriarch, not in accordance with the ordinances of the Holy Fathers and the Apostles.

The same year *Knyaz* Kostyantin Dmitrievich came to Novgorod from Moscow. And by the grace of God and with the blessing of *Vladyka* Simeon the men of Novgorod received him with all hónour on February 25 in great congregation. And they granted him the appanages which had been Lugven's,[4] and allowed him to make a tax collection over all Novgorod districts. And this is why he was in Novgorod, because his brother the *Veliki Knyaz* Vasili wished to make him kiss the Cross in submission to his son Vasili; and not wishing to be under his nephew, *Knyaz* Vasili, he[5] cast on him his displeasure and deprived him of all his patrimony, seized his *Boyars* and appropriated their cattle and villages.

A.D. 1420. A.M. 6928.   The men of Novgorod began to trade with silver coins, and sold the *artugs*[6] to the *Nemtsy*, having traded with them nine years.

[1] Northmen, or Norwegians.
[2] *Korilsky*.
[3] *Pogost*, villages, settlements, small colonies or outposts.
[4] sc. *Knyaz* Simeon Olgerdovich of Lithuania.
[5] sc. the *Veliki Knyaz*.
[6] Swedish copper coins.

190 THE CHRONICLE OF NOVGOROD

There was a great plague in Pskov.

The same autumn an envoy from the Master Selivester from the *Nemtsy* arrived in Novgorod, the Commander Gostilo of Velyad, with Timofei, the Master's nephew, and the *Voyevoda* of Rugodiv,[1] and they agreed with *Knyaz* Kostyantin and with all Great Novgorod to meet at a conference with the Master and *Knyaz;* Kostyantin and Novgorod to send their *Boyars* and they sent *Knyaz* Fedor Patrikeyevich, lieutenant of the *Veliki Knyaz, Posadnik* Vasili Esifovich of Novgorod, *Posadnik* Afonosi Fedorovich, Yakov Dmitrievich, Mikhail Yurievich, and Naum Ivanovich. And they met the Master at Narova and took perpetual peace on the old terms, as it was under the *Veliki Knyaz* Alexander Yaroslavich.

A.D. 1421. A.M. 6929. *Knyaz* Kostyantin departed from Great Novgorod, and *Vladyka* Simeon, the *Posadniks* and the *Tysyatskis* and the *Boyars* of Novgorod bestowing gifts on him sent him off with honour.

The same year the water was big in the Volkhov; and washed away the great bridge, also the Neredich and the Zhilotug bridges.[2] At Kolomentsa[3] it carried away the Church of the Holy Trinity, and in Shchilova, Sokolnitsa, and Radokovitsi [Streets] and in the Resurrection in the Lyudin quarter service in the churches was performed only on raised platforms, and in the different quarters it washed away dwellings with all their stores; and it was so great that it poured out through the town gates to Rybniki.[4]

The same year on May 19, during Peter's Fast, there was a great storm by night in the skies; clouds came up from the south, and in the north thunder and fiery lightning came from the skies with frightful noise, and purple rain fell with stones and hail. And *Vladyka* Simeon going at dawn on Monday into St. Sophia with the hierarchy and choir, ordered prayers to be sung to the Holy Mother of God for the whole Christian race, to avert the wrath of God.

The same year the two *Posadniks*, Fedor Timofeyevich and Olexander Fominich, died in monks' orders.

The same year on June 15, the day of the holy Prophet Amos, Simeon, *Vladyka* of Novgorod, died, he was *Vladyka* five years and three months short of five days, or six years altogether. The same year the men of Novgorod having deliberated in *Veche* in Yaro-

---

[1] i.e. Narva.
[2] Bridges over small tributaries of the Volkhov in Novgorod.
[3] Kolmovo, near Novgorod.
[4] The Fisheries.

slav's Court, and having held a *Veche* at St. Sophia placed three written lots on the altar in St. Sophia; *Igumen* Feodosi of the Holy Trinity at Klopsko, *Igumen* Zakhari of the Annunciation of the Holy Mother of God, and Arseni, the *Vladyka's* steward from Lisitsa[1] Hill; and on conclusion of holy service, the priest Trifan brought out first the lot of Arseni, then that of Zakhari, and Feodosi's lot remained on the altar. And *Posadnik* Timofei Vasilievich and the *Tysyatski* Kuzma Terentievich with the men of Novgorod raised *Igumen* Feodosi honourably to the threshold[2] of the house of St. Sophia on Monday, September 1, the day of the holy father Simeon Stylites.

The same year were completed three stone churches: the Manifestation of our Lord in the Field, the Resurrection in the monastery of the Annunciation, and of Ioan the Merciful in the Lyudin quarter; and the men of Novgorod kissed the Cross to be as one brother.

During these two years there were great famine and plague, and three public graves were filled with the dead, one behind the altar in St. Sophia and two by the Nativity in the field.[3]

A.D. 1423. A.M. 6931. There was a sign in the sun. The same year they completed two stone churches: of the Holy Mother of God at Kolmovo,[4] and of St. Yakov on the Luzhitsa.

A.D. 1424. A.M. 6932. The men of Novgorod sent away Feodosi to his own monastery, for he had sat two years in the threshold[2] in the House of St. Sophia, and in the same year they raised Emelian by lot to the altar in St. Sophia.

The same year they minted money in Pskov, and began to trade with coin throughout all the Russian Land.

There was a plague in the Korel Land. The same year there was a plague with glands and with spitting of blood in Novgorod.

Eufemi was appointed *Vladyka* by the Metropolitan Foti in Moscow. Two stone churches were completed; St. Luke in Lyubyanitsa [Street], and SS. Boris and Gleb on the [stream] Gzen. The same year *Vladyka* Eufemi built a church to St. Saviour the Merciful behind the altar of St. Sophia.

The same year the *Veliki Knyaz* Vasili Dmitrievich died.

[1] " Fox."
[2] cf. p. 123.
[3] No record for 1422.
[4] Near Novgorod.

A.D. 1425. A.M. 6933. The commercial side was burnt and the whole of the Lyudin quarter.

The same year the people of Ustyug ravaged the country beyond the *Volok*, and the men of Novgorod went to war against them to Ustyug and took a ransom on that place of fifty squirrel skins and six forties of sable.

The same year *Knyaz* Ivan Mikhailovich of Tver died.

Igumen Feodosi of the Holy Trinity died in his own monastery on September 29.

A.D. 1426. A.M. 6934. Vitovt stood under Voronach three weeks and withdrew without taking it.

A.D. 1427. A.M. 6935. The stone Church of St. Saviour the Merciful was completed by *Vladyka* Eufemi; and it was wonderfully fitted up with pictures and with books.

A.D. 1428. A.M. 6936. *Knyaz* Vitovt came to Porkhov with an armed force and the men of Porkhov agreed [to pay] for themselves 5,000 of silver; and then *Vladyka* Eufemi went to Porkhov with Novgorod envoys and paid Vitovt another 5,000 of silver and a sixth thousand for captives.

A.D. 1429. A.M. 6937. *Vladyka* Eufemi died on November 1, SS. Kuzma-Demyan Day, having been *Vladyka* five years and five weeks, and as monk he had sat at the threshold[1] one year and two weeks.

On the 13th of the same month the holy monk Eufemi of Lisitsa Hill was elected by lot and raised to the threshold[1] in the House of St. Sophia.

The same year the Church of the Holy Fathers in the *Knyaz's* Court collapsed.

A.D. 1430. A.M. 6938. They put up the Church of the Holy Fathers in stone in the same place in the *Knyaz's* Court.

The same year the men of Novgorod built another stone wall round Porkhov.

The same year there was a summons to Novgorod on the people for the building up of a wall; every fourth man furnished a fifth.

The same autumn *Knyaz* Vitovt of Lithuania died, and in his stead there took his seat on the throne *Knyaz* Svetrigailo.[2]

[1] cf. p. 123.
[2] Svidrigailo.

The same autumn the water was exceeding low; the soil and the forests burned, and very much smoke, some times people could not see each other, and fishes and birds died from that smoke; the fish stank of the smoke, for two years.

A.D. 1431. A.M. 6939.   The Metropolitan Foti[1] died in Moscow.
            The Russian *Knyazes* Yuri Dmitrevich and Vasili Vasilievich went to the Horde this year.

A.D. 1432. A.M. 6940.   The Russian *Knyazes* came away from the Horde, without the title of *Veliki Knyaz*.
A wooden church was erected to the Holy Apostles in Chudinets Street by the holy monk *Vladyka* Eufemi.
Knyaz Yuri Simeonovich arrived in Novgorod from Lithuania in the autumn.
The *Vladyka's* Court and all the surrounding quarter were burnt down in the same autumn.
A stone Church of St. Yuri was founded in Borkhov Street.

A.D. 1432. A.M. 6940.[2] The Russian *Knyazes* Vasili Vasilievich and Yuri Dmitrievich came away from the Horde; *Tsar* Mahmed gave the title of *Veliki Knyaz* over the whole Russian Land to *Knyaz* Vasili Vasilievich.
The same autumn *Knyaz* Yuri Simeonovich with his wife arrived in Novgorod from the Lithuanian country.

A.D. 1433. A.M. 6941.   A fire broke out in the spring in Yanev Street, spreading over the suburban quarter and the Lyudin quarter, as far as Lukin Street.
The same year the people of Borkhov Street completed the stone Church of St. Georgi.
The same year the most reverend *Vladyka*-elect Eufemi built himself a house in his court and it had thirty doors; and Nemetski masters from oversea made it with masters of Novgorod.

A.D. 1434. A.M. 6942.   *Knyaz* Yuri Dmitrievich seized the town of Moscow and took his seat as *Veliki Knyaz*.
And the same year, in the spring, on April 1, in Holy Week, the *Veliki Knyaz* Vasili Vasilievich came to Novgorod.
And on April 5, at the same time, in Holy Week, all Great Novgorod went out in arms into the country the other side of the river

[1] Photius.
[2] Year repeated.

O

towards the Zhilotug [stream] and *Knyaz* Vasili was then in the *Gorodishche*[1]; and nothing happened to the men of Novgorod.

The same year the *Veliki Knyaz* Yuri Dmitrievich died.

The same spring Eufemi of Novgorod went to Smolensk on April 11 to be confirmed by the Metropolitan Gerasim, and *Knyaz* Vasili left for Moscow on April 26.

The same spring the former house in the *Vladyka's* Court was painted. *Vladyka* Eufemi returned to Novgorod on May 26, confirmed and blessed by the Metropolitan Gerasim.

The same year *Knyaz* Vasili Yurievich came to Novgorod when the *Vladyka* Eufemi was there. That autumn *Knyaz* Vasili Yurievich left Novgorod, committing much robbery along the Msta,[2] in Bezhitsy, and in the country beyond the *Volok*. Much mischief was suffered through him.

The same autumn a stone church was erected in the Ioan Zlatoust[3] district on an old foundation by *Posadnik* Gregori Kirilovich and Esif Ondreyanovich, grandson of Goroshkov.

A.D. 1435. A.M. 6943. The following *Voyevodas* of Novgorod went out in the winter; the *Posadnik* of Novgorod Ivan Vasilievich, *Posadnik* Gregori Kyurilovich, the *Tysyatski* Fedor Oliseyevich, Esif Vasilievich, Annai Simeonovich, Ostafi Esifovich, and many other *Boyars* and men of Novgorod, with Fedor Ostafev, Mikhail Buinosov of Russa, and others of Porkhov, and they went by three different ways and punished the men of Rzheva, and burnt all the villages along the Rzheva river, along the borders of Pleskov, and by God's help returned all well to Novgorod with their plunder.

The same winter the *Veliki Knyaz* Vasili Vasilievich kissed the Cross to the men of Novgorod, and the men of Novgorod kissed the Cross likewise to the *Veliki Knyaz*, the *Veliki Knyaz* to relinquish the Novgorod patrimony, Bezhitsy, and at the Lamsk *Volok*, and in Vologda; and the *Boyars* of Novgorod to give up the lands of the *Knyaz* wheresoever such may be. The *Veliki Knyaz* engaged to send his *Boyars* for the delimitation of the lands, on Peter Day,[4] and the men of Novgorod were to send their own *Boyars*.

The same year Eufemi, *Vladyka* of Novgorod, erected a stone

---

[1] Near Novgorod.
[2] A river flowing into lake Ilmen from the E.
[3] John Chrysostom.
[4] July 11.

church to St. Ioan Zlatoust at the gates of his court. In that autumn they completed that church; but the masters[1] only just left the church and in that instant it collapsed.

A.D. 1436. A.M. 6944. *Knyaz* Vasili Yurievich was blinded by *Knyaz* Vasili Vasilievich in Moscow.

The same year the men of Novgorod sent their *Posadnik* Gregori Kyurilovich and Ivan Maksimov with the men of property Kuzma Tarasin, and Ivan Maksimov to Bezhitsy and others to the Lamsk *Volok* and to Vologda to carry out the delimitation of land, but the *Veliki Knyaz* did not send his own *Boyars*, and he did not cede any of the Novgorod patrimonies anywhere to the men of Novgorod, nor did he make any reparation.

The same year *Vladyka* Eufemi, *Vladyka* of Novgorod, again finished the Church of St. Ioan Zlatoust and he put up a sounding clock over his palace.

The same year *Vladyka* Eufemi founded a stone church to St. Nikola at Vezhishchi.[2]

The same autumn by God's sufferance a frost struck the crops during harvest throughout the entire Novgorod province; and in the same autumn the water was big, and on a frosty night the ice carried away seven stays of the great bridge, and the little Zhilotug[3] bridge was carried away.

The same winter the men of Novgorod sent their *Posadnik* Gregori Kyurilovich to Zhidimont,[4] and *Knyaz* Zhidimont of Lithuania kissed the Cross to the Novgorod envoys, and they took peace.

A.D. 1437. A.M. 6945. *Knyaz* Yuri Patrakievich arrived in Novgorod from Moscow demanding on behalf of the *Veliki Knyaz* Vasili Vasilievich a tax on the common people, and the men of Novgorod gave him the tax, and *Knyaz* Yuri Patrikievich left Novgorod.

The same spring the Church of St. Ioan Zlatoust at the gates of the *Vladyka's* Court was painted.

The same spring the Metropolitan Sidor, a Greek, arrived in Moscow from *Tsargrad* from the Patriarch Joseph, as Metropolitan.

[1] sc. builders.
[2] Near Novgorod.
[3] A stream in Novgorod.
[4] Sigismund, King of Poland.

The same spring the water washed away the wall of the *Detinets*,[1] and the earth from the wall slipped down and the stone wall fell together with the belfry [undermined] by the Volkhov. The same year the Church of St. Nikola collapsed at Vezhishchi.

The same year, at a *Veche*, *Vladyka* Eufemi in his vestments blessed with the Cross the *Posadniks* and the *Tysyatskis* and all Great Novgorod on Sunday, and on July 7, on the holy Father Thomas' Day, he went to Moscow to the Metropolitan Sidor.

The same year *Vladyka* Eufemi erected a stone church to St. Peter at the gates of his court, and he demolished the old church. The same year they completed the great bridge.

That autumn on October 9 the Metropolitan Sidor the Greek arrived from Moscow in Novgorod; and the *Vladyka*, and the *Posadniks* and the *Boyars* and the merchants and all Great Novgorod honoured him; and in the winter the Metropolitan went to Pskov on his way to *Tsargrad*. And in Pskov he appointed Gelasi, the Archimandrite [as their *Vladyka*], and gave him *Vladyka's* jurisdiction and all the taxes.

A.D. 1438. A.M. 6946. *Knyaz* Yuri Simeonovich arrived in Novgorod in the spring on March 3.

The same year the Church of St. Nikola at Vezhishchi was again erected of stone on the old foundations.

A.D. 1439. A.M. 6947. *Vladyka* Eufemi, *Vladyka* of Novgorod, built a stone granary. The same year he plastered the whole Church of St. Sophia with lime. The same year *Vladyka* Eufemi erected a stone belfry on the wall on the old place where it had fallen to its foundation.

The same year the body of the *Vladyka* Ioan was found, in whose time the men of Suzdal had been before Novgorod.[2]

The same year *Vladyka* Eufemi gilded the tomb of *Knyaz* Volodimir, the grandson of the great Volodimir, and had it inscribed, and also had the tomb of his mother inscribed, and a canopy was raised over it; he ordained a commemoration of them to be held on October 4 every year.

A.D. 1440. A.M. 6948. The *Veliki Knyaz* Zhidimont[3] Kestutievich of Lithuania was murdered in Lithuania by

1 Citadel.
2 sc. at war.
3 Sigismund.

Olexänder Chertoriski[1] and his brother Ivan: he had ruled nine years. This *Knyaz* was cruel and unmerciful, and moreover a covetous man; he ruined many Lithuanian *Knyazes*, drowning some and putting others to the sword. And he destroyed not a few of the *Boyars* and landowners mercilessly; for that reason did God send him this cruel death. And so because of his wickedness they did not support his son Mikhail, and all the Lithuanian and Russian towns chose Kasimir, Yagoilo's[2] son, for their *Veliki Knyaz*, and they set him on the throne in Vilna quietly and without any disturbance.

The same year Poltesk[3] was entirely burnt down.

And *Knyaz* Yuri Simeonovich left Novgorod the Great for Lithuania, and the *Veliki Knyaz* Kasimir gave him back all his patrimony: Mstislavl and Krichev, and not a few other towns and districts; but having grown proud, he occupied Smolensk and Polochesk[3] and Vitebsk, which brought him no advantage, and the people broke out in great tumult and conflict. The same autumn he took fright seeing his own audacity, that he had acted unwisely, and fled to Moscow.

The same year the *Vladyka* erected a stone church to St. Anastasia, and he built a smaller stone house.

A.D. 1441. A.M. 6949. In the winter the *Veliki Knyaz* Vasili Vasilievich of Moscow turned his wrath on Novgorod the Great; he sent a declaration of war and ravaged many Novgorod districts. And the men of Novgorod sent out *Vladyka* Eufemi with *Boyars* and men of property who fell in with him in Dereva near the town of Demyan, and concluded peace with him on the old terms, and gave him 8,000 *roubles*.

And the men of Pskov aided the *Veliki Knyaz* Vasili in ravaging the Novgorod lands and they did no little damage.

At that same time Novgorod *Voyevodas* with men from the country beyond the *Volok* ravaged many lands of the *Veliki Knyaz* for those he had ravaged of the districts of Novgorod.

The same winter the Metropolitan Isidor returned to Russia from the Eighth *Veche* in Rome, and began calling himself *Legatos* from the rib of the Apostolic seat of Roman power, and Roman Metropolitan: he also began the naming of the Pope of Rome in his services, and other new things which we had never heard since the

[1] Alexander Czartoryski.
[2] Jagiello Olgerdovich, King of Poland.
[3] Polotsk.

baptism of the Russian Land; and he ordered Russian priests to perform his services in the Polish[1] churches, and chaplains to serve in Russian churches. But Lithuania and Russia did not support this.

The same year by order of the most holy *Vladyka* of Great Novgorod, *Vladyka* Eufemi, the Church of St. Nikola at Vezhishchi was painted, the same year the large palace of the *Vladyka* was painted, and the front porch was painted.

The same year *Vladyka* Eufemi erected the Church of SS. Boris and Gleb in the Okolotok,[2] on the old foundations, and the men of Novgorod were his helpers.

A.D. 1442. A.M. 6950.   The Metropolitan returned to Moscow from Lithuania, and the *Veliki Knyaz* Vasili Vasilievich ordered him to serve; and hearing him in the service cite the Pope of Rome and not the Patriarch of *Tsargrad*, and many other things not according to the custom of the Russian Land, the *Veliki Knyaz* said: " Under our brethren, the *Veliki Knyazes* of the Russian Land, this has never been, and I do not wish to hear it." And he ordered the Metropolitan to live in a monastery and ordered warders to guard him; but he escaped to Tver and thence to Lithuania.

The same year the *Veliki Knyaz* of Moscow cast his displeasure on *Knyaz* Dmitri Yurievich, and pursued him; and he escaped to the Novgorod [territories of] Bezhitsy, and he did much harm to the districts, and sent an envoy to Novgorod: " Receive me on your own conditions." And the men of Novgorod replied: " Thou mayst come if thou wilt, or not, *Knyaz*, as thou likest."

The same year the pious *Vladyka* of Novgorod, *Vladyka* Eufemi, erected the church and monastery of the Transfiguration of the Holy Saviour on the old foundations in Russa, and the men of Novgorod and of Russa helped him, and it was completed on September 13.   On the same day the *Vladyka* came from Novgorod and ordered an all-night vigil because of the Lord's Festival, and put on his full ecclesiastic vestments, and attended by all the clerics of St. Sophia, he commanded the *Igumens* and priests of Russa to perform service with him; and he himself consecrated it on the Festival of the Exaltation of the honourable Cross, and finishing the holy liturgy, the holy (man) rejoiced in his heart and soul in beholding the temple of the Holy Saviour and the beginning of his work brought to good completion, which he had built to his own

---

[1] *Lyadski.*
[2] lit. " District," a part of Novgorod.

everlasting memory and for the remission of sins, a refuge and a joy
to all Christians and a joy and gladness to the faithful, and a cause of
praise of the *Vladyka* by the people entering the house of the Holy
Saviour, beholding the church, saying: " Blessed be God who put
it into the heart of our lord to create the supremely first temple of
the Holy Saviour." And he ornamented it well and had the pictures
well painted on gold and other requisite places well finished, as is
proper for the beautifying of a church; and he had church vessels
made of silver, and other silver vessels for use in the monastery. At
that time Ivan Vasilievich was *Posadnik* of Novgorod and held the
Posadnik-ship of Russa, and was consecrated under *Igumen* Ivan
of the Holy Saviour.

The same year *Vladyka* Eufemi erected the stone Church of St.
Nikola in his court.

The same year they erected the stone Church of St. Prokopi in
Belaya.[1] The same year *Vladyka* Eufemi built a stone kitchen and
a stone room in his court.

The same year a fire broke out in the Carpenters' quarter.[2] The
fire began in Shchitna[3] Street on May 4. A half of Konyukhov[4]
Street was burnt and the whole of Zapolskaya[5] [Street], and passing
beyond the town the fire extended to the Antonov monastery.

And again on the 11th of the same month of May, the day of the
holy Martyr Moki, a fire broke out in Podol[6]; and it was terrible and
people suffered much harm, and twelve stone churches were burnt;
and God knows how many Christian souls were burnt; and the
entire quarter was burnt as far as St. Georgi; and here the fire
stopped at the Lyubyanitsa [Street]. After a short time in the
same month Mikitin Street in the Zapole quarter was burnt, and
great harm was inflicted on people who went into them[7] with their
belongings. These fires occur because of our sins, in order that we
might repent of our evil ways. At that time some people in their
distress at those great conflagrations seized some men, saying to
them in the confusion of their fury: " Ye walk secretly and do not
show yourselves to men and set fire to the town and destroy people."
And some of them they burned, and others they cast from the

---

[1] " White," a place on the river Msta, q.v.
[2] *Plotniki.*
[3] " Shieldmakers."
[4] " Grooms."
[5] " Beyond the fields."
[6] The Lower town.
[7] sc. the churches.

bridge. But God knows, who tests the hearts of men, whether that is true that was said.

A.D. 1443. A.M. 6951. *Vladyka* Eufemi, *Vladyka* of Great Novgorod, built a sacristy of stone and a warder's room of stone in his court.

In the same year they erected a stone church to St. Nikola at Krecheva in Russa.

A.D. 1444. A.M. 6952. *Knyaz* Ivan Volodimirovich came to Novgorod on September 14 at the invitation of Novgorod, to [take possession of] the dependencies which had been held by Lugven[1] and his son Yuri; and *Knyaz* Yuri Lugvenich went to the *Nemtsy* and the *Nemtsy* gave him no road, and he went away to Moscow.

The same autumn the *Nemtsy* came to Yam,[2] burned the outskirts and ravaged the coast, and sent to Novgorod: " We are not warring against you; it is *Knyaz* Gregori of Klev from oversea to avenge his *Voyevoda* Itolk of Rugodiv."[3] But the *Nemtsy* lied in all this.

The same autumn people from the *Veliki Knyaz's* patrimony of Tver ravaged many lands and villages of Novgorod, Bezhitsy, the country beyond Borov, and all the districts of Novi-torg. And from Lithuania the *Veliki Knyaz* Kazimir sent to Novgorod, saying thus: " Receive my lieutenants into the *Gorodishche;* I shall defend you. And on your account I have not taken peace with the *Knyaz* of Moscow." And the men of Novgorod did not agree to this.

The same winter the men of Novgorod went to the country of the *Nemtsy* beyond the Narova, with *Knyaz* Ivan Volodimirovich; and took much plunder and burnt much round Rugodiv[3] as far as the Purdozna river, along the Narova and up to the Chud lake.[4]

The same year the *Nemtsy* with the Master and all his forces came to Yam[2] town and bombarded it with guns for five days; they also plundered and burnt the Vod lands and those along the Izhera and the Neva. But God and the Holy *Archistrategos* Mikhail protected the town, so they did not take it; but a great many *Nemtsy* fell before the town, and others returned to their own country wounded.

At that time *Knyaz* Vasili Yurievich, one of the Suzdal *Knyazes*, was in the town of Yam. And the men of Novgorod sent the

[1] Simeon Olgerdovich *Knyaz* of Lithuania.
[2] sc. Yamburg.
[3] Narva.
[4] Lake Chudskoe or Peipus.

Luga villagers and the Vod and Izhera *Boyars* in advance, themselves intending to march with them and with *Knyaz* Ivan Volodimirovich beyond the Narova. But for our sins at that very time the horses began to die in great numbers in the town and in the districts, so the men of Novgorod returned and did not go beyond the Narova.

At that time the men of Pskov sent envoys to Novgorod about peace, and saw that horses were dying in Novgorod in great numbers, and that the men of Novgorod had not gone beyond the Narova, and left without coming to terms of peace.

The same year the Korel people attacked the Murman people, slaughtered them, and ravaged their lands, and returned with plunder in good health.

A.D. 1445. A.M. 6953. *Vladyka* Eufemi, *Vladyka* of Great Novgorod, erected a stone church at Khutin to St. Varlam, with a belfry on the top. The same year Eufemi, *Vladyka* of Great Novgorod, founded the monastery of St. Georgi in Gorodok; he repaired the stone wall, and renovated the Church of St. Georgi in parts which had fallen away, and had it painted, and roofed it with shingle; and it was a refuge for Christians.

The same year *Knyaz* Yuri Lugvenevich came to Novgorod from Moscow, and the men of Novgorod gave him maintenance: grain from the districts, but they gave him no appanages; and the *Knyaz* went away to Lithuania.

The same winter the *Veliki Knyaz* Vasili sent two Tartar princes[1] against the Lithuanian towns Vyazma and Bryansk and others, by surprise; and they made great havoc, burning, and taking many captives, nearly up to Smolensk. And hearing of this, *Knyaz* Kazimir of Lithuania sent out his *Boyars* and soldiers against Mozhaisk and other towns; and they took five towns and seized much territory, and there was great ruin to Christians.

The same winter the *Veliki Knyaz* Vasili went against the Tartar *Tsar* Mahmed; many Christians died from cold, others were slain by the Tartars who laid waste the country. But God aided the *Veliki Knyaz* Vasili, and the Tartars fled, others being slain.

The same winter *Knyaz* Boris of Tver seized fifty Novgorod districts, ravaging Bezhitsy and the country about Torzhok, and he took Torzhok.

The same winter the men of Novgorod sent *Knyaz* Yuri with

[1] *Tsarevitsa.*

Boyars and merchants to a conference with the *Nemtsy* and the Master; but the Master wanted the town of Ostrov, so they all dispersed without peace.

Bread was dear in Novgorod, and not only this year but during ten whole years: one *poltina*[1] for two *korobyas*[2]; sometimes a little more, sometimes less; sometimes there was none to be bought anywhere. And amongst the Christians there was great grief and distress; only crying and sobbing were to be heard in the streets and market place, and many people fell down dead from hunger, children before their parents, fathers and mothers before their children; and many dispersed, some to Lithuania, others passed over to Latinism, and others to the *Besermeny*[3] and to the Jews, giving themselves to the traders for bread.

At the same time there was no law or justice in Novgorod; calumniators arose and turned obligations and accounts and oaths to falsehood[4]; and began to rob in the town and in the villages and districts; we were exposed to the rebukes of our neighbours, who were around us. There was much confiscation, frequent demands for money, throughout the districts, with weeping and anguish and with outcries and curses on all sides against our seniors and our town: because there was no grace in us, nor justice.

The same year *Vladyka* Eufemi erected a warm stone church to St. Eufemi at his Court, and he painted it and decorated it with pictures; and all that was done in four months.

The same year the people of Knyazhna erected the stone Church of the Holy-Women-who-brought-Myrrh, on the old foundation.

The same year the stone Church of St. Dmitri was built in Russa.

The same year Vasili Shenkurskoi and Mikhail Yakol, *Voyevodas* of Novgorod, with three thousand men from beyond the *Volok* went against the Yugra people, and after capturing many Yugra men with their wives and children, disbanded. And the Yugra people succeeded in deceiving them, saying thus: " We will pay you tribute, and we will count our numbers and show you our camps, settlements and islands and natural boundaries." At the same time they collected and attacked Vasili's fortress, killing many good men, *Boyars'* sons, and eighty other brave men. It was terrible to hear their destruction, but Vasili escaped with his son

[1] Half-Rouble.
[2] " Baskets."
[3] sc. Mussulmans.
[4] sc. repudiated.

Semeon and a small party, and others fled into the forest and dispersed. The other *Voyevoda* Mikhail Yakol was then on another river, and coming to Vasili's fortress and finding it demolished and his fellows killed and others scattered, he set about seeking his own people along the river. And Vasili and his son and the others joining him, they all returned to their own country.

The same year the Murman *Svei*[1] came in force by surprise to the Dvina[2] beyond the *Volok*, to Nenoksa, plundering and burning, killing people and making many captives. And the people of the Dvina having heard, came up quickly, slew some and sent about forty to Novgorod, putting to death their *Voyevodas* Ivor and Peter and a third one; a few others jumping into their boats escaped.

The same year there was a great sign in the town of Suzdal in the Cathedral Church of the Holy Mother of God, on April 20, the eve of the Wednesday of the fourth week after Easter, in the presence of the *Veliki Knyaz* Vasili Vasilievich and of Avram, Bishop of Suzdal: the tombs of the Saints began suddenly to burn inside and to fall to pieces; and on the morrow, the very day of middle term,[3] the Cathedral Church of the Holy Mother of God collapsed.

The same year the *Veliki Knyaz* Vasili gathered his forces and went against that same Mahmed; he reached Suzdal, and while he was in the Eufemi monastery the Tartars came upon him by surprise, and the *Veliki Knyaz* had a fierce fight with the Tartars, and for our sins the *Veliki Knyaz* was defeated; and having captured him the Tartars took him to the Horde and with him *Knyaz* Mikhail Ondreyevich and a great many *Boyars* and monks and nuns and young people, and many others they slew. And *Knyaz* Ivan Ondreyevich and *Knyaz* Vasili Yaroslavich escaped wounded, with a small following.

And after this defeat by the Tartars there was the following calamity: six days afterwards, when from all sides the remainder of the people had hastened into Moscow with all their possessions, the inside of the town of Moscow took fire: and was entirely burnt, and about seven hundred Christians perished and all the property was burnt, and the cupola of the Cathedral Church of St. Mikhail fell in, and another church collapsed, that of the Exaltation of the honourable Cross.

The same year, on August 7, the *Vladyka* of Great Novgorod, *Vladyka* Eufemi, having blessed his children the *Posadniks* and the *Tysyatskis* and all Great Novgorod, went beyond the *Volok*

[1] Norsemen.
[2] The Northern Dvina (White Sea).
[3] i.e. half-way between Easter and Pentecost.

to bless the patrimony of Novgorod and his children and his diocese.

The same year, on August 22, *Knyaz* Boris of Tver sent his *Voyevodas* against Torzhok, and drove out the remainder of the people to rob them, others he destroyed, and from others he exacted ransom. He took away to Tver forty cartloads of goods and belongings of people of Moscow, of Novgorod and of Novi-torg; other cartloads of goods were lost in the river. And in two years he ravaged Bezhitsy and eighty districts beyond Borov.

A.D. 1446. A.M. 6954. *Tsar* Mahmed let the *Veliki Knyaz* Vasili return to the Russian Land, taking a ransom of two hundred thousand *roubles;* and what else, God knows, and they.

That same year the people began to find fault with the silver coinage, till all the men of Novgorod looked one at the other; there was tumult and rebellion and animosity amongst them.

And the *Posadnik* and the *Tysyatski* and all Novgorod appointed five minters, and they began to re-mould the old coins and to mint new coins of the same value: of the same weight of four *pochki*, and half a *denga* was taken off the new *grivna*. There was much distress and loss among the Christians in the town and in the districts. And this will not be forgotten even in the last generations.

The same year, on January 3, there were heavy clouds with rain, and wheat and rye and corn were beaten down altogether,[1] both in the fields, and in the forests, all round the town for five *versts* from the Volkhovets [river], and as far as the Msta river, for fifteen *versts*. The people bore into the town whatever they could gather up; and the townspeople collected to see this curious marvel, whence and how it came.

The same winter, on January 23, the *Vladyka* returned to Novgorod from the country beyond the *Volok*, and on the 30th of the same month, the day of the three holy Bishops Vasili the Great, Grigori the Theologian, and Ioan Zlatoust,[2] *Vladyka* Eufemi in congregation consecrated the warm Church of St. Eufemi.[3]

A.D. 1446.   The same year three *Knyazes*: Dmitri Yurievich, Ivan Andreyevich of Mozhaisk and Boris Alexandrovich of Tver, with two of the *Tsar's* envoys,

---

[1] sc. the autumn-sown crops.
[2] John Chrysostom.
[3] Here this text ends; the following is added from another text.

conspired together; they ordered the levy of a contribution and took the money.

The same year those same three *Knyazes* caught the *Veliki Knyaz* Vasili Vasilievich in the Trinity monastery, behind the Sergiev tomb, and blinded him; and Dmitri Yurievich became *Veliki Knyaz*.[1]

[A.D. 1471. A.M. 6979. The *Veliki Knyaz* Ioan Vasilievich marched with a force against Novgorod the Great because of its wrong doing and lapsing into Latinism.[2]

Concerning these[3] this is a copy of the introductory words to the narrative of the first taking [of Novgorod] by the *Veliki Knyaz* Ioan Vasilievich of all Russia, the grandfather of the *Veliki Knyaz* Ioan Vasilievich[4] of all Russia, when there were dissensions in Great Novgorod.

King of kings, and Lord of lords, God supreme and ruling and strong, Owner and Creator of all, our Lord Jesus Christ, keep everlasting kingdom, having neither beginning nor end. That one only is all powerful whom the Creator of Heaven and earth and all else may create of His own will; power and glory he is pleased to give to him, the sceptres of empire He entrusts him with, and by His mercifulness establishes all virtue, and pours his grace on all who fear him. It is written in the old books as it was said: " A country wishing to be ruled in the face of God sets up a prince who is pious and just, regardful of his kingdom and of the governing the land, and loving justice and truth." Of those, it is said, who in goodness build earthly [kingdoms] receive also a heavenly one. Truly has the Lord God of His unspeakable mercy with His life-bearing right hand raised a chief over the God-loved Russian Land, who maintains it in truth and piety, whose honourable head is filled with wisdom, who has organized it like to a lamp of illumination of piety, a promoter of truth, a guardian of godly law, a strong champion of Orthodoxy, the honourable, pious and trusty *Veliki Knyaz* Ioan Vasilievich of all Russia. The Lord God and the most pure Mother of God by their unspeakable mercy have committed to him the prosperity and

[1] Here ends the Chronicle proper. The record for the year 1471 (edited in the sixteenth century, under Ivan the Terrible) has been added, because it gives a detailed account of the final suppression of the independence of Novgorod by Ivan III ' the Great' of Moscow.

[2] From Number Two Chronicle: Ivan Vasilievich the *Veliki Knyaz* came to Novgorod with an armed force; he camped on the river Shelon, and took a ransom of 16,000 *Roubles*.

[3] sc. the people of Novgorod.

[4] Ivan IV "the Terrible," (*Grozny*.)

the strengthening of all; extending their godly mercy through shedding the light of religion over Russian Lands.

Likewise it is written: Length of days, and long life and peace shall be added to thee, and he found favour and was beloved for his righteous acts, the *Veliki Knyaz* of all Russia, Ioan Vasilievich; yet the deceitful people would not submit to him; stirred by a savage pride, the men of Novgorod would not obey their sovereign *Veliki Knyaz*, until they were reminded of the great piety of old times told to them. For that reason did their fame abate, and their face was covered with shame: by reason of the men of Novgorod leaving the light and giving themselves over in their pride to the darkness of ignorance, saying that they would draw away and attach themselves to the Latins.

Thus have these inclined away from their sovereign the *Veliki Knyaz*, wishing to give themselves over to the Latin king, bringing evil to all Orthodoxy. The pious sovereign and *Veliki Knyaz* of all Russia, Ioan Vasilievich, has frequently sent his messengers to them, calling on them to keep his patrimony from all harm, to improve themselves in all things within his ancestral estates, and to live according to old custom. He suffered much in these things from their vexatious ways and contumacy within his paternal domains, while he expected from them a thorough amendment of their conduct towards himself and a respectful submission.

And again when the Novgorod *Posadnik* Vasili Ananin came as envoy from Great Novgorod, the patrimony of the *Veliki Knyaz*, laying before him all the affairs of Novgorod, he did not say a single word of the ill-behaviour of the men of Novgorod and of their failure to amend their ways, but in reply to the *Boyars* of the *Veliki Knyaz* Vasili he said: " Under that head I have no instructions from Great Novgorod, and I have no orders to speak." The sovereign *Veliki Knyaz* was sorely aggrieved by their churlishness, who, while sending to him men from his patrimonial domains to implore favours, bear themselves with insolence and are unmindful of their misbehaviour. Therefore has the *Veliki Knyaz* laid his anger upon them, upon the land of his inheritance, upon Great Novgorod, and he has commanded Vasili, the Novgorod envoy, to tell Great Novgorod: " Mend your ways towards me, my patrimony, and recognize us; encroach not on my lands and my waters, and keep my name of *Veliki Knyaz* in strictness and in honour as of old; and send to me, the *Veliki Knyaz*, representatives to do homage and to make settlement. I desire to keep you, my patrimony, in good favour, on the old conditions." With that he dismissed him, informing his patrimony that his power of endurance was exhausted, and that he would not suffer their misbehaviour and contumacy any longer.

The *Veliki Knyaz* sent also to Pskov, his patrimony, repeating the same words and with commands to acquaint Pskov with the opposition to him of his patrimony Great Novgorod, and to say: " If you send to me, the *Veliki Knyaz*, with due homage, then I will hold them in my favour; but if my patrimony, Great Novgorod, fails in so doing, then must you be ready to act against them with me." And after this the *Vladyka* Iona of Great Novgorod and of Pskov died amongst them, and the men of Novgorod chose the monk Feofil[1] as their father to occupy his place, without reference to the *Veliki Knyaz* Ivan Vasilievich of all Russia. And it was after this selection that they sent their *Boyar*, Nikita Savin, to the *Veliki Knyaz* Ivan Vasilievich of all Russia to ask on behalf of Great Novgorod, the patrimony of the *Veliki Knyaz*, for letters of safe conduct; and Nikita in the name also of all Great Novgorod prayed Filip the Metropolitan of all Russia and the spiritual father of the *Veliki Knyaz*, as well as the *Knyaginya* Marya, the mother of the *Veliki Knyaz*, to intercede for them with the *Veliki Knyaz*, in obtaining guarantee of security in submitting their petition for Feofil whom the men of Novgorod had nominated, for the *Posadniks* and *Tysyatskis* and *Boyars* who would come to Moscow to do homage to the *Veliki Knyaz* and to obtain confirmation of Feofil as *Vladyka* of Novgorod the Great and of Pskov, with the white hood, that they might all depart again in freedom. The *Veliki Knyaz* acceding to the solicitations of his spiritual father the Metropolitan and of his mother the *Knyaginya* Marya, granted letters of security and withdrew his displeasure from his patrimony Great Novgorod. Yet the men of Novgorod, gone mentally astray, and forgetful of this, went not in fear of God's words spoken to the whole congregation of the children of Israel.

Those ancient Israelites hearkened not to the words of God, and they did not obey his commandments; they were therefore deprived of the promised land and were scattered over many countries. Thus also the people of Novgorod, enraged by the pride in them, followed in the ways of the old desertion and have been false to their sovereign the *Veliki Knyaz*, choosing to have a Latin ruler as their sovereign, and having before that accepted from him in Great Novgorod the *Knyaz* Mikhail Alexandrovich of Kiev, keeping

[1] Theophilus.

him a long time in Novgorod, doing offence in this wise to their sovereign Ivan Vasilievich the *Veliki Knyaz* of all Russia. By their artful devices they won over evilly inclined men, who were thus caught in the nets of the snarer and destroyer of the soul of man, the many-headed beast and cunning enemy, the devil; like a living hell has he devoured them by his evil counsel.

That tempter the devil entered in their midst into the wily Marfa[1] Boretskaya, widow of Isaak Boretski, and that accursed [woman] entangled herself in words of guile with the Lithuanian *Knyaz* Mikhail. On his persuasion she intended to marry a Lithuanian *Boyar*, to become Queen, meaning to bring him to Great Novgorod and to rule with him under the suzerainty of the King over the whole of the Novgorod region.

This accursed Marfa like to them beguiled the people, diverting them from the right way to Latinism, for the dark deceits of Latinism blinded her soul's eyes through the wiles of the cunning devil and the wicked imaginings of· the Lithuanian *Knyaz*. And being of one mind with her, prompted to evil by the proud devil Satan, Pimin the monk and the almoner of the old *Vladyka*, the cunning [man], engaged with her in secret whispering and helped her in every wickedness, seeking to take the place of his lord as *Vladyka* of Great Novgorod during his life, having suffered much punishment for his rogueries; his desire had not been gratified, inasmuch as the Lord God had not favoured him in the drawing of the lot, and he was not, therefore, accepted by the people for the high office. That wicked man is like Peter the Stammerer, the first perverter of the faith, or like the ancient *Farmos*, those originators of the Latin heresies; and they were followed in our time by the apostate Metropolitan Isidor who attended the eighth *Veche* of Rome at Florence, tempted by the Pope's gold and coveting a cardinalship, seceding to Latinism. Among these is also Grigori, his apostate pupil, who is now in Kiev called Metropolitan; but he is not received into our great Orthodox church of the Russian Land, but excluded.

This cunning monk Pimin sought his appointment by the apostate Grigori, spreading it among the people that he should be sent to Kiev where he would receive his confirmation, being unmindful of the words in the Holy Gospels spoken by the lips of our Lord: " He that entereth not by the door into the sheep-fold, but climbeth up some other way, the same is a thief and a robber." Now this cunning man not only sought like a wolf to climb over the fence into the sheep-fold of the house of Israel, but to scatter and to

[1] i.e. Martha.

destroy God's church; and he in this wise ruined the whole of the Novgorod land, the accursed one. According to the Prophet: "He made not God his strength, but trusted in the abundance of his riches and strengthened himself in his wickedness." This Pimin did similarly trust in the abundance of his riches, giving of them also to the crafty woman Marfa, and ordering many people to give money to her to buy over the people to their will; and this accursed wicked serpent fearing not God and having no shame before man, has spread destruction throughout all the Novgorod land and destroyed many souls.

The most venerable priest-monk Feofil, their spiritual father, nominated to the *Vladyka*-ship, exhorted them to refrain from their wicked ways, but they would not hearken to him, and he tried many times to withdraw to his cell in his own monastery, but they would not let him go, while they persevered in their wicked design.

The *Veliki Knyaz* Ioan Vasilievich, hearing of what was doing in his patrimony, Novgorod the Great, of the uncurbed outrages of his people who were like the waves of the sea, bethought him of these occurrences in the goodness of his heart, yet he did not hasten to show his wrath, but quieted his most honest soul with a goodly patience, filled, like the Apostle, with the fear of God, and in remembrance of the holy light of the righteous Son, of Christ's merciful long-suffering, when the word of God came down from heaven and humbling himself, he descended to the earth, taking the form of a servant for the salvation of mankind; the *Veliki Knyaz* allowed them sufficient time, saying to himself: "Thou art just, O Lord, and thy judgments are correct; and as the Lord is just, so may I, loving justice, be just in His sight." Thinking thus, being favourably inclined towards his patrimony, and not being desirous of witnessing the shedding of Christian blood, he said to himself: "Even as the waves dash into foam against the rocks and come to naught, so also our people the men of Novgorod have more than once acted treasonably towards us, and the Lord God will subdue them." With this view he commanded his [spiritual] father Filip, the Metropolitan of all Russia, to write to them in his name, admonishing them, and instructing them not to draw away from the light of piety, to abandon their evil designs, and to withstand the darkness of the Latin allurements. The Metropolitan of all Russia did repeatedly write to Novgorod the Great, sending his blessing and writing instructions from the sacred Book: "It has come to my hearing, my sons, that some among you are endeavouring to cause

P

a great rebellion and to produce dissent in God's holy church, to renounce the Orthodox Christian faith, and to pass over to the Latins. You must disadvise those wicked people among you from their evil inclinations, for, my sons, theirs is false and godless work; for by abandoning the light of piety they will unwittingly bring down upon themselves the future judgment of God and many eternal torments; let them be guided by a godly wisdom and by God's commandments. Stand in fear of the wrath of God, and in dread of the awful scythe which was seen by the great prophet Zachariah descending from heaven upon the unruly; you must punish those who make tumult and sow dissension among you, and teach them to walk in the old ways of their fathers and to dwell in the former ways of peace and piety. Cruel and irremediable will be the effects of these beginnings, if you neglect the new law of piety and salvation of the testament of the living God, and adhere to Latinism. The Lord God will call to account all the godl s perverters of the faithful, so that you must restrain the evil-doers according to the words: 'Fly from sin as from a foe; fly from deceit as from the face of a serpent, that it may not sting thy soul with the barb of eternal perdition.' You know, my sons, how many cities, countries and places of mighty kingdoms have been ruined and desolated in former times for breaking the law and for disobeying the Prophets and for not following the teachings of the Apostles and the holy Fathers; that countries and cities which did no mit to God and to their sovereign were destroyed. The once pio s and great Imperial city of Constantinople perished because of that same Latinism; it fell through impiety, and is now possessed by the heathen Turk. Fear the wrath of God, ye sons of God's world, it is not only one or two among you who are working to depart from the truth and to turn from the right way, forgetting your past greatness and the laws of your fore-fathers; but the whole multitude of your people are in commotion. Submit yourselves, my sons, to him under whose strong arm God has placed you and the God-serving land of Russia, the *Veliki Knyaz* Ioan Vasilievich our ɫ editary ruler, according to the direction of Christ's Apostle Paul tne teacher of the universe, who said: 'Whosoever submits to the power of God, obeys His ordinances, but whosoever resisteth the power, resisteth the ordinance of God;' and again: 'Fear God and obey the king.' The minister of God beareth not the sword in vain as an avenger, but also in de fence of the godly. Ponder, therefore, my children, over these things, and humble yourselves, and may the God of peace be with you."

They remained, however, not only implacable, but also stone-hearted, and gave no attention to the above writing, and were as deaf as adders, closing their ears to the voice, as it were, of the charmers. So these men of Novgorod giving no heed to the writing, nor accepting the benediction, and continuing in their evil courses, could not be compacted [in the right]. The pious sovereign and *Veliki Knyaz* of all Russia Ioan Vasilievich being still gracious to them, sent to Great Novgorod, his patrimony, his servant Ioan Fedorovich Tovarkov with fair words, saying: " His patrimony should not abandon the Orthodox faith, but cast the evil thought from off their hearts, and should not adhere to Latinism; that the great sovereign holds the men of Novgorod in favour and in his regards as of old." But the wicked people minded him not, and clung to the intention of abandoning Orthodoxy and giving themselves over to the king. We will state the accusation against them.

The *Veliki Knyaz* being informed of the unceasing evil doings of the men of Novgorod, dispatched to Novgorod the Great a challenge in writing, exposing the malpractices of the people and their treason, and announcing that he was himself marching with a force against them. The *Veliki Knyaz* had first sent his *Voyevodas* Vasili Fedorovich Obrazets and Boris Matveyevich Tyushtev with his men of Ustyug, of Vyatka and of the Vologda district, to the Dvina and the country beyond the *Volok*, and into all the territories of Novgorod in those parts. In advance of his own force the *Veliki Knyaz* sent an army under his *Voyevodas*, *Knyaz* Danilo Dmitrievich Kholmski and his *Boyar* Fedor Davidovich, accompanied by many others of his court; they were ordered to scour the country around Novgorod, towards Russa beyond the Ilmen lake and to burn all places of habitation. To his patrimony Pskov the *Veliki Knyaz* sent to say that the men of Pskov should release themselves from their engagement on oath to Great Novgorod, and take to horse in his service against Novgorod which had abjured Orthodoxy and was giving itself to the Latin king. They issued forth at once with all the men of the country of Pskov, and at the instance of the *Veliki Knyaz* they revoked their oath on the Cross to Novgorod the Great.

The pious sovereign and *Veliki Knyaz* Ioan Vasilievich prayed to God and to the most pure Mother of God, shedding many tears before them, beseeching their mercy for the pacification of the world, and for the well-being of God's holy churches and the Orthodox faith.

His heart filled with sorrow, he said to himself: " It is known to Thee, Almighty God and everlasting King, who knowest the secrets of all men's hearts, it is not of my own desire and will that I dare to do this which may cause much shedding of Christian blood upon this earth.   I stand by the godly laws of the holy Apostles and holy Fathers and for the true Orthodox faith of the Russian Land, also for my patrimony and against their renunciation of the true faith and adoption of Latinism."   And praying thus, the pious worker invoked to his aid the great defender and speedy helper in war, the *Voyevoda* of the celestial forces, the *Archistrategos* Mikhail, and the great unconquerable sufferers for Christ, Dmitri of *Selun*,[1] Georgi the Brave and Feodor Stratilat,[2] also his saintly and Orthodox ancestors St. Vladimir and his two sons Boris and Gleb; and putting his trust in the prayers of the Saints, of the great sanctifier Ioan Zlatoust,[3] the Bishop of *Tsargrad*,[4] the miracle-worker Nikola, Peter the Russian Metropolitan, Alexis the miracle-worker and Russian Metropolitan, St. Leonti the miracle-worker and Bishop of Rostov, and the Saints and miracle-workers Sergei, Varlam, and Kiril, and Nikita the almoner of the miracle-worker of Pereyaslavl. By their prayers might he be strengthened and established for many years by the Lord God with His help from on high.

And so putting his trust in God, the *Veliki Knyaz* mounted his horse; and in the house of the Most Pure Mother of God and of the great Sanctifier Peter the miracle-worker, he left his son the faithful and pious *Veliki Knyaz* Ioan Ioanovich to sit in his throne in Moscow in guard of his patrimony and to govern the land of Russia; he left his younger brother *Knyaz* Andrei Vasilievich with him, and he commanded his son to retain by him the *Tsarevich* Murtasa, the son of *Tsar* Mustafa, with his *Knyazes* and *Kazaks*,[5] to serve him on any emergency.

The *Veliki Knyaz* took along with him his younger brother *Knyaz* Yuri Vasilievich and his youngest brothers Andrei and Boris Vasilievich, also *Knyaz* Mikhail Andreyevich with his son Vasili, with a large number of other *Knyazes* in his service, and *Boyars* and *Voyevodas;* he took with him also the son of *Tsar* Aldayaras Kasimovich of the Meshcher country with his *Kazaks* and retinue. The men of Pskov joined their forces from the borders of their country.

[1] Salonika.
[2] Theodore *Stratelates*.
[3] John Chrysostom.
[4] Constantinople.   [5] Bodyguard.

Thus did the *Veliki Knyaz* advance with all his host against his patrimonial domain Novgorod the Great because of the rebellious spirit of the people, their pride and their conversion to Latinism. With a numerous and overpowering force he occupied the entire Novgorod country from border to border, visiting every part of it with the dread powers of his fire and sword. As in ancient times Jeremiah prophesied of Nebuchadnezzar, King of Jerusalem: " From the rumbling and thunder of his chariots and from the neighing of his horses the earth shall tremble; " and so by the mercy and aid of God shall the same prophecy be fulfilled in our time over the wicked men of the Novgorod country, through the pious sovereign *Veliki Knyaz* Ioan Vasilievich of all Russia, for their abjuration of the faith and for their wrong-doing.

The Novgorod country is filled with lakes and swamps, for which reason mounted forces were never employed against Novgorod by former *Veliki Knyazes* and the wicked people in their wonted contumacy dwelled in security during the summer after, following their own evil ways from the autumn to the winter, and even up to spring time, by reason of the inundation of the lands.

By the beneficence of God, vouchsafed by God from on high to the *Veliki Knyaz* Ioan Vasilievich of all Russia to the detriment of the Novgorod land, not a drop of rain had fallen during the summer, from the month of May to the month of September the land was dry and the heat of the sun had dried up all the swamps. The troops of the *Veliki Knyaz* found no impediments and could ride in every direction over the country, driving the cattle over dried ground; thus did the Lord God through this desiccation punish the men of Novgorod for their evil-doing and subject them to the strong hand of the pious sovereign and *Veliki Knyaz* Ioan Vasilievich of all Russia. When the men of Novgorod heard that the *Veliki Knyaz* was marching upon them with a large army, those cunning men sent to him professions of duty and again asked for guarantees of security while proceeding with their evil doing. At the same time they sent forces from Novgorod the Great by the Ilmen lake in boats against the advancing columns of the *Veliki Knyaz*, and fought them; but God aided the *Voyevodas* of the *Veliki Knyaz*, and 500 men of Novgorod were killed and others were captured or drowned, while others fled back to the town informing the townsmen that they had been defeated by the *Voyevodas* of the *Veliki Knyaz*. Thrown into great agitation, the men of Novgorod, after deliberation, dispatched another messenger to the *Veliki Knyaz*, *Posadnik* Luka

Klementievich, doing homage and again asking for guarantee of security and ignoring the defeated force which had passed down in boats, declared that as yet no men from the town had fought with those of the *Veliki Knyaz*.

Without waiting for the return of their venturesome envoy the crafty people conceived a great wicked design; the rebel *Posadniks* and *Tysyatskis*, the *Boyars*, well-to-do men, the merchants and the whole of Great Novgorod collected together forming a fighting body of fully 30,000 men, being unaware that the sword of God was sharpened against them, and mounting their horses, rode quickly out of the town to fall upon the advance force of the *Veliki Knyaz* which was led by *Knyaz* Danilo Dmitrievich and by Fedor Davidovich. Here befell what was said by David the Prophet: "By the morning shall all the wicked of the earth be slain; I shall destroy all the lawless of the city." When the watchers and the scouts informed the *Voyevodas* that a large force of mounted men was advancing from Novgorod, and that an auxiliary force was coming in boats, into the Shelon river, then the *Voyevodas* of the *Veliki Knyaz* began to acknowledge the justice of the *Knyaz's* cause and the perfidy of the men of Novgorod and, praying to the Lord God and to the most pure Mother of God, and reposing their trust in God, they said to their company: " It is our duty, brothers, to serve our sovereign the *Veliki Knyaz* Ioan Vasilievich of all Russia, and were they 300,000 strong we should all the same lay down our lives in fighting for the cause of our sovereign *Veliki Knyaz*; and God and the holy Mother of God know that the cause of the *Veliki Knyaz* is a just cause."

Early on the morning of July 14, the day of the Apostle St. Kuld, the entire force of the men of Novgorod was ranged on the Shelon river, and the opposing armies faced each other across the river.

When they saw the forces of the men of Novgorod the troops of the *Veliki Knyaz* precipitated themselves into the river on their horses, not one of their horses stumbling in descending the steep bank, nor floundering in the water, and closing up they rushed upon the whole body of the men of Novgorod and they joined in battle. And here was fulfilled what was said by the Prophet: " Like drunken men did they stagger and fall into confusion, and all their understanding was swallowed up; " and again: " As in drowsiness they mounted their horses, terrible art Thou, O Lord; who can stand against Thee? "

Thus was God's favour bestowed on the troops of the *Veliki*

Knyaz, maintaining his just cause; even as God helped Gideon against the Midianites, and Abraham against the king *Hodologo-mor* of Sodom, so did he aid the *Voyevodas* of the *Veliki Knyaz* against these unrighteous backsliders, the men of Novgorod. Although they rebelled and arrayed themselves against the troops of the *Veliki Knyaz*, yet they could not raise strong hands against them, but themselves fell into confusion from the stretching of their arrowed bows, and from the weapons of their hands.   Thus likewise did God in his goodness turn their faces in an hour's time, as they threw down their arms and fled back whence they had come; they ran in disgrace, casting away their armour to relieve their horses of weight, and a great number of them fell dead, for their lawlessness and for their rebellion against their sovereign the *Veliki Knyaz*. It did not appear to them that they were stricken by men's hands, but by the invisible power of the Living God and by the aid of the great *Archistrategos* Mikhail, the leader of the heavenly forces.   All were in great terror and many fell dead with their faces to the earth, while others throwing themselves off their horses ran into the forests where they strayed like cattle in their separate ways,—being there no married men amongst them,—but hearing on all sides the shout of " Moskva "[1] from the troops of the *Veliki Knyaz*.

So did the Lord fill their wicked souls with dread that they strayed in the forests not knowing their own country.   The troops of the righteous sovereign and *Veliki Knyaz* triumphing over them by God's mercy, chased the wicked men of Novgorod twenty *poprishche*[2] killing many and taking others alive, while others were drowned in their boats in the Shelon river.

The troops on the field of battle proclaimed their victory by trumpet sound and kissed the sacred images, glorifying God for their victory over their presumptuous enemies.

And searching in the transport they found a writing which was the draft of an agreement between Novgorod and the king.[3]   This was a surprise, and it caused astonishment, and the papers were forthwith sent to the *Veliki Knyaz* Ioan Vasilievich by the hand of the *Boyar* Ivan Vasilievich Zamyatin; he was to report that a large army of Novgorod men had advanced against them with banners with the best men among them, and had fought desperately, but that God had aided the *Voyevodas* of the *Veliki Knyaz*, that the great Novgorod army was completely defeated, that many Nov-

[1] Moscow.
[2] About 20 versts.   [3] Of Poland.

gorod men had fallen, and many had been captured, to the number of 1,700; that here were the copies of a treaty with the King of Poland, and with these they sent a prisoner, the man who had written out the draft, to serve the *Veliki Knyaz* in his accusation of the crafty men of Novgorod.

The pious *Veliki Knyaz* was gladdened by the unspeakable mercy of God in the aid given to him from on high against his cunning enemies. Praising God and the most pure Mother of God for having frustrated their wicked design of corrupting the sacred churches of God, of causing agitations and of producing hostilities between great sovereigns to the utter discomfiture of all Orthodoxy. He found among the documents the draft of a treaty with the king, by the terms of which the men of Novgorod agreed to surrender all the towns and districts of the *Veliki Knyaz*, with his lands and waters and with all the taxes of Novgorod the Great, setting forth the names of the envoys to be sent to the king—Panfili Selifontov and Kurila Ivanov, son of Makar—and naming him "our honourable king and sovereign." It is written, that their sickness shall turn upon their heads and their untruth shall descend upon them. So may it be with them for their craftiness and evil counsels.

The pious *Veliki Knyaz* of all Russia Ioan Vasilievich, having prayed to God and to the most pure Mother of God, went forward in his great work to Novgorod the Great, with his younger brothers *Knyaz* Yuri Vasilievich and *Knyaz* Andrei Vasilievich and *Knyaz* Boris Vasilievich, with the [Tartar] *Tsarevich*, with all his *Knyazes* and *Voyevodas* and with all the people of his lands, hastening to his *Voyevodas* and to his advance army.

When the men of Novgorod were brought before the *Veliki Knyaz*, he, the pious one, with a godly wisdom accused the crafty men of their cunning and dishonourable proceedings, of departing from the light of true worship and giving themselves up to Latinism, of surrendering themselves to the Latin king while being the patrimony of him the *Veliki Knyaz;* and of surrendering to the Latin king according to the draft of a treaty with him all the towns, districts, lands and waters which belonged to him the *Veliki Knyaz* of Moscow, together with the taxes. Having found them guilty of all this, and being thus stirred against the men of Novgorod, he ordered them to execution by the sword, the chief *Posadniks*, among whom was Dmitri the eldest son of the charming Marfa, the town *Posadnik;* and she was also to lose her life by decapitation; together with these Vasili Seleznev Guba, Kiprian Arzubiev and

Ieremia were also beheaded for their conspiracy and crime in seeking to take to Latinism. Many other *Posadniks, Tysyatskis, Boyars* and men of substance of Novgorod were sent away to various towns or thrown into prisons, while others were retained in the fortress under charge to bide their time.

When God's aid came down from on high, with the leader of the heavenly host, the great *Archistrategos* Mikhail, in that hour Great Novgorod trembled before the wrath of God, and the *Posadniks*, the *Tysyatskis*, the men of substance, the *Boyars*, the merchants, and all the land of Novgorod turned their hearts towards good.

So did those men of Novgorod come unanimously to one decision; taking with them the priest-hermit Feofil, nominated *Vladyka* of Novgorod the Great and of Pskov, the Archimandrites, and *Igumens*, the worthy fathers and hermits, the priests from all the seven cathedral churches, and a great number of the best men of the town, they went to the pious sovereign and *Veliki Knyaz* of all Russia Ioan Vasilievich, and all of them prostrating themselves before him, they repented them with tears and in great sorrow of their crimes, praying: "Merciful lord and *Veliki Knyaz* of all Russia Ioan Vasilievich, for the Lord's sake pardon us guilty men of Novgorod the Great your patrimony; grant us, Lord, your favour, withdraw your anger, hold back your sword and extinguish your fires, silence your thunders, spare the land from ruin, be merciful and let your irresponsible people see the light."

And they all came on many days to his brothers, *Knyaz* Yuri Vasilievich, *Knyaz* Andrei Vasilievich, and to *Knyaz* Boris Vasilievich, humbling themselves before them and praying them to plead for them to their elder brother, the *Veliki Knyaz* Ioan Vasilievich; and on many days they likewise visited the *Boyars*, the *Knyazes* and *Voyevodas*, beseeching them because of the sorrows of all Great Novgorod to plead for them, before the *Veliki Knyaz*. The gracious brothers of the *Veliki Knyaz*, *Knyaz* Yuri Vasilievich, *Knyaz* Andrei Vasilievich, and *Knyaz* Boris Vasilievich, favoured them as of their patrimony, and compassionating them, and together with all the *Knyazes* and *Boyars*, did plead for them before their brother the *Veliki Knyaz* of all Russia, praying him to have regard for them of his patrimony and to lay aside the wrath in his heart. The gracious and intelligent sovereign *Veliki Knyaz* of all Russia, Ioan Vasilievich, seeing before him such a multitude of penitent people, and among them his own priests, the hermit priest Feofil, the *Vladyka*-elect of Novgorod the Great and of Pskov, who had grieved sore many days, as also his brothers and the *Boyars* and *Knyazes* in supplication before him, and the righteous *Veliki Knyaz* being also mindful of the writing he had received from his spiritual father Filip, Metropolitan of all Russia in which as pastor and teacher of Christ's flock the Metropolitan entreated the *Veliki Knyaz*, with his blessing, to be merciful to the people of his patrimony, those many Orthodox Christians for whose souls he grieved, and for the sake of Christian peace to accept their petitions, and remembering also the words which came from the mouth of our Lord: " Be merciful even as our Father in heaven, forgive man's trespasses as your Father will forgive yours," and again: " Blessed is the merciful," so because of these words spoken by God, and of all these intercessions, the *Veliki Knyaz* granted grace to his patrimony, to Feofil the *Vladyka*-elect of Novgorod the Great and of Pskov, to the *Posadniks*, *Tysyatskis*, merchants and to the whole of Novgorod the Great: he withdrew from them the anger of his heart, withheld his sword and his menace over the land, and commanded that all the captives should be freed without ransom.   He put a termination to the war and to plunder; and as to taxes and tribute, he settled them all in writing, on oath, after which the *Veliki Knyaz* withdrew from his patrimonial domains of Novgorod peacefully with his brothers, his *Boyars*, with the *Knyazes* and *Voyevodas* and with all his armed forces.

From his *Voyevodas* operating on the Dvina the *Veliki Knyaz* received communications to the effect that they had defeated *Knyaz* Vasili Shuiski, the servant of Great Novgorod, who with men from the country beyond the *Volok*, from the Dvina country and from the Korel region had advanced in large numbers and had fought with them great battles from morning to night on land and on water, but that God had aided the forces of the *Veliki Knyaz* under *Voyevoda* Vasili Fedorovich and his comrades, that a large number of the men of Novgorod were slain and others captured; so were the men of Novgorod overcome with fatigue and staggered in battle that they could not move their hands or turn their heads; that their *Knyaz* was wounded by an arrow and was taken away in a boat by his men, being barely alive, and that the towns on the Dvina had been burned and demolished.   Thus did God's grace and mercy descend from on high in aid of the right of our sovereign the righteous and pious *Veliki Knyaz* Ioan Vasilievich of all Russia.   On receipt of this intelligence the pious *Veliki Knyaz* gave praise to God and to the most pure Mother of God for those great mercies, and returned to his throne in the God-protected city of Moscow on the 1st day of September of the new year 6980 (1472).

Having received their liberty from their sovereign Ioan Vasilievich the *Veliki Knyaz* of all Russia, the men of Novgorod at once dispersed from out of the town to their several homes. A large number of people proceeded to Russa in big vessels, and to the Volkhov river with their wives and children and possessions; their cattle and with their movable houses, going to the places of their residence by the Ilmen lake, or by way of the Russa lake, the breadth from shore to shore on all sides being sixty *poprishche*.[1] When their numerous big vessels reached the middle of the lake, a storm with a hurricane of wind broke suddenly upon them, and tore their sails; there was terrible thunder and heavy rain with hail, and waves of mountain height, and dreadful, broke up their barges and all their big vessels in the middle of that frightful lake. There was in that hour an overwhelming terror and a raging storm, with shrieking and crying, many people clinging to each other, bitterly bewailing their peril, and in their agony tearing their clothes; mothers embracing their infants, fathers their sons, while shedding many tears and praying: " Lord save us, in the hour of our destruction and of our separation from the evils of this world." Sadness and woe to those who take to evil! This was not within sight of their friends, and they got no help from them; unless it came from on high, because of the straits of the great city and the angry spirit pervading it; the while that the big vessels were being shattered and wrecked, and all the men and women with their children were perishing in the deep waters separating from each other and tumbling about at the will of the waves which left nothing living in the waters, but all drowned and put to death. It was heard afterwards that the number of drowned in the lake was 7,000. Thus did God punish his people of the Novgorod country for their wicked imaginings, those evil-minded men, even for relinquishing their faith and inclining to Latinism. When it came to the ears of Great Novgorod that on the Dvina the *Voyevodas* of the *Veliki Knyaz* had beaten *Knyaz* Vasili Shuiski and the Novgorod men, while a large multitude had been drowned in the lake, then tears were added to tears, and wailings to wailings, realizing that the whole of the Novgorod country was by the wrath of the *Veliki Knyaz* of all Russia, Ioan Vasilievich, burned and laid waste by war, with its best men driven out, which had never happened to them before. But all this evil and ruin they had brought

[1] About 40 miles.

upon themselves by their cunning and faithlessness and for their going over to Latinism, having allowed themselves to be misled by cunning people and rebels; and that civic disaster and human blood shall they be made to account for by the Almighty God, according to the writing: " Lord! destroy the provokers of strife; and let the consequences fall on the heads of the traitors and on their souls in this world and in the next. amen."

APPENDIX.

Grivna was the old Russian equivalent of "pound"; the word originally seems to have meant a circular ingot of silver.

Kuny (nom. pl. from *Kuna* = a marten) came to mean money in general, which took the form in earliest times of the heads of martens or squirrels; *grivna kun* (gen. pl.) meant a monetary pound, a pound of martens.

The *grivna* contained twenty *nogaty* (nom. pl. from *nogata*), or twenty-five *Kuny*, or fifty *rezany* (nom. pl. from *rezana*)—all names of monetary units in the shape of paws, heads, or skins of various animals.

There existed also metallic *Kuny*, and $2\frac{1}{2}$ of these equalled one fur *nogata* in the twelfth century. The *grivna* in the tenth century was actually about $\frac{1}{3}$, in the eleventh and earlier twelfth centuries about $\frac{1}{2}$, and in the later twelfth and thirteenth centuries only a $\frac{1}{4}$, of a lb.

The *Rouble* was in the fifteenth century a bar of silver weighing about $\frac{1}{4}$lb. and was worth approximately ten *roubles* of the present day, i.e., about £1 sterling. One *rouble* contained 100 *dengi*, a small silver coin worth about ten *kopeks* of the present day, or $2\frac{1}{2}$d. One *denga* (a Tartar word, meaning "money") contained four *pochki* (*pochka*, lit. kidney, the smallest unit in old Russian weights).

Kad is the same as the *osminka*, which latter contained four *chetveriki*, equal to about $11\frac{1}{2}$ pecks.

A *Verst* or *poprishche* is about two-thirds of a mile, or 1,067 metres.

NOTE ON THE BIBLIOGRAPHY

The best general critical accounts of the Republic of Novgorod, its organization and its life, are perhaps by (1) V. O. Klyuchevsky *History of Russia*, Vol. I, Chs. xix-xx (English trans., C. J. Hogarth, 1911, pp. 319-368 of Vol. I); (2) K. Bestujev-Ryumin, *History of Russia*, Vol. I, Ch. vi (German trans., T. Schiemann, 1877, Vol. I, pp. 230-274).

The reader may also refer to N. Karamzin, *History of Russia*, and S. Solovev, *History of Russia*. Karamzin, after his manner, does not devote any particular section to Novgorod, but refers to the history of the Republic in nearly every chapter of Vols. II, III, IV, V (e.g., Vol. II, Chs. 2, 7, 9, 10, 12-16; Vol. III, Chs. 1, 3-8; Vol. IV, Chs. 1-11; Vol. V, Chs. 1-4 [only 4 chs. in vol.] See also references in notes to the Introduction of this vol., *e.g.* pp. xxvii, xxviii.)

The following works, additional to those cited in the text, and in the preceding paragraphs, in many cases studies on particular aspects of Novgorod life and history, mostly un-translated, are among the chief authorities:

Andreevski, *On the Trade of Novgorod with the German Towns from 1270;*
  Antiquités Russes, esp. Vol. II;
  Barsov, *Materials for the Historical Geography of the Slavs;*
  Belaev, *Narratives from Russian History*, 1863;
  Documents of Russian Livonia, 1868;
  Eugenius the Metropolitan, *Discourses on Old Novgorod;*
  Kazan Academy Journal, 1863, *Remarks on the Organization of the Old Novgorod Hierarchy;*
  Kostomarov, *North Russian Communities*, 1863, and *Origins of Russia;*
  Krazov, *On the Position of Old Novgorod*, 1851;
  Kunizin, *History of the Old Law of Russia;*
  Malkovski, *Critical Researches on the Origin of Great Novgorod;*
  Muravev, *Historical Researches on Old Novgorod*, 1828;
  Nikitski, *Pictures of the Life of Great Novgorod;*
  Passek, *Independent Novgorod;*
  Slavenski, *Survey of the Trade Relations of Novgorod;*
  Solovev, *Relations of Novgorod with the Grand Princes of Russia;*
  Zamyslovski, *Russian Historical Atlas.*

All these are only to be had in Russian.   To them add:

Behrmann, *De Skra von Nougarten;*

Ewers, *Studien zur grundlichen Kenntniss der Vorzeit Russlands;*

Lindner (Theodor), *Die deutsche Hanse,* Leipzig, 1911;

Müller, *Kurze Nachrichten über die Anfänge Nowgorods;*

Riesenkampf, *Der deutsche Hof zu Nowgorod;*

Urkunden über die Beziehungen des N.-W. Russland . . . und den Hanse-Städten, 1857.

INDEX

Q

[1] Pronounced *Fjódor*=Theodore, similarly Feofil=Theophilus, etc.

Q2

Letchworth: At the Arden Press